Philanthropy in Europe
A rich past, a promising future

EDITORS

Norine MacDonald +
Luc Tayart de Borms

ALLIANCE
PUBLISHING
TRUST

ISBN 978 0 9558804 0 7

Alliance Publishing Trust
1st Floor, 25 Corsham Street
London N1 6DR
UK

publishing@alliancemagazine.org
www.alliancemagazine.org

Registered charity number: 1116744
Company registration number: 5935154

A catalogue record for this book is available from the
British Library.

Typeset in Grotesque MT
Design by Benedict Richards
Printed and bound by Hobbs the Printers, Totton,
Hampshire, UK
This book is printed on FSC approved paper.

Contents

Foreword **5**
Editors' commentary **7**

Profiles

1 Stefan Batory Foundation *Dianna Rienstra* **21**

2 Robert Bosch Stiftung *David Watkiss* **37**

3 Compagnia di San Paolo *Anna Cantaluppi and David Watkiss* **53**

4 European Cultural Foundation *Gottfried Wagner* **69**

5 Fondation de France *Dianna Rienstra* **85**

6 Institusjonen Fritt Ord *David Watkiss* **99**

7 Calouste Gulbenkian Foundation *António José Teixeira* **115**

8 Impetus Trust *Dianna Rienstra* **129**

9 Stavros Niarchos Foundation *Hildy Simmons* **143**

10 Sabancı Foundation *Filiz Bikmen* **157**

11 Stephan Schmidheiny *Dianna Rienstra* **173**

12 Van Leer Foundation Group *Dianna Rienstra* **189**

13 Wellcome Trust *David Watkiss* **205**

Essays – the diverse roles played by European foundations

14 The rich history of philanthropy in Turkey: a paradox of tradition and modernity *Filiz Bikmen* **223**

15 Encouraging change: European foundations funding research *Wilhelm Krull* **235**

16 European foundations' support for civil society: a means to an end or an end in itself? *Caroline Hartnell* **245**

17 Foundations and policy influence in Europe *Diana Leat* **259**

18 Engaged philanthropy and market-based solutions *Maximilian Martin* **273**

19 The importance of there being a European foundation statute *Gerry Salole* **289**

About the contributors **300**
Index **302**

Foreword

The purpose of this book is to showcase the rich diversity of the European foundation sector and to profile some of the personalities behind its evolution. We achieve this in the profiles, although the foundations featured in these pages are just a very few examples of the thousands across Europe. Special attention is given to Turkey as it prepares for the upcoming negotiations with the European Union and the role of foundations in the past, present and future.

Through the essays, we invite readers to explore some of the complex dynamics of the sector, although we do not intend this endeavour to be strictly academic or comprehensive. We believe the essays shed some light on the various theories of change that foundations are following in their approach to civil society, science and research, and the market.

There is an abundance of literature about US philanthropy, which could lead to a belief that the methodologies and strategies used by our American colleagues are the benchmark for philanthropy around the world. We hope to demonstrate that continental European philanthropy is a different animal; because of the various models of civil society in Europe and the role played by the state, the Anglo-Saxon style philanthropy found in the US is actually the exception. Foundation leaders in Africa, Asia and Latin America are also developing their own approach to philanthropy.

We believe the reader will be able to get a very clear impression of the rich variety and diversity Europe has to offer by looking through the prism of a few well-chosen examples. Of course, many others could be chosen, and we trust that in coming years more European foundations will make efforts to share their stories with a wider public. We have tried to illustrate the diversity of the sector by choosing older foundations, going back as far as the 16th century, and new philanthropic ventures.

We looked for geographic spread and foundations that use various and often innovative methodologies. We take full responsibility for our choices, but apologize to our colleagues whose interesting and inspiring work does not appear in this book. This means there is much more work to be done in profiling the good work being done across the continent.

We also make a plea for the long-overdue European foundation statute to become a reality, and call on national governments to implement the necessary legal and fiscal framework that will enable foundations to fulfil their mandate – to create value for society.

Success has many parents. As does this book. First and foremost, the editors would like to thank Gerry Salole, Chief Executive of the European Foundation Centre. He was the lead parent in this exercise, for it was his idea to showcase some of the sector's achievements through a storytelling lens rather than an academic treatise. We thank Dianna Rienstra who took the lead on the writing, as well as the other writers who worked on the profiles. Every book needs a good publisher. We thank Alliance Publishing Trust and particularly Caroline Hartnell for fulfilling this role. We would also like to thank our colleagues who took the time to contribute to this endeavour by writing what we believe are thought-provoking essays.

Norine MacDonald
Luc Tayart de Borms

NORINE MACDONALD + LUC TAYART DE BORMS

Editors' commentary

Why this book?

As the title of this book suggests, philanthropy in Europe is rooted in a rich past and is moving towards a promising future. The diversity of philanthropic impulses, a *leitmotif* that has fuelled the dynamism of the sector throughout history, is expressed here in just a few examples of European foundations. This dynamism continues today, following – sometimes shaping – the contours of Europe's evolving social, political and economic fabric. This dynamism was born within Europe's different religious contexts and has moved forward in tandem with its secularization. As church and state separated – in most countries – philanthropy has found its place in modern societies in different ways.

One of the primary points we hope to illustrate with this book is that throughout history, foundations have played an important role in the development and strengthening of European societies. Today and in the future, the sector has an even more critical role to play within the European landscape, both within and across national borders, and internationally. However, the sector's potential is being held back, among other things, by the EU's single market, which does not include foundations. In effect, foundations are operating in an environment of unfair competition arising from differences between the tax systems in the 27 EU Member States. Hence the essay by Gerry Salole, Chief Executive of the European Foundation Centre, which makes a plea for Europe's institutional machinery to get into gear and facilitate the sector's ability to participate properly on the European stage by moving forward with a European foundation statute.

Such a statute – on and off the back burner for years – would at once complement national legislation and create an enabling environment for foundations' work locally, regionally, nationally and globally. At the same time, in many EU Member States, foundations need a more modern legal and fiscal environment if they are to live up to their potential to create real value.

In this commentary, we explore Europe's various civil society models and how foundations work within them. The journey takes us across a philanthropic landscape that is colourful, complex and compelling, peopled by some quixotic characters and pragmatic visionaries. In the essay section of this book, we introduce the reader to several of the 'thinkers' in the field who offer valuable insights into the past, present and future of the sector. We also take stock of the accomplishments of foundations and outline some challenges facing the sector that only foundations themselves can meet.

Models of civil society

The Anglo-Saxon model In Anglo-Saxon societies, civil society organizations (CSOs) are viewed as being a counterweight to government and the state. In an ideal world, they foster pluralism in their societies and cast themselves in the role of critics of the state and advocates of reform. There is usually a strong culture of volunteerism and foundations support civil society and fund issues that governments do not. There is also an enabling legal and fiscal infrastructure that encourages donations and gifts. The most obvious examples are the United States and the United Kingdom.

The Rhine model This includes Belgium, Germany and the Netherlands and is characterized by strong CSOs that are institution-like and often receive contracts from the state in a form of 'societal corporatism', rather than operating as a counterweight to the state. They function much like subcontractors in sectors such as healthcare and education. Paradoxically, they are independent from the state, but predominantly publicly funded. Because of this interdependent relationship and dependence on government funding, the fiscal and legal climate does not strongly favour donations and gifts. In this space, foundations are only recently being recognized as important players, particularly corporate foundations.

The Latin/Mediterranean model Here the role of the state is strong with a clear division between church and state. Traditionally,

Exploring the context in which foundations create value

Foundations – to fulfil their obligations to create value – must fully understand the context in which they assume their various roles and how best to meet the economic, cultural and social needs of the societies in which they operate, whether in their own communities or beyond. To do this, foundations must take into consideration the policy environment in which they work. In defining this environment – and responding to it through grantmaking or operational programmes, projects and initiatives – it is critical to evaluate the interplay of roles among the state, the market and civil society.

We see in the foundations profiled in this book that the various expressions of the philanthropic impulse differ according to the societal context. This may appear obvious, but US/Anglo-Saxon literature about the sector often gives the impression that the American Anglo-Saxon model is the benchmark not only for Europe and the United States but also for the

the church does charity work and the state is responsible for delivering goods and social services. The state is a strong economic actor and the relationship between the state and market is different from that in other models. CSOs face a challenge in being accepted as independent and autonomous. There is an effort to control organizations and associations politically, either through representation on boards or by legal measures, such as what happened in Italy with the attempt to bring the banking foundations under political control.[1] Gifts and donations are not encouraged by the fiscal system and volunteerism is viewed as a threat to the job market. Foundations have difficulty moving into their role of complementarity – supporting and funding what government does not, thereby fostering pluralism in civil society – because when they move into what is perceived as political territory, they are challenged by politicians who question their mandate.

The Scandinavian model Here the state traditionally plays a strong role, but because of the Protestant roots in these countries, personal initiative is viewed as a positive. There is a strong welfare state, but at the same time volunteerism is a powerful force. CSOs typically thrive and fulfil a complementarity role to bridge the gaps in the system. Civil society often identifies a need, which is later filled by government. Gifts and donations are not strongly promoted in the fiscal system. In this environment, foundations have a very strong relationship with government and government agencies.[2]

rest of the world. This book certainly dispels this notion. We see through the profiles that foundations are operating in very different societal contexts, which inevitably means they are actors within a framework created by different models of civil society. They are also using a broad range of creative methodologies that go beyond traditional grantmaking to taking on operational roles such as advocacy, communications strategies and running their own scientific and cultural institutions. This theme is further explored in the essays.

Civil society is quite a different animal in the north of Europe from in the south, as it is responding to different realities and cultural paradigms. Consider that despite the forces of secularization and post-modernism that have swept across Europe, cultural paradigms die hard, which in part accounts for the different civil society models in Europe. For example, southern European society is still characterized by a very Catholic paradigm, while in northern Europe Protestant ethics generally prevail.

Three models of civil society can be identified across Europe outside the Anglo-Saxon model: the Rhine, the Latin/Mediterranean and the Scandinavian models (see box on pp8–9). These models are of course evolving and changing, as are our societies, but distinctive characteristics can be identified.

The reality of these different civil society models begs the question of whether the standardized methodological approach sometimes taken by foundations is really effective, particularly as such an approach often does not see past the Anglo-Saxon model. It also begs the question of whether a standardized methodological approach is appropriate in the face of the inescapable fact that globalization is creating new cross-border, regional and international challenges. The methodologies of the foundations profiled here indicate that many are reaching beyond the standard approaches to create value in a creative, innovative way, which reflects their diverse responses to change.

This is not to say that the Anglo-Saxon model does not work in societies where civil society is positioned as it is within this particular model, as the profiles of the Wellcome Trust and Impetus Trust show. It is to point out that for many non-Anglo-Saxon foundations, the roles they play are completely different. For example, continental European foundations mostly trust the state to work within international institutions and frameworks to adequately address issues such as human rights and climate change.

We see throughout the profiles a rich diversity in the *raison d'être* of foundations within various civil society models, as well as how they fulfil their various mandates today against the backdrop of globalization, whose only constant is change. To further complicate the mix, the role of the state – and thus the relationship between the state and foundations – is constantly changing. These dynamics are also explored in the essays.

These profiles and essays do not attempt to classify the various foundations into rigid parameters, but certain themes and trends do emerge that reflect the civil society models in the various countries. One of the issues we hope to showcase in this book is that European societies are changing, which results in often overlapping models of civil society – and it is these very differences that are creating the richness and diversity of the sector as foundations are permanently adapting to the changing socioeconomic context. At the same time, we believe this richness and diversity could be deepened and extended by increased regional and global cooperation between and among foundations working in partnership.

Diversity within different socioeconomic contexts

It is illuminating to compare the socioeconomic context within which the foundations profiled were founded and how the context has evolved and relates to their work today. Norway's Fritt Ord focuses on freedom of expression, springing from painful memories of Nazi occupation and repression in Norway exacerbated by the Cold War and fears of communist totalitarianism. The Stefan Batory Foundation has helped to guide Poland through tumultuous political, economic and social changes in the wake of the collapse of the Soviet Union and is now helping to guide the country through the changes brought on by its accession to the European club in 2004.

Armenian Calouste Sarkis Gulbenkian launched the oil economy and became one of the world's wealthiest individuals. His legacy – the Calouste Gulbenkian Foundation, founded after his death in the 1950s during a dictatorial regime – played an important role in its first decades in combating Portugal's enormous shortcomings in the areas of education, health, culture and science. Shipping tycoon Stavros Niarchos passed away in the same decade and left a legacy that requires the eponymous foundation to spend half its funds in Greece – shoring up critical educational, healthcare, social welfare and cultural provision – and the other half on supporting projects outside the country.

The Sabancı Foundation, deeply rooted in the socioeconomic, political and philanthropic history of Turkey, has evolved from meeting the urgent needs of society in the areas of education, healthcare and social welfare to one of the largest foundations in the country, which is today realigning its strategy to better meet the dynamic context and shifting mandates of Turkish society and the consequent changes in the philanthropic landscape. A landscape, as we read in the essay, that has dramatically changed since the first foundations were established before the Ottoman Era in the context of a tradition where pious Muslims could realize – in perpetuity – their religious obligations. 'Modern' foundations are playing a role in service delivery and shaping the policy agenda, as well as dealing with the 'software' of sweeping social change.

Sabancı's role also underscores the role of foundations in the EU accession process, which has commonalities with the role of the Stefan Batory Foundation in Poland's transition to becoming a member of the European Union. Interestingly, although Turkey and the EU are struggling with the potential accession of Turkey, the fundamental framework – rule of law, individual freedoms and rights, gender equality and improvement of basic services – are essential for the country's future prosperity.

The Compagnia di San Paolo has for more than four centuries had a rich, complex history of service to its city, its region, the Italian state and the world. Today, the Compagnia is structured as a 'not-for-profit group' operating primarily in Italy, but its activities reach across Europe and extend worldwide, often in partnership with other foundations. This history, together with the Compagnia's institutional and operational transformations, illustrates the creative way in which foundations are constantly adapting themselves to changing societal contexts.

Fondation de France is an example of a foundation with institutional origins, created by General Charles de Gaulle's Ministers of Culture and Finance to act as an engine of foundation development in a barren philanthropic landscape scarred by the practices of France's *Ancien Régime*, under which legacies and donations were subject to royal approval. Although created by the state, it is today a private non-profit organization that has fulfilled its mandate to foster philanthropy in the country and continues to work for the benefit of French society at local level, as well as supporting some international initiatives.

The European Cultural Foundation is the oldest pan-European foundation. It is the brainchild of a group of prominent European personalities who took the prescient step of establishing an independent foundation to focus on the cultural aspects of Europe's interdependencies in the wake of World War Two. The Foundation believes that cultural diversity is a resource and seeks to bring people closer together through cultural cooperation and creative activities. A strange animal in the family of European foundations, it is neither a national foundation nor a corporate foundation; it is not a community foundation nor is it endowed. It is private, but works for the public benefit at European level.

When reading the rich history of the European foundation sector, it becomes apparent how resilient foundations are. They have evolved, transformed and changed over time. Some have survived regime change, others have survived invasion. Foundations are obviously very capable of adapting to the socio-economic and political environment they are operating in because they are contextually grounded.

Diversity of the philanthropic impulse

From the philanthropic impulses of wealthy business entrepreneurs come some of Europe's most successful foundations: Gulbenkian, Stavros Niarchos and Stefan Batory (started by the Hungarian-born American philanthropist and financier George Soros), but also Henry Wellcome, Robert Bosch, Bernard van Leer and, more recently, Stephan Schmidheiny and Stephen Dawson. Although the work of the various foundations differs, according to the legacy of the founder and the context in which they operate, they are all the result of visionaries who basically want – or wanted – to make the world a better place.

Henry Wellcome lived a remarkable life, driven by a brilliant entrepreneurial spirit and care for indigenous peoples. Today, the UK's Wellcome Trust's mission to foster and promote research with the aim of improving human and animal health is being fulfilled, and so is the legacy of its founder in the diversity of the Trust's activities in science, technology transfer, history of medicine, ethics, public engagement and art.

The Robert Bosch Stiftung holds the stock of the industrial giant Bosch and is fulfilling the broadly defined mandate of its founder. Robert Bosch was a man whose substantial gifts and endowments during his lifetime were complemented by his financial and personal support of peace and reconciliation before World War Two. His broad mandate to 'promote health, education, talent, international understanding and the like' is being fulfilled through the Foundation's programme areas with multiple focuses that change over time.

The enigmatic Bernard van Leer – an industrialist, benefactor and circus director – left behind a money-making corporation and a charitable fund. His rather vague philanthropic impulse was insightfully executed by his son, who decided to focus on the educational challenges of environmentally disadvantaged children and youth. Today, the Foundation is multifaceted with a grantmaking programme focusing on early childhood care and development. Its activities in Israel support the Jewish people and a democratic society, as well as projects to build bridges with Palestinians.

Two contemporary entrepreneurs – Stephan Schmidheiny and Stephen Dawson – express their philanthropic impulses in different ways but they are both visionaries who have found innovative methodologies to make a difference. Entrepreneur Schmidheiny has been driven by his passion for both the environment and global issues and by a deep belief that achievement and wealth bring with them a responsibility to be involved in the issues facing society. Venture capitalist Dawson wanted to go beyond chequebook philanthropy to ensure that charities were using money effectively and efficiently. Both are using instruments that work in the private sector to boost and strengthen civil society.

The challenges and opportunities ahead

Within this fascinating and diverse tapestry of European philanthropy, we find a number of common threads that intersect at the crossroads of the public perception of foundations – a brand that inspires trust but also brings with it challenges. For what is a foundation? For the greater public and decision-makers, the term 'foundation' may still be unclear.

There are many other types of organization other than public-benefit foundations operating as foundations. There are political foundations linked to political parties that have played roles in Eastern Europe and are playing an important role in helping to create the political infrastructure in new democracies. There are also foundations created by governments or the European Union and primarily controlled by their founders. An example of this is the Anna Lindt Foundation.

Incidents such as the recent Lichtenstein scandal in early 2008 involving banks acting as tax havens and private foundations raise questions in the minds of citizens. Private money used for public benefit raises as many questions as it does concerns. Questions about the proper role of foundations in a modern democracy; concerns about transparency, effectiveness and accountability.

There is clearly a need to define exactly what constitutes a foundation. If we do not do this for public-benefit foundations within a European foundation statute and within national legal and fiscal frameworks, we risk draconian measures from governments with a penchant to over-react with regulation. We also need specific legal models for other types of foundation as well.

The European Foundation Centre has a central role to play as the philanthropic sector in continental Europe is not very well known compared to other parts of the world, notably across the Atlantic. The public, policymakers and politicians are largely unaware of the immense amount of assets at play in the sector, which are due to increase exponentially in the future with the wealth transfer of the current generation. They are also largely unaware that the grants, the project development and advocacy work from foundations create employment and strengthen our communities. Foundations rarely if ever seek a high profile in the media and, according to European tradition, individual philanthropists do not like to display their wealth. The European relationship with money is also quite different. In most European countries, citizens are obliged to show their social solidarity through the tax system.

Another reason for this low profile is that in the European environment today, foundations are perceived as relatively small players compared to what governments and other actors are achieving. However, many foundations are playing the role of catalyst, facilitator or convenor, and working closely with civil society organizations, governments, scientific and cultural institutions, and other actors. Despite the fact that foundations are playing a critical role, the sector does not work on taking a higher profile as they don't want to overshadow the accomplishments of other players or to undermine the role of foundations as convenors or as providing neutral platforms for debate, dialogue and action.

What these profiles and essays clearly demonstrate is that foundations have a brilliant track record. They are imaginative and creative and have fulfilled their mandates in innovative ways. Many are working cross-border to help meet the challenges of issues such as migration, science, culture, human trafficking, HIV/AIDS and poverty. The sector has earned a lot of credibility in myriad areas, but we must do more.

Therein lies our conundrum – the challenges ahead demand that we become even more European and more global, while working in closer partnership with other organizations and foundations. But our operating environment is restricted, something that could be remedied to a large degree within the parameters of a European foundation statute.

But a European foundation statute is not a silver bullet, nor is it a panacea for everything that challenges the sector and limits its potential. Yes, a statute will clarify the role of foundations and create a framework for citizens to pool their expertise and financial resources for projects of public benefit and European interest. Yes, a statute will be a public-benefit legal tool governed by European law and complemented by existing national laws. Yes, a statute is a logical extension of the political idea that Europe should be a Europe without frontiers.

All of this holds true. But at the end of the day, the sector must also consider some of the challenges it is facing, including those posed by the rich ethnic, religious and cultural diversity that is Europe. We discuss some of the challenges here, but this list is just a beginning.

Challenges ahead

Work more in partnership

Working in partnerships is often necessary if foundations are to meet today's complex challenges. Such challenges almost always involve a wide range of different actors who can play key roles in meeting them. This is a rather new paradigm in philanthropy, but one that has already proved its value. Working in partnership is not only more effective but will go far to reaffirm the legitimacy of foundations as valuable players in their societies.

The Network of European Foundations for Innovative Cooperation (NEF) is a prominent force for European foundation collaboration around key policy issues. NEF is not a membership organization but a 'platform' to enable joint projects to get off the ground, involving 62 foundations (in 2007) participating in one or more projects, including work on integration and migration, deliberative democracy, and the European Fund for the Balkans. This combination of convening, research and participation is characteristic of the way in which NEF tends to work.

This type of collaboration is a good start, but working in partnership – when feasible – should become the norm rather than the exception.

Bridge the gender gap

When it comes to foundations and gender, European women are facing a glass ceiling. In 2005, among the European Foundation Centre's 173 voting members, 49 had a female primary contact (28 per cent). Primary contacts are mostly the head of the organization. On the Governing Council, 6 out of 30 members have a woman as primary contact (20 per cent). Some concerned EFC members set up a Gender Strategy Group in 2005 to address the lack of gender balance among EFC members and governing bodies, on EFC conference panels and so on. Among its aims is to encourage the EFC to follow the policy of the European Union and its institutions and adopt a target of at least 40 per cent women on each committee, group or platform. The EFC initiative is laudable, but change must come from within individual foundations.

Reach out to become more European and more global

Despite the reservoir of resources and talent at their disposal, many foundation leaders feel overwhelmed and disempowered in the face of

the daunting challenges we face today. As they wring their hands over
how best to deploy these resources, they often end up doing what they
know and hiding behind the strictest interpretations of their mandate. We
believe – and it is proved within the chapters of this book – that they need to
mobilize innovative methodologies strategically to create impact and effect
meaningful change. There are many areas to work in where they can make
a difference, either individually or in partnership, be it in science, better
governance or migration, to name a few.

Collect more data
The foundation sector needs to invest in better data collection. There is
a serious lack of up-to-date, credible data from the 27 EU countries. As
illustrated in the final essay of this book regarding the need for a European
foundation statute, existing data is outdated and limited to certain
countries. Data is critical to transparency, but also to help us make a
convincing argument to decision-makers about the need for a statute.
We need data about how many foundations actually exist, about their
endowments and budgets, about the numbers of employees and volunteers
in philanthropy, and we need an inventory of the issues the sector is tackling.
Some question the need for data or get lost in academic detail. But if the
philanthropic sector is to be given the weight it deserves – and we want to
lobby for a European foundation statute – we need the numbers.

Pay more attention to dialogue and cultural differences
As the title of this book graphically depicts, Europe is a mosaic of languages.
There is an increasing trend to view dialogue as a simple matter of
translation, but this is far too simplistic. Behind each and every language
is a long tradition of culturally intertwined concepts, beliefs and practices.
This is increasingly presenting a challenge in a world where English is
becoming the *lingua franca*.

Concepts such as social justice, social economy, social
entrepreneurship, leadership, community and volunteer work – to name a
few – are not necessarily understood in the same way in different parts of
Europe, whether it be in the north, south, east or west. At the same time, the
lingua franca is often being simplified into a type of shorthand, which risks
leaving out nuances and meanings behind it. We need to be consciously
aware of this intercultural learning challenge as we branch out into doing
cross-border or international work.

[1] The Italian government in 2001 introduced reform measures to a bill that would ensure the majority of seats on the boards of foundations would go to representatives of local authorities. The European Foundation Centre argued that the changes in the law undermined the independence of foundations of banking origin, thereby affecting their capacity to act for the social and economic development, well-being and progress of their communities at local, regional and European levels. In 2003, the Italian Constitutional Court declared that some of the changes to the law were unconstitutional.

[2] Based on L Tayart de Borms, *Foundations: Creating impact in a globalised world*, UK: John Wiley, 2005, pp40-45.

Profiles

DIANNA RIENSTRA

1 Stefan Batory Foundation
Laying a foundation for democracy

Since the Stefan Batory Foundation was established in 1998, it has lived up to its mission to support the development of an open, democratic society in Poland and other Central and Eastern European countries. Named after a 16th century Hungarian-born Polish king, the Foundation has accompanied the country through the tumultuous decades in the wake of the collapse of the Soviet Union. From 1998 to 2007, it has distributed 11,200 grants and 5,500 scholarships for a total amount of €63 million and €21 million for projects implemented directly by the Foundation.[1]

The list of founders of the Stefan Batory Foundation reads like a 'who's who' of Poland's resistance movements in the 1970s and 1980s. Members of KOR (the Workers Defence Committee) and the Solidarity Movement, they were political prisoners, leaders of the democratic opposition and anti-communist underground, editors of uncensored magazines and *samizdat*,[2] independent thinkers, trade union activists and lecturers of the Flying University, who from October 1977 to June 1979 gave lectures in private homes on literature, history, economics, politics and sociology, with the stated objective of unveiling the lies of communist party propaganda and filling the gaps in the official education.

Today, the Warsaw-based Stefan Batory Foundation plays a multifaceted role in Polish society, but it is primarily the country's most important grantmaker supporting the political and social changes that have unfolded in the country since June 1989 with the collapse of the Soviet Union. At the same time, it is helping Polish society to deal with the

Secret teachings of the Flying University

The original 'Flying University' in Poland began in 1883. There were no campuses, land or buildings – each class was held in a different private apartment. It was an alternative to official academic teachings, which were considered distorted by suppressions, taboos and lies, especially in the social and human sciences.

It offered some of the first opportunities for women in Warsaw and Eastern Poland to attend higher education, and women made up about 70 per cent of the student body. Between 1883 and 1905, about 3,000 women received diplomas. One of the Flying University's more famous students was Marie Sklodowska Curie, the first woman to receive a Nobel Prize, who studied sciences there after graduating from high school in 1883.

The greatest illegal educational activity took place during World War Two, with the Underground Alma Mater (1939–45). A full educational system was created underground, consisting of elementary, middle and university levels, which worked parallel to the official educational system. The main aim of the *tajne nauczanie* (secret teaching) was to prepare educated people for life after the war. It was important as Poland's then-enemies (Germany and the Soviet Union) killed the best scientists and educated people.[3]

changes and challenges in the country since it joined the European Union in May 2004.

The activities of the Stefan Batory Foundation are funded by George Soros's Open Society Institute, the Ford Foundation, Charles Stewart Mott Foundation, Trust for Civil Society in Central and Eastern Europe, Robert Bosch Stiftung, the Commercial Union of Poland, and other individual and institutional donors in Poland and abroad.

Promoting the process of democratic transformation

The Stefan Batory Foundation was established in 1988 by financier and philanthropist George Soros, founder and chairman of a network of foundations that promote, among other things, the creation of open, democratic societies based upon the rule of law, market economies, transparent and accountable governance, freedom of the press, and respect for human rights.

The Hungarian-born Soros was prescient. In spring 1989, negotiations between Poland's communist Prime Minister Wojciech Jaruzelski's regime and democratic opposition leaders brought about the free parliamentary elections of June 1989. In a letter written in September 2002, urging people to support the Foundation during the country's run-up to EU accession, Soros writes:

'I established the Warsaw-based Stefan Batory Foundation in 1988 with the cooperation of a group of Polish dissidents and intellectuals. Our mission was to promote the process of democratic transformation in Poland. Since then, the foundation has grown to become one of the largest philanthropies in Poland.

'The organization's support for grassroots programs and innovative projects, its transparent grantmaking policies, and its carefully considered governance structure have earned the Batory Foundation respect and recognition throughout Central and Eastern Europe and beyond. The foundation has attracted funding from both Polish and foreign donors, including many US organizations. For many, it serves as the model for grantmaking in Central Europe.

'For fourteen years the Foundation has actively supported the development of civil society, democracy, the rule of law, and the market economy in Poland and other countries in the region. Today, with Poland's anticipated accession to the European Union, new challenges and responsibilities arise. To meet these challenges, the Foundation is working to identify the areas where its activities can have the greatest impact. It must also seek new and diverse sources of funding, both to develop new programs and to build an endowment to secure its future.

'As the founder and principle funder of the Foundation, I strongly support its ambitious efforts to create a stable, independent and lasting resource for the people of Poland and Eastern Europe. For all who are committed to the ongoing process of transformation in the region, the Stefan Batory Foundation can serve as a reliable and honest partner. I urge you to support the foundation in its current efforts.'[4]

Anna Rozicka, Executive Director of the Stefan Batory Foundation since 2001, has witnessed a sea change. She started working at the Foundation as a programme officer in 1990. 'Since the very beginning we have been laying a foundation for democracy. At the beginning of transformation [in 1989] we had a weak state with no money,' she explains. 'In the first years of the Foundation's operation, we invested mostly in people: hundreds of assorted scholarships and travel grants were issued to economists, bankers, physicians, teachers, and local government activists. In this way, we took a hand in the preparation of cadres for the market economy and democratic system taking root in Poland.'

She adds: 'We also tried to counteract some of the negative aspects of transformation, including bankruptcy of state enterprises, inflation and increase of prices, unemployment, rising social discrepancies, growing marginalization of whole social groups. In addition, we were working with problems that were not sufficiently present in the public awareness such as domestic violence, child abuse, palliative care, the rights of ethnic minorities and the disabled.'

Rozicka says the Stefan Batory Foundation has always functioned as a non-partisan institution, promoting civic engagement and responsibility. It has run campaigns for transparent and accountable government and voting in the elections. It also serves as an independent

Named after a partisan who became a king

Stephen Báthory (Stefan Batory) was born in Somlyo, the son of Stefan Batory (born in 1534). His father was a partisan of John Zapolya, who claimed the crown of Hungary in opposition to the Habsburg claimant Ferdinand I, and had been appointed Prince of Transylvania.

Stephen Báthory, the son, won fame as a valiant lord-marcher, and as a skilful diplomat at the imperial court. His advocacy for the rights

of Zapolya's son John Sigismund incurred the wrath of Roman Emperor Maximilian II, who kept Báthory in prison for two years.

Batory became a Prince of Translyvania and was elected king of the Polish-Lithuanian Commonwealth in 1576. In 1581 Stephen and his army invaded the heart of Russia and on 22 August they laid siege to the city of Pskov, which lasted until February 1582. The Siege of Pskov was unsuccessful, but he successfully blockaded the city of Pskov during the final stage of the Livonian War of 1558–83. The Livonian War was a lengthy military conflict between the Tsardom of Russia and a variable coalition of Denmark, the Grand Duchy of Lithuania, the Kingdom of Poland (later the Polish-Lithuanian Commonwealth) and Sweden for control of Greater Livonia (the territory of the present-day Estonia and Latvia).

Stephen Báthory.

forum for public debates on important foreign and domestic issues for people of different outlooks, views and opinions.

A 'liberal' foundation

The Foundation was labelled 'liberal' by Poland's extreme right-wing Roman Catholic station Radio Maryja (pronounced Maria), which gained international notoriety in 2006 when the Vatican ordered the Polish Catholic church to clamp down on the station's mix of prayer and politics after Maryja's vitriolic condemnation of Jewish groups seeking compensation for property expropriated during World War Two. (The station likened their efforts to a 'Holocaust industry'.[5])

Rozicka says that in the eyes of Radio Maryja, 'liberal means devilish', and chauvinist and xenophobic circles in Poland used to see in the Stefan Batory Foundation either a 'plant by the Jewish Mafia' or a US agent in Poland.

Rozicka admits that the Batory Foundation is liberal in the sense that it embraces a broad array of ideas related to individual rights, protection of minority rights, equality of opportunity, freedom of speech, rule of law, transparent system of governance, balance of powers. Aleksander Smolar, the President of the Foundation, wrote in his article for the Foundation's 15th anniversary: 'The Foundation is not a homogeneous environment in terms of ideology – and this variety is what we consider to be of great value. In our grantmaking decisions we never followed any ideological, political, ethnic or religious criteria. The aim of the Foundation is to participate in building a Poland that would be open and tolerant and that would respect its diversity.'[6]

The mission of the Stefan Batory Foundation is to support the development of an open, democratic society in Poland and other Central and Eastern European countries. Its key programme areas are: strengthening civil society, promoting civil liberties and the rule of law, and developing international cooperation and solidarity. The Foundation works proactively to encourage long-term thinking, partnership between the public and private sectors, innovative approaches, and coalition building.

It also serves as a forum for activity, organizing conferences, debates and training seminars, publishing policy papers and reports, and initiating public awareness campaigns. The Stefan Batory Foundation also encourages solidarity and generosity by offering administration of named funds and corporate funds to support initiatives that serve the public interest.

A reborn tradition of giving

The Foundation is operating in a landscape with no shortage of actors – today, there are 55,000 associations and 8,000 foundations in the country. There is not much difference between the two. Typically, foundations are established by one person and an association by 5 to 15. There is no established tradition of grantmaking, but there is a strong tradition of giving and charity in the country as people have always given to the church.

Charities have a long tradition in Poland. The first was established in the 11th century. However, after World War Two, all independent institutions were destroyed under the communist regime. Associations, allowed by the state, were under its full control and there were no foundations operating as the law forbade their creation. But there were thriving illegal civic groups, such as those whose leaders helped launch the Stefan Batory Foundation. The rebirth of the sector started in 1989.

Executive Director Anna Rozicka notes that Polish citizens are willing to support charities that focus on people with disabilities, poverty or humanitarian assistance, but less willing to support programmes to promote civic engagement, fight corruption or strengthen the rule of law. 'This activity is new in Poland. The Poles are a generous people,' she says. 'But they are unaccustomed to giving to support activities that do not involve charity.'

The Foundation has also been receiving funds from individuals, mainly for its equal opportunities programme addressed to impoverished and disabled people. But in 2007 the Foundation received a donation of €50 for its anti-corruption programme. 'It's a very small amount, but for us even such small donations are important,' Rozicka adds.

Enhancing the role and development of civil society

The Foundation is committed to supporting the building of civil society in Poland and throughout the region. It aims to create a society in which citizens have a sense of shared responsibility for the democratic process and do not expect all their concerns to be addressed by the state but to organize themselves around their own needs, opinions and desires. To this end programmes support a variety of public initiatives, mainly independent non-governmental groups (NGOs), which are active wherever the role or capacity of the state is limited, and which contribute to increased public participation in public affairs and create equal opportunities for marginalized citizens and those with disabilities.

The Stefan Batory Foundation is the only organization in Poland providing core support to civil society organizations, says Anna Rozicka. 'Our grants are aimed to help organizations run their core activity, and can be used both for the implementation of projects and conducting their programmes and for the development of their infrastructure, improving human resource qualifications, diversifying funding sources and improving management. More than 400 organizations have been awarded one-year or multi-year core support grants. Our grantees include experienced NGOs with extensive achievements as well as relatively new organizations only beginning their activities. But all of them play a significant role and have had a vital impact on the functioning of the civil sector.'

Much attention is also focused on local communities. Acting on the premise that democracy and civil society cannot exist without active involvement of the citizenry, the Foundation disburses hundreds of micro-grants towards various civic initiatives, contributing to the establishment of many local organizations. It also conducts the 'Your vote, your choice' programme, with the aim of encouraging citizens' involvement in local community affairs, including voting in the elections.

The programme started in 2006, sparked by the low turnout at elections and an increasingly disengaged electorate – particularly young people. Poland has the lowest turnout among EU countries. The campaign conducted before the local election in 2006 involved 339 non-profits from 224 areas, including associations, foundations, student organizations, economic chambers and industry organizations. It resulted in a 5 per cent higher turnout. Before the 2007 parliamentary elections, the Foundation, in a coalition with the Federation of Polish Private Employees and the Civic Development Forum, launched a get-out-the-vote campaign addressed to young people.

'It was huge campaign supported by more than 150 local organizations from all over Poland and very well received by almost all media,' Rozicka explains. 'Our polling revealed that we reached 80 per cent of the population through the campaign and influenced 20 per cent of voters to vote.' The election turnout neared 54 per cent, the highest since 1989. Among voters 20–40 years old, the campaign's target group, the growth in turnout was quite dramatic, with over 48 per cent of that age cohort voting, whereas 32 per cent voted in 2005.'

Promoting civil liberties and the rule of law

The Foundation considers that respect for the rule of law, the transparency of public life, protection of civil liberties, minority rights, and the rights of women, children and people with disabilities, immigrants and refugees are the cornerstone of democracy, which it wants to promote in Poland and across the region. It supports projects that enhance legal or civic education and measures to improve public access to legal aid and justice. It also promotes projects to strengthen the understanding and methodology of public scrutiny of administration and the protection of the rights of individuals against any forms of abuse of power.

In 2007, the Foundation supported 14 projects that concern civic scrutiny over access to public information, use of public funds, transparency and functioning of administrative units, monitoring of prisons, access to psychiatric services, as well as monitoring of education reform. For example, it supported the Association of Leaders of Local Civic Groups to develop a web portal to collect and disseminate information about the experiences of watchdog organizations in Poland, in Central Europe and in developed democracies.

The Foundation also supported organizations and institutions providing free legal counselling, as well as lawyers' NGOs that are working to increase access to legal aid and justice, curtail discriminatory regulations and practices in Polish legislation, and increase the transparency and efficiency of the justice system. Grants were made to 14 projects that provide legal counselling to at-risk or socially discriminated against groups, use and promote mediation, and analyse the practice of pre-trial detention by Polish courts. Support was also given to the Legal Clinics Foundation and a network of Citizens Advice Bureaux that offer free legal information and advice.

Developing international cooperation and solidarity

Since the 'transformation' of the country in 1989, the Stefan Batory Foundation has been looking beyond its borders. Nations and societies should interact with and enrich each other, Rozicka explains. The Foundation supports projects that foster the exchange of experiences of political transition to democracy, build civil society, and solve social problems in Central and Eastern European countries.

According to the Foundation website: 'We are active towards rapprochement between the East and West and we object to the re-establishment of a new "iron curtain" on the eastern border of Poland.

A friendly EU border

Since 2002, the Stefan Batory Foundation has been supporting activities to liberalize the visa policy of Poland and other EU Member States towards citizens of Eastern Europe, as well as to improve the standards of border services on the EU's eastern frontier. Together with a group of NGOs from Poland, Russia and Ukraine, in 2002–03 the Foundation conducted monitoring of the Polish border crossing to record the behaviour of officers towards citizens from outside the European Community. In 2003–04, they monitored Polish visa policy, and from 2005 to 2006 they monitored EU Member States' procedures for issuing visas to citizens of Eastern Europe. The monitoring resulted in a report, *Visa Policies of the European Union Member States*, and recommendations, *Neighbours and Visas: Recommendations for a Friendly Union Visa Policy*.

We seek the strengthening of the role of civic initiative in international relations and unity in the search for democracy and human rights.'[7]

In 2006, for example, the Foundation convened a discussion of 55 experts in Warsaw. The meeting – 'Awakening? Ten days before the presidential election in Belarus' – brought together Belarusian experts and journalists as well as analysts from Poland and the Czech Republic. The discussion focused on the current situation, possible political events, and EU and EU Member States' policy towards the regime in Minsk. A similar debate was held several days after the election and a series of expert seminars on the subject were organized in other capitals, including Prague, Budapest and Bratislava.

In 2007, Stefan Batory funded 36 cross-border cooperation projects, primarily addressing Poland's eastern neighbours. Projects include cooperation between local government and civic organizations, assistance to marginalized groups, informal education, increased standards of education, and monitoring access to public information. Several projects involving organizations from different Central and Eastern European countries deal with transparency in public life, the social economy, challenges faced by people with disabilities, and development aid policy.

Most projects are implemented jointly with partner organizations from eastern countries, especially Ukraine, but also Moldova, Russia, Central Asia and Caucasian countries.

'We are the only organization in Poland that provides core support not only to organizations in Poland, but also to organizations in Ukraine and Belarus,' Rozicka explains. 'This way we reach across borders to create partnership, which strengthens the region as a whole.'

Overcoming an old enmity

There has been a long history of enmity between Russia and Poland. The Stefan Batory Foundation is determined to change that relationship by creating ties between people in an 'east-east' partnership. 'We believe there is plenty of space for the Foundation to work with civil society organizations in the Russian Federation,' Rozicka says.

The aim of the Russia in Europe project, initiated in 2006, is to inspire Polish and European dialogue about the changes occurring in Russia and EU policy towards Russia. In November 2006, an international conference on 'Putin's Russia' was organized in Warsaw, with the participation of outstanding experts on Russian affairs from Russia, Finland, France, Poland and Britain. In May 2007, the Foundation held a conference on 'EU – Russia: Energy game in common neighbourhood', during which the speakers – specialists in international relations and energy issues from the EU, Poland, Russia, Ukraine and the US – discussed the situation in the energy sector and the energy policy of Ukraine, Belarus, Moldova and Russia. In November 2007, together with the German Institute for International and Security Affairs (SWP), the Foundation organized a seminar in Berlin on 'Russia as a challenge for the EU: the German and Polish perspective', which included discussions among some 30 participants about energy issues in EU-Russian relations, Russia's attitude towards the EU and the shared neighbouring states (Belarus, Ukraine, Moldova), and Russia's role in resolving global problems.

A Batory Foundation representative was invited to take part in the recently established EU ISS Russia Task Force, run by the Paris-based European Union Institute for Security Studies. The first meeting of the group, 'Russia as a difficult EU partner', was held in April 2007. The goal of the taskforce is to exchange opinions regarding the situation within Russia, its foreign policy, and EU policy towards Russia. Participants included experts and diplomats from EU Member States and representatives of the European Council and Commission.

Creating more transparency at local level

The concept of watchdog organizations is relatively new in Poland. Located on a leafy side-street in downtown Warsaw, the new office of the Association of Leaders of Local Civic Groups (SLLGO) is abuzz with activity. Young, enthusiastic activists are eager to explain their organization's role in helping to strengthen democracy across the country by expanding civil watch over the activities of local authorities. This is done by local community members, who are trained through the Watchdog School Project.

SLLGO was launched at the end of 2003. The organization was born under the wing of the Stefan Batory Foundation's anti-corruption programme in 2000, but expanded when it empowered itself. 'We learned that it is necessary to raise public awareness by training watchdogs to operate on the local level, and the best trainers are the practitioners in this area,' explains SLLGO President Katarzyna Batko-Toluc. 'Top-down training is a good idea sometimes, but we also found it more effective to engage citizens where they live and to work with them as a follow-up of the training.'

Perhaps easier said than done, as people often have their own political agendas for engaging with local government, but over the past four years SLLGO has developed its own course based on practical experience. It includes an 80-hour training workshop covering the

The Watchdog School Project trains local community members
to monitor the activities of local authorities.

knowledge and skills required to control the activities of local government institutions.

The organization's second call for applications attracted 50 local activists, 20 of whom will be given the opportunity to take part in a course. SLLGO also provides assistance to new watchdog organizations by experienced Local Civic Group members in the form of direct and individual consultations. SLLGO's Budget Monitoring Laboratory aims to help citizens monitor the procedures related to drawing up a budget, monitor its implementation, and control budget processes better.

The objective of SLLGO's NGO Centre on Access to Public Information is to improve the practice of providing citizens with information that concerns public issues. The target groups are citizens and local administration officers. The organization fosters the development of watchdog organizations and has launched an information portal, or online resource centre, to bring together the experiences of organizations from Poland and other Central European countries. SLLGO also holds an annual seminar for watchdog organizations.

Batko-Toluc points to the 'culture of secrecy' in Polish society, which is strangely enough exposed by 'big scandals about the secrecy'. SLLGO's aim is for Poland to be as open as possible. 'Openness needs to be the rule, not the exception,' she says. 'But many people in local government authorities are threatened by civic control, they think the monitors are not well intentioned.'

She believes that the level of civic engagement is increasing across the country, and points out that in a small community there are always a few people willing to engage in civic activity. SLLGO's membership has grown to 30 watchdog organizations. 'Watchdog activity is difficult – it is hard work and is not always fruitful,' Batko-Toluc comments. 'But increasing transparency in public life is critical. For this reason, many people are very committed to engaging in watchdog work. We have people from all ages who have formed groups and we are very proud of that mix.'

Batko-Toluc notes that it took considerable work to obtain grants and support from Stefan Batory. 'We had no clear strategy, so the Foundation supported us to develop one,' she recalls. 'They gave us a lot of freedom, but kept us under control at the same time.' She describes 2005 as a 'year of trial and error', but says that today SLLGO is involved in 'real action'. Stefan Batory provides about 25 per cent of SLLGO's budget; the remainder is financed by other foundations, grants and EU programmes.

A change in direction

In its first decade of operation the Stefan Batory Foundation operated more than 30 programmes and awarded thousands of small grants and scholarships in the areas of democratic institutions, the market economy and public administration. In its second decade of operation, a new strategy was devised to prepare for Poland's EU membership. The 30 programmes were streamlined to a dozen, organized under three priority areas, and the staff was cut in half from 60 to 30. Today, the Board and staff are already working on a new strategy for 2010 and beyond.

The Foundation has enjoyed considerable support from Soros's Open Society Institute since its creation (€67 million), including €8 million for a building that the Foundation occupies and rents out. In the first decade, Soros's funds represented about 90 per cent of the Foundation's resources. From 2000 to 2007, the figure was 55 per cent. The Foundation is now focusing on growing its endowment, a project started in 2001. The initial capital of €4.4 million has grown to €34 million, thanks to support from other foundations and individual gifts as well as income from interest on investments and sales of investments.[8]

The rental income from the building pays for administration costs and contributes to the endowment. The Foundation has ambitions to boost the endowment to €40 million by 2010, to be held in a mixture of stocks and bonds and other safe instruments. The next decade will be different because the Foundation will fund projects using its own money generated by the endowment, Rozicka explains.

And so will future challenges in Poland be different.

Meeting future challenges

Rozicka sees several main challenges on the horizon. The first is that the majority of Polish youth are 'totally market oriented' and do not participate in public life. 'They don't want to be part of the democratic process,' she explains. 'You can't really blame them when you look at the quality of the country's political elites. They have no one to look up to, no role models.' To address this issue, she says, a civic education programme should be devised with new models, frameworks and tools for young people.

A second challenge is civic engagement at all levels, particularly now that Poland is within the EU framework. 'We need to be more involved in the transformation of the EU. Poland has 54 Members in the European Parliament, but it's not enough to guarantee citizen participation.' Citizens

– and politicians – need to learn how to communicate, consult and compromise as they work on decisions for the 'common good'.

She adds: 'In Poland we have quite a well-established social dialogue with government, workers and employers, but civil society in our country has always worked in opposition to the government. There has been no tradition of dialogue and no platform for dialogue in the public interest. Through dialogue, we can strengthen democracy.'

Another challenge for Poland is to build social diplomacy in the context of international relations, particularly with the Russian Federation. Rozicka believes that relationships between nations depend not only on governments but also very much on people. 'Often, people can build better bridges,' she says. 'People-to-people diplomacy is powerful.'

Rozicka says the Foundation is still 'in the process of defining its new niche' for the next decade and that she does not 'know yet the headlines'. But she is confident that the Stefan Batory Foundation will continue its legacy to be on the frontlines of change, strengthening democracy, boosting civil society and building bridges.

'A major influence'

'In the spheres of the Foundation's activity there were issues, which probably all of us encounter on an everyday basis. By educating teachers and local government employees, it stimulates local communities to work for social self-assistance. By supporting organizations acting for human rights, women's rights, ethnic minorities, by publishing numerous basic papers on freedom and democracy, the Foundation has become an important, or even main factor in Poland behind the increasing involvement of the non-government sector for transformations in our country. The Stefan Batory Foundation's activity has had a major influence on Polish politicians, on Polish institutions, and on the civic society that was shaping.'

Former Polish President Aleksander Kwasniewski praising the Stefan Batory Foundation during the ceremony of awarding George Soros the title of Man of the Year 2000, quoted in newspaper Gazeta Wyborcza, *9 May 2000.*

[1] Funds in PLN were converted into euros in March 2008. From 1998 to 2007, the Stefan Batory Foundation has distributed 11,200 grants and 5,500 scholarships for a total amount of PLN238 million and PLN80 million for projects implemented directly by the Foundation.

[2] A Russian word referring to the clandestine copying and distribution of government-suppressed literature or other media in Soviet-bloc countries.

[3] http://sg.geocities.com/theflyinguniversity/history.htm

[4] From the archives of the Stefan Batory Foundation.

[5] Andrew Purvis, *Time* Magazine, 'Volume on High', 16 April 2006.

[6] From the archives of the Stefan Batory Foundation.

[7] www.batory.org.pl

[8] US funds were converted into euros in March 2008.

DAVID WATKISS

2 Robert Bosch Stiftung
Industrial giant funding good works

The mission of the Robert Bosch Stiftung is to alleviate 'all kinds of hardship and promote the moral, physical, and intellectual development of the people'. The Foundation continues the legacy of democrat and internationalist Robert Bosch. It has provided about €850 million in funding to projects and programmes in Germany, France, Central and Eastern Europe, Turkey and the United States, and more recently in China, India and Japan.

The Bosch Group, consisting of Robert Bosch GmbH and its subsidiaries, is a leading worldwide supplier of automotive, industrial and building technology and several lines of famous consumer products. Founded by German industrialist and philanthropist Robert Bosch (1861–1942) in Stuttgart in 1886, the Bosch Group today employs about 270,000 people in more than 280 subsidiaries in more than 50 countries. The Bosch Group invests heavily in research and development and is the worldwide leader in the number of patents in the field of automotive technology.

Following the principles in Robert Bosch's will, today 92 per cent of the stock of Robert Bosch GmbH is held by the Robert Bosch Stiftung GmbH, a charitable foundation created in 1964.

The Foundation has its headquarters in Stuttgart and an office in Berlin. In 2007, its assets totalled about €5 billion. Its nine-member Board of Trustees and its staff of approximately 100 oversee approximately 800 projects each year. Annual programme and grant expenditure totals approximately €58 million. Most of this expenditure goes to the creation and operation of the Foundation's own multifaceted programmes, but some external projects are funded by grants.

Foundation support goes mainly to awards and prizes, conferences and seminars, curriculum development, fellowships, publications, scholarships and commissions.

Robert Bosch – entrepreneur and philanthropist

Robert Bosch was born in September 1861 in the village of Albeck in southern Germany, the eleventh of 12 children. According to his biographer and later West German President Theodor Heuss, Robert Bosch 'came from a wealthy peasant-bourgeois family that had never known want. The family had worked their property actively and had maintained a sense of frugality. It was natural for them to include those who were less fortunate, and they did so with a matter-of-factness that came from an inborn goodness or good nature.'[1]

Bosch attended a secondary technical school in Ulm and was then apprenticed as a mechanic. His dissatisfaction with his own education would lead him to emphasize improvement of education and apprenticeships in his activities both as an industrialist and as a philanthropist.

Bosch spent several years working for companies in Germany, in the US where he worked for Thomas Edison, and in the UK where he worked for Siemens. In 1886, he founded his Workshop for Precision Mechanics and Electrical Engineering in Stuttgart and soon made a significant and commercially successful improvement to an unpatented magneto ignition device that generates the electric spark required to ignite the fuel and air mixture in a stationary combustion engine. A year later, Bosch adapted the magneto ignition device for a vehicle engine, thereby solving one of the most significant technical challenges confronting the automobile industry. In 1902, an engineer employed by Bosch invented a high-voltage spark plug enabling the development of the internal combustion engine.

The company began international operations in 1898 and by 1913 had operations in the Americas, Asia, Africa and Australia. It continued to produce innovations for the automotive industry, such as diesel fuel injection. By the end of the 1920s, the company had evolved from a small automotive supplier into a multinational group.

Bosch's personal life mixed happiness and tragedy. He and his first wife had three children, two successful daughters and one son. His son died at the age of 30 after suffering for a decade with an incurable paralysis. His death plunged Bosch's first wife into depression. Divorce followed. Bosch

Robert Bosch as a young man.

remarried in his sixties. His second marriage was a happy one, and he and his second wife had a son and a daughter.

From the early days of his company, Bosch exhibited concern for corporate social responsibility, promoting occupational training and the wellbeing of his employees. He introduced the eight-hour workday in 1906, established a workshop for apprentices in 1913, paid high wages and provided retirement benefits, and supported industrial arbitration. His attitude towards his employees is suggested by his remark: 'I don't pay good wages because I am rich. I am rich because I pay good wages.'[2]

The philanthropist

Robert Bosch's 'virtually incomparable philanthropy'[3] began in 1910, when he made a large donation to the Stuttgart Technical University. This was followed by numerous gifts during World War One for relief efforts, hospitals, sanitary housing and public works. Bosch used the profits the company had made from armaments contracts during World War One for good causes. One philanthropic impulse stemming from Bosch's lifelong commitment to homeopathy was his gift of a hospital, Robert-Bosch-Krankenhaus, to the citizens of Stuttgart.

During his lifetime, Bosch made dozens of substantial gifts and endowments. His biographer, Theodor Heuss, analyses Bosch's attitudes and motivations as follows:

'For Bosch, what mattered was having the desire and the ability to give concrete assistance. He desired neither honor nor honors, neither power nor influence, and he was not motivated by a sentimental desire to do good deeds. The splendid freedom with which Bosch . . . would make available both small and very large sums for purposes of the common good sprang from his sovereign attitude toward money and from the sense of his duty as a citizen to make his growing wealth fruitful for the welfare of the people, in the broadest sense. Bosch's contributions were unsystematic at first; later, they came to reflect a certain type of giving. . . . [T]he breadth and variety of what Bosch accomplished is astonishing.'[4]

Robert Bosch in later years.

The democrat and internationalist

After World War One, Robert Bosch played an active role in building German democracy. He made a substantial donation to the Deutsche Liga für den Völkerbund (German Federation for the League of Nations). Concerned about the self-destructive tendencies of the Weimar Republic, Bosch became a founding member of Bund der Erneuerung des Reiches (Federation for the Renewal of the Empire), which aimed to stabilize the republic on the basis of the Weimar Constitution.

Bosch's engagement with European politics focused on reconciliation between Germany and France, a cause he supported financially and with strong personal dedication. Bosch believed that reconciliation would bring lasting peace to Europe and lead to a European economic area without customs barriers. This focus also led him to join the Pan-European Movement of Richard von Coudenhouve-Kalergi. In December 1932, Bosch appealed for international reconciliation in an article published in several newspapers.

The Nazi regime brought Bosch's peacemaking efforts to an end. His company accepted arms contracts and employed forced labour during World War Two. Robert Bosch, like many other Germans, was reduced to public silence.

Bosch, however, supported the resistance and, with his close associates, saved Jews and other Nazi persecution victims from deportation. He had a long-time commitment to German-Jewish causes.

Together with two colleagues, Bosch founded the Stuttgart branch of the Verein zur Abwehr des Antisemitismus (Association against Anti-Semitism) in 1926. From 1936 onwards, he provided support for Jewish charities. In 1937, he gave a consulting contract to Carl Goerdeler, who the conspirators that attempted to assassinate Hitler on 20 July 1944 intended should become the German Chancellor. Goerdeler maintained contact with the German resistance with Bosch's knowledge and support.

Between 1938 and 1940, Hans Walz, Bosch's private secretary and his successor as CEO of the company, donated substantial sums to the Jüdische Mittelstelle, an organization in Stuttgart that helped Jewish citizens to escape Germany. Bosch also employed victims of Nazi persecution in his factories.

Bosch's philanthropic vision

Robert Bosch died in 1942. Before his death he directed that his estate be used to alleviate hardship and promote the moral, physical and intellectual development of the people. In his guidelines, Bosch provided that his philanthropic vision be fulfilled through the promotion of 'health, education, talent, international understanding and the like'.

Rather than delegate his goals to a state-chartered and supervised charity under civil law, he entrusted his associates on the board of a non-profit company, then called Vermögensverwaltung Bosch GmbH, to serve as administrators of his will and to determine, within a statutory period of 30 years, if and when Bosch's interest in the manufacturing company would be transferred. Between 1962 and 1964, the administrators found a way to advance both Bosch's commercial interests and his philanthropic goals. Robert Bosch Stiftung, the foundation, a non-profit limited liability company, received 92 per cent of the capital stock of Robert Bosch GmbH, without voting rights; the Bosch family retained 7.99 per cent of the capital stock with 7 per cent of the voting rights, and a holding company, Robert Bosch Industrietreuhand KG, received 0.01 per cent of the capital stock and 93 per cent of the voting rights.

Thus, Robert Bosch GmbH is unusual. It is a very large and profitable privately held corporation almost entirely owned by a not-for-profit limited liability organization. Most of the profits of the corporation are reinvested to sustain future growth. Nearly all of the profits distributed to shareholders, however, are devoted to philanthropic purposes. The members of the Board of Trustees of Robert Bosch Stiftung, as shareholders, make most of the decisions regarding the deployment of the Foundation's resources.

Dieter Berg, formerly General Counsel of Robert Bosch GmbH, has served as Chairman of the Foundation's Board of Management since 2000. According to Berg, the structure of Robert Bosch Stiftung provides for great flexibility. Berg also notes the significant contribution made by Robert Bosch's heirs, who gave up most of their interest in the company at a steep discount.

Dr Christof Bosch, one of Robert Bosch's grandchildren and a Trustee of the Foundation, expresses the Bosch family's satisfaction with this structure. 'What was established in 1964 was the best approximation, the best adaptation of my grandfather's last will to the situation. We are happy that the whole thing survived and survived well.'[5] He continues:

'[My grandfather] believed that his company was his biggest contribution to society. So, the company in itself should be run in a way that really supports society. That was his primary thinking. So, when there is more profit than actually needed for the survival of the company, for the flowering of the company, or for his family to have a good life, when there is a surplus, then this should be spent for the alleviation of need, for international understanding, things like that.'[6]

The Robert Bosch Stiftung today

Consistent with Robert Bosch's vision, the Foundation's charter defines its main objectives to be the promotion of:

'Public health care, in particular through operation of the Robert Bosch Krankenhaus, the Dr Margarete Fischer-Bosch-Institut für klinische Pharmakologie [Clinical Pharmacology], and the Institut für Geschichte der Medizin [History of Medicine]; further aims: international understanding, public welfare, education, the arts and culture, and research and teaching in the humanities and the social and natural sciences.'

According to Dieter Berg, among German foundations, the Robert Bosch Stiftung devotes the largest amounts of money to promoting international understanding.

Robert Bosch Stiftung pursues its objectives through six programme areas, each with multiple focuses that change over time.[7]

Science and research

This area seeks to stimulate and support young people's interest in science and technology, raise public awareness of science, and promote dialogue between researchers and journalists. The Foundation operates research programmes on selected topics, such as sustainable use of natural resources and geriatric medicine. It is also responsible for the research conducted at the Foundation's research facilities at the Robert Bosch Hospital, the Dr Margarete Fischer-Bosch-Institute for Clinical Pharmacology, and the Institute for the History of Medicine.

Health and humanitarian aid

This area promotes health science and training in a wide range of therapeutic, social and medical-technical professions. It also focuses on the multifaceted challenges of life in old age. Humanitarian projects in Central and Eastern Europe encourage self-help through training in traditional trades, agriculture and the health and social sectors. The topics addressed include Perspectives on Health, Ageing and Demographic Shift, and Social Issues.

International relations: Western Europe, America

The Foundation's work in this area seeks to strengthen relations between Germany, on the one hand, and France, the US and Turkey on the other, as well as Japan and India. It does this through initiatives to enhance the capacity of young international leaders for international cooperation and communications. Activities include programmes for journalists, teachers and government officials.

International relations: Central and Eastern Europe

Aiming to foster understanding between Germany and the countries of Central and Eastern Europe, the Foundation focuses on culture, languages, literature, translations, higher education, academic exchange, media and information, young academic elites, youth and volunteering, and civil initiatives. Recently, programmes involving China and the Balkans have also been initiated.

Education and society

This area addresses issues regarding the sustainability of German society and institutions in light of profound demographic changes, particularly declining birth rates. Special emphasis is given to proposals to strengthen the family and early childhood education and school reform. Programmes also promote young talent from immigrant communities and integration from an educational perspective.

Society and culture
This new programme area expands on previous initiatives in migration, integration and coexistence of citizens of diverse backgrounds. The Foundation fosters civic involvement in Germany and encourages initiatives in historical-political education. It supports literature and film in an intercultural context and pedagogic cooperation between museums and schools.

The breadth of the Robert Bosch Stiftung's activities is suggested by these ongoing projects representing each of the Foundation's six programme areas.

NaT-Working: High School Students, Teachers and Scientists Network in the Natural Sciences and Technology
'The goal of NaT-Working is to inspire students with an enthusiasm for the natural sciences and technology, and to introduce them and their teachers to state-of-the-art research,' reports Dr Ingrid Wünning Tschol, Head of the Department of Science and Research at Robert Bosch Stiftung. The programme connects schools and researchers through personal partnerships forming the basis for joint projects. 'This approach undertakes school reform from the bottom up,' adds Tschol. Currently, scientists and researchers volunteer in more than 100 NaT-Working projects throughout Germany. Scientists, teachers and students test new formats that put scientific methods and new findings at the core of science teaching.

Aktion Demenz – Working Together for a Better Life with Dementia
The likelihood of developing dementia increases with advancing age. Today, as many as 1 million people in Germany suffer from the disease, a number that is rising with each passing year. In light of this pressing health challenge, the Robert Bosch Stiftung 'considers care for dementia a concern of everyone in society', notes Health and Humanitarian Aid Department Head, Dr Almut Satrapa-Schill. Working with experts, the Foundation performs international studies and training programmes to improve the competence of personal and professional caregivers and to base dementia care on firm scientific foundations.

Robert Bosch Foundation Fellowship Programme
Robert Bosch's long-time commitment to improving international understanding as a means to avoid war is continued through several Foundation initiatives. 'Perhaps the most prominent of these is the Robert Bosch Fellowship Programme for future American leaders,' observes

Dr Peter Theiner, Department Head for International Relations: Western Europe, America.

Established in 1984 at a time of difficulties in the relationship between Germany and the US, the goal of the Fellowship Programme is to foster a group of young Americans with first-hand professional experience of Germany and Europe who, in later years in leadership positions in the US, will actively promote German-American relations. Up to 20 fellowship recipients are selected each year. During a 9–12 month stay in Germany, Bosch Fellows work in their professional fields in high-level placements in the federal government and the private sector in Germany and they attend intensive seminars addressing contemporary issues facing Germany and the European Union. Eligible candidates are young Americans with a university degree, preferably in law, political science, economics or journalism, and relevant professional experience. Since its inception, the Programme has produced more than 400 Bosch Fellows.

Robert Bosch cultural managers

Under this programme, young German 'cultural managers' work for two to three years at institutions in Central and Eastern Europe. With local colleagues and supported by the German Foreign Office, they develop cultural and educational activities. Through fundraising, public relations, concept development and networking, they enhance both the institutions to which they are assigned and their own skills. German cultural managers are currently working in Romania, Poland, Czech Republic, Kosovo, Macedonia, Moldova, Slovakia, Hungary, Bulgaria and Ukraine.

In 2004, the Foundation launched a parallel programme, 'Cultural Managers from Central and Eastern Europe', under which cultural managers from Central, Eastern and South-east Europe work in institutions in Germany.

Since 2005, Robert Bosch cultural managers have also been working in institutions in Egypt, Morocco and Lebanon. According to Dr Joachim Rogall, Head of International Relations: Central and Eastern Europe Department, 'the aim is to intensify dialogue and build trust between young people from the Islamic world and the West.'

Der Deutsche Schulpreis (The German School Prize)

In 2006, the Robert Bosch Stiftung and another German foundation established by Robert Bosch's heirs, the Heidehof Stiftung, in cooperation with the German weekly Stern and the ZDF television network, created this annual prize honouring outstanding pedagogic work by German schools.

The winning school receives a €100,000 prize and four other schools each receive €25,000. Eligible schools are public and private general education institutions at all levels. A jury of experts assesses schools using six quality benchmarks: academic achievement, dealing with diversity, quality of instruction, responsibility, school culture, and the school as a learning institution.

'In addition to the monetary prize, the winning school participates in a school development academy,' notes Mr Günter Gerstberger, Department Head for the Education and Society Programme Area. 'This participation provides opportunities for mutual exchange and transfer of good practice,' he adds.

LISA – Local Initiatives to Integrate Young Resettled Ethnic Germans in Vocational Training and Professional Life
Established in 2005, the goal of the LISA competition was initially to identify and support local projects designed to help Russian-speaking young people in Germany take advantage of education and training opportunities for a smooth transition from school to professional life. According to Dr Olaf Hahn, Robert Bosch Stiftung Department Head for Society and Culture, such a transition 'is a prerequisite of successful integration'. The programme has now been broadened to include immigrants to Germany from many ethnic backgrounds. The LISA competition seeks to identify, reinforce and disseminate good local practice in professional guidance and training. Currently, the Foundation is providing support to 20 local projects through this grant programme.

The hospital and research institutes
The Robert Bosch Stiftung owns and operates a major hospital and two important research institutes. Robert Bosch endowed the Robert-Bosch-Krankenhaus in 1936; it first opened in Stuttgart in 1940. Bosch's motto for the hospital is: 'May everyone contribute for everyone's benefit.' The facilities have been remodelled several times. The Foundation and the hospital management jointly decide on medical, therapeutic and nursing strategies. The Foundation funds medical research and operations. Between 2002 and 2007, €190 million was invested in an extensive modernization project. Since 1978, the hospital has served as a teaching hospital for interns. It currently has over 850 beds and a staff of more than 1,350.

In 1973, Robert Bosch's eldest daughter endowed the Dr Margarete Fischer-Bosch-Institute for Clinical Pharmacology. The largest private

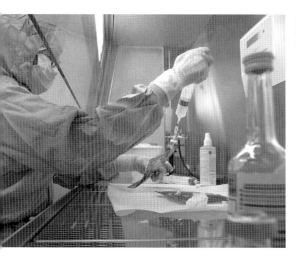

Medical research at the Robert Bosch Hospital in Stuttgart.

institution devoted to clinical pharmacology in Germany, it works in cooperation with the Robert-Bosch-Krankenhaus and external partners to improve the efficacy of pharmaceuticals. The Institute's work currently focuses on oncology and pharmacogenomics, with emphasis on leukaemia in children, inhibition of the growth of 'immortal' cancer cells, prevention of undesirable side-effects of drugs, and treatment of chronic gastrointestinal illnesses.

The Institut für Geschichte der Medizin der Robert Bosch Stiftung, founded in 1980, is the only research institute for the history of medicine in Germany not affiliated with a university. It owes its existence to Robert Bosch's keen interest in public health and homeopathy.

A large number of research projects are undertaken jointly by the Foundation, the hospital and the two research institutions. Since 1964, over €106 million has been expended on research at the hospital and the research institutes.

Addressing future challenges

As a non-partisan private foundation, the Robert Bosch Stiftung generally maintains a low profile on controversial political and economic issues. Two exceptions involve initiatives to address pressing challenges of demographic shifts in Germany and the European Union's relationship with the Balkans. In each of these two cases, the Foundation supported expert commissions charged with making policy recommendations.

Expert Commission on Family and Demographic Shift
The Foundation organized an expert commission, headed by the former
Minister President of Saxony, Professor Kurt Biedenkopf, to address
the issues underlying low birth rates in Germany. In December 2005, the
Commission published its final report recommending basic reforms to
strengthen families in Germany, including dismantling discriminatory
German tax and social security regulations, improvements in the
educational system, stronger legal safeguards for families, and measures
to help people reconcile the demands of family and professional life.

The report recommends ways to help young adults break out of
the 'biographical tailback' – the situation of 20–39 year olds confronting
decisive milestones of life relating to education, career and marriage at
the same time – that delays parenthood. The work of the Commission has
been followed by subsequent reports and recommendations, all devoted to
strengthening German families and increasing the birth rate.

International Commission on the Balkans
In 2003, the Robert Bosch Stiftung, in partnership with the German
Marshall Fund of the United States, the King Baudouin Foundation and the
Charles Stewart Mott Foundation, launched an International Commission
on the Balkans. In 2005, the Commission, chaired by former Italian Prime
Minister Giuliano Amato, published its report, *The Balkans in Europe's
Future*, presenting recommendations and a vision for the integration of the
countries of South-east Europe into the European Union.[8] The Commission
argued that 'the status quo in the Western Balkans was dangerous and
unsustainable and that European integration is the only way to bring
development and prosperity to the region.'[9] In May 2006, the Commission
issued a declaration warning the EU of the dangers of failing to give 'clear
membership perspective to the countries of the Western Balkans'. The
Commission called on the EU to 'live up to its promise' to 'offer a realistic
route for membership to the countries and societies from the Balkans'. It
urged the EU to 'develop policies that will guarantee free visas, educational
opportunities and freedom of movement for the younger generation . . . [in]
the Western Balkans'. In the absence of such measures, the Commission
warned, 'all efforts of the EU to build trust and hope in the European future
of the region are doomed to fail'.

Following up on the work of the Commission, the Robert Bosch
Stiftung, with other European foundations, including Compagnia di San
Paolo, the King Baudouin Foundation, and Die ERSTE Österreichische
Spar-Casse Privatstiftung, established the European Fund for the Balkans.

The Fund, with an annual budget of €1 million per year from 2007 through 2010, is designed to engage European foundations to become more involved in South-east Europe and prepare the countries of the region for their future in the EU. The Fund is both operational and grantmaking, supporting initiatives in Albania, Bosnia and Herzegovina, Croatia, Macedonia, Montenegro and Serbia (including Kosovo), aimed at bringing the Western Balkans closer to the EU.

Commenting on the Foundation's strategy for its work in the Balkans, Dieter Berg notes: 'We are looking to support young professionals, to establish a fellowship programme for young government officials, and to support projects promoting reconciliation between the countries of the region.'

Looking to the east

Consistent with Robert Bosch's dedication to promoting international understanding and dialogue, the Foundation, since its early days, has devoted the bulk of its funding to improving relations between Germany and other nations. The focus of these efforts has evolved with the political and economic changes that have reshaped the world over the last 40 years.

In the 1970s, the Foundation's focus was on German-French and German-Polish relations. The 1980s saw initiatives to improve German-American relations. With the fall of the Berlin Wall and the opening of countries of Eastern Europe, the Foundation launched programmes in East Germany, and Central and Eastern Europe. More recently, the Foundation has supported projects seeking to build lasting and peaceful collaboration between Germany and the Russian Federation. To date, these projects have been hindered by lack of reciprocal funding from Russian partners, notes Dieter Berg. However, he remains optimistic that the 'Russian side will improve funding in the future'.

Another recent focus is relations between Germany and Turkey. The aim of the Foundation's work is to promote intercultural exchange independent of whether or not Turkey becomes a member of the EU. A key motivation here is to promote better communications with Muslim societies.

As China, India and Japan assume ever-greater prominence in world affairs, the Foundation intends to extend its programmes in the region. 'We are looking for ways to establish sustainable programmes between these countries and Germany,' notes Dieter Berg. 'We will probably create exchange programmes for journalists, students and researchers,' he adds.

The Robert Bosch Stiftung supported the King Baudouin Foundation-led European Citizens' Consultation, which gave members of the public from all EU Member States the opportunity to debate the future of Europe. In February 2007, 200 people worked together for two days at the Berlin Federal Foreign Office to prepare the 'German Citizens' Perspective on the Future of Europe'.

Lessons learned

When Robert Bosch died in 1942, the objectives of his philanthropic vision were reasonably clear. However, given the uncertainties created by the war then ravaging Europe, the means for accomplishing those objectives were not. By entrusting his company and his vision to able administrators and a supportive family, a philanthropic organization of significant financial means and operational flexibility was created in 1964. Since then, a wide variety of good works has been supported to address changing medical, social and international challenges.

Commenting on the lessons learned during the life of Robert Bosch Stiftung, Dieter Berg and his colleagues on the Board of Management write:

'Experience teaches us that if an effort is to really have an impact and change practice, it must be carefully thought out and prepared, and requires time for its effects to unfold in the medium and long term. That is why many of our programmes evince a high level of perseverance and commitment. We shall continue to use our constructive potential in the future to help solve urgent social issues.'[10]

[1] Theodor Heuss, *Robert Bosch: His life and achievements*, translated Susan Gillespie and Jennifer Kapczynski, Henry Holt and Company, New York, 1994, pp156–57.

[2] Ibid, p380.

[3] Ibid, p162.

[4] Ibid, p165.

[5] Suzy Bibko, 'Firm foundation. Focus: Robert Bosch Stiftung, *Families in Business*, March–April 2007, p32.

[6] Ibid.

[7] *Robert Bosch Stiftung Profile*, Robert Bosch Stiftung GmbH, Stuttgart, May 2006.

[8] Available at www.balkans-commission.org/activities/Report.pdf

[9] www.balkan-commission.org/activities/n-7.htm

[10] Robert Bosch Stiftung Profile, p5.

ANNA CANTALUPPI AND DAVID WATKISS

··

3 Compagnia di San Paolo
Philanthropy and banking – four and a half centuries of service

**Founded as a lay charitable Catholic brotherhood in 1563 by seven
'very zealous citizens' of Turin, inspired to protect the Catholic
church against the threat of the Reformation and to help the needy,[1]
the Compagnia di San Paolo (Brotherhood of St Paul) for over four
centuries has had a rich, complex history of service to its city, its
region, the Italian state and the world.**

During its long history, the Compagnia has combined charitable and
banking activities and experienced several institutional transformations. In
1991, as a result of legislative changes in Italy and the restructuring of the
San Paolo Bank Group, the Compagnia became a foundation and no longer
holds a controlling interest in the privatized bank.

Today, the Compagnia is structured as a 'not-for-profit group' with
assets exceeding €9 billion. Annually, it gives approximately €150 million in
grants and spends €25 million in support of its own 'instrumental bodies'. It
operates primarily in Italy, but its activities reach across Europe and extend
worldwide, often in partnership with other foundations.

The Compagnia's broad mission today is to 'pursue goals of
social utility with the purpose of fostering civic, cultural and economic
development'[2] in the following fields:

- scientific, economic and juridical research;
- education;
- art;
- preserving and valuing cultural heritage and activities, and
  environmental resources;

- health;
- assistance to socially deprived people.[3]

This mission is advanced by grants to third-party non-profit organizations and the activities of seven permanent operating 'instrumental bodies':

- **Consorzio Collegio Carlo Alberto** was created by the Compagnia and the University of Turin in 2004. Its mission is to promote research in economics, institutions and politics and to provide postgraduate training. It has its own research fellows and professors and acts as an interface between Italian and international centres specializing in research and public affairs. These centres perform research in such areas as the economics of the welfare system, the economics of the family, labour economics, European governance, mobility and local services.
- **Fondazione per L'Arte** works in the areas of training, research and the management and promotion of cultural heritage and museum acquisitions. These activities are conducted in partnership with national and regional governments, universities and other foundations. Among other things, it has supported the Turin Egyptian Museum, organized an exhibition of treasures from Afghanistan, acquired pieces of Japanese, Chinese and Indian art for loan to the Turin Museum of Oriental Art, and supported the refurbishment of the National Museum of the *Risorgimento*.[4]
- **Fondazione per la Scuola** is the historical successor to earlier Compagnia educational entities. Today, it works in cooperation with educational bodies, national and local authorities and other organizations to bring Italian schools up to the highest European standards; to promote understanding of the European Union and the meaning of being citizens of Europe and to stimulate interest in the European project; and to enhance employment through the acquisition of knowledge and skills. The Fondazione benefits from the work of the Compagnia in other fields such as art and cultural heritage, health and scientific research.
- **Istituto Superiore Mario Boella**, founded in 2000 by the Compagnia and the Turin Polytechnic, is a centre of excellence for information and communication technologies (ICT). Its industry partners include Motorola, SKF, STMicroelectronics and Telecom Italia. Its aim is to promote interdisciplinary research, training and technological development programmes, particularly in the field of wireless technologies.

- **Istituto Superiore sui Sistemi Territoriali per l'Innovazione** (SiTI) (Advanced Institute for Territorial Systems of Innovation), established in 2002 by the Compagnia and the Turin Polytechnic, carries out research and higher education aimed at socioeconomic growth. Its areas of specialization include: cities, territories, landscape and environment, innovation and development, architecture and heritage, infrastructure and transport, and integrated security systems. With a wide range of relationships in Italy and abroad, SiTI advances strategic and innovative projects supporting economic development, environmental protection, sustainability and quality of life.
- **Ufficio Pio** (Pious Office), first established in 1595, continues the long charitable tradition of the Compagnia by providing direct relief to the poor, emergency social services and vocational training. Its work is assisted by a network of volunteers who report cases of need. The Ufficio Pio provides monetary grants to the needy, but also funds initiatives to help marginalized people achieve autonomy and reintegration into social, school and work life.
- **Human Genetics Foundation**, established with the University and Polytechnic of Turin in 2007, seeks to create a critical mass of researchers in Italy in the field of genomic research.

A long and rich history
The Brotherhood (1563–1852)
In the late 16th century, the Duchy of Savoy – later the Kingdom of Sardinia, and eventually the core of the Kingdom of Italy – included regions today called Piedmont, Savoy and the city of Nice. The Duchy straddled the present border between Italy and France to include most of the western Alps. This strategic position enabled the Duchy to play an active role in the European arena, but also exposed it to conflicts and tensions associated with the religious and political struggles that followed the Protestant Reformation. Geneva, the capital of Calvinism, was just around the corner; as was the strong Huguenot presence in south-eastern France. The only surviving medieval 'heretic' group, the Waldenses, who were to join the Protestant camp, lived in the Duchy and adjoining valleys. These valleys would later be annexed to Piedmont, establishing the only important Protestant minority in Italy.

An important fault line crossed Europe exactly here, where the Dukes of Savoy were attempting to rebuild a state – restoring public finances, redefining loyalties, reshaping power relationships and reducing

Saint Peter and Saint Paul: print from the first history of Compagnia di San Paolo, written by Emanuele Tesauro.

the autonomy of city governments – after 30 years of French domination. Duke Emmanuel Philibert was a pivotal figure. After leading the Imperial armies to victories against the French, he regained the territories ruled by the House of Savoy before the French conquest, formally establishing the capital of the Duchy of Savoy in Turin in 1563.

On 25 January 1563, amidst bitter social and religious tension, seven citizens of Turin – two lawyers, a notary, a soldier, a merchant, an artisan and a priest – founded the Compagnia. What motivated these devout Catholics to donate money and establish a new religious brotherhood is not completely clear. Piety and power, charitable impulses and a desire for social recognition have all been identified by a leading historian[5] as important motivations. The pitiful sight of growing urban poverty, associated with the inflow of immigrants from the countryside ravaged by wars, surely played a role, as did preoccupation with expansion of the Protestant Reformation.

The Catholic Church was attempting to win back the hearts and souls of the faithful through new forms of social presence and civic action.

The Compagnia's initial operations focused on poverty. Assistance to the poor and sick was provided by collecting and discreetly distributing alms. The brotherhood's increasing membership included merchants, lawyers, state officials and craftsmen. From the end of the 16th century, its activities were organized by setting up *opere* – 'operating charities'.

The first of these was the reopening in 1579 of the city's pawnbroking institute, the Monte di Pietà. This was an old tool of social assistance, established by the Franciscans in the 14th century, an early form of microcredit – providing small, interest-free loans against a pledge to social groups that would otherwise have been denied credit without incurring the sin of usury. The Monte later became the core of a fully-fledged bank that for centuries bore the name of the brotherhood and today still includes San Paolo in its name.

This early period also saw the start of assistance to women. The economic and social condition of women during those times was subordinated and vulnerable, especially on the death of the head of the family. The Casa del Soccorso (House of Relief), founded in 1589, took in 'poor girls of good families' who could not receive an education befitting their station and who risked falling victim to those who would exploit their situation. In those times, marriage was the only avenue for such girls for a decent secular life. Accordingly, the assisted young women were given a dowry at the end of their stay at the Casa.

To meet numerous requests for dowries from the poor, the Ufficio Pio (Pious Office) was set up in 1595. Soon it assumed all the Compagnia's activities of providing assistance: to the impoverished nobility; to the 'shamefaced poor' who would not beg; to the sick and to beggars; to young women for dowries and for the payment of fees to the Casa del Soccorso. Later, in 1683, the Casa del Deposito was founded to take in women who wished 'to abandon dishonesty' – prostitutes and public concubines. Over time, these two institutes for women evolved into educational establishments where paying boarders were also accepted. The instruction focused on domestic duties and religious education.

The Compagnia also supported male education. It helped establish the Collegio dei Nobili Convittori (College for the Young Noblemen) to educate the sons of the wealthy classes. The Compagnia supported the Albergo di Virtù (Hostel of Virtues) to train young beggars and those today called 'youth at risk' in mechanical and manufacturing skills according to plans to introduce silk manufacture into the Piedmont region.

In the mid-17th century Compagnia brethren helped found a charitable hospital and continued its support through management assistance, loans and gifts. In the following century, it provided a considerable sum for the building of what was known in those days as a lunatic asylum.

During the 17th century, the Compagnia gained ever-larger influence and reputation. Membership included some of the most influential members of court and government, while the bequests from leading Piedmontese families, as well as small legacies, increased its patrimony. Hundreds of donations are recorded in the Compagnia's archives. This period reflects the establishment and growth of a community foundation, where donors were motivated both by civic pride and by a religiously inspired sense of charity.

As a result of its growing wealth, the Compagnia moved beyond the financial activities of the Monte di Pietà; it began investing its endowment in real estate and stocks and making loans to the state, the city government and the aristocracy. This financial role assumed political and institutional relevance, reaching its height in 1653 when administration of the ducal public debt was entrusted to the Monte di Pietà.

By the mid-18th century, the Compagnia had attained its maximum expansion, following the parallel growth of the Savoy-Piedmont state (then known as the Kingdom of Sardinia) and the increasing importance of Turin, one of the fastest-growing Italian capitals. Thereafter, the Compagnia suffered the effects of a general economic crisis. War erupted again between 1792 and 1796 when Revolutionary France became an enemy of the Kingdom of Sardinia. Taxation imposed to cover war expenditures put a heavy burden on the Compagnia's wealth.

During the French occupation of Piedmont, which in 1800 became part of the French Empire, the Compagnia lost the management of operating charities and the possession of its property. Like many *Ancien Régime* institutions, the Compagnia became a target of Napoleonic reforms aimed at centralizing power and resources in a rational, state-controlled bureaucracy. In 1802, the venerable brotherhood was dissolved, and replaced by publicly appointed boards in charge of the various charitable operations. However, several members of the new Beneficence Committees were former Compagnia officers, who helped ensure continuity with their previous experience. The Monte di Pietà was reopened in 1804 and reorganized along the lines of the Parisian Institute, which had a stronger banking emphasis.

With the restoration of the House of Savoy in 1814, the Compagnia reacquired its functions and properties, with an important change that enabled some of the features of the Napoleonic reforms to survive. A

The interior of the Opere Pie di San Paolo headquarters in via Monte di Pietà in the early 20th century.

pawnbroking institute that charged interest was established, alongside the old interest-free Monte. As the Uffcio Pio resumed its charitable assistance activities, the Compagnia was entrusted from 1814 to 1851 with providing health services to the poor of the city of Turin. These services were not limited to basic medical treatment, as in traditional public health structures, but included pharmaceutical and specialist services.

Opere Pie di San Paolo (1852–1932)

Having survived almost three centuries, the Compagnia went through a profound transformation during the Italian *Risorgimento*.[6] With the spread of liberal ideas and the new Constitution of 1848, Turin's secularized political circles came to believe that religious congregations should be dissolved and their properties confiscated to serve public purposes. In 1852, King Victor Emmanuel II decreed that the Compagnia's activities be restricted to the religious sphere, and entrusted its endowment and the management of its charitable services and credit activities to a board appointed mainly by public bodies.

This new entity, with a strong sense of historical continuity, the Opere Pie di San Paolo (Charitable Institutions of Saint Paul), gave greater impetus to the credit sector. Giovanni Giolitti, the future great Italian statesman, was appointed a Royal Commissioner of the Opere in 1879. He described the Monte di Pietà as a fully-fledged credit institute, with a regular current accounts service, in which pledge-based loans represented less than one-tenth of the business. In 1867, the Opere commenced mortgage lending operations. This move, which coincided with agrarian reform and the expansion of building activity in the city of Turin, inaugurated a sector that would have an important role in the bank's later business.

The Opere Pie di San Paolo began a period of rapid expansion which coincided with the industrial development of Turin and Piedmont. The institution's policies were prudent and conservative, allowing it to pass unscathed through the 1887–94 financial crisis and the great crash of 1929. In 1928, the government recognized the Monte di Pietà as a 'prevalently banking business'. The institution provided loans to public bodies, especially municipalities, and participated in new financial organizations, such as the consortium for grants for industrial development, the federal institute for agricultural credit for Piedmont, and the national consortium for agricultural improvement credit.

At the end of the 1920s, the international economic crisis caused the bankruptcy of several Piedmontese industrial groups and the banks that financed them. For the Opere Pie di San Paolo, the crisis was an opportunity for growth, permitting it to acquire branches of a failed bank in Piedmont, Liguria and western Lombardy.

While its banking business grew, San Paolo's philanthropic activities continued and were transformed. After the institutional change in 1852, the Ufficio Pio converted legacies for dowries into educational grants. The Monte di Pietà paid out part of its income to support Turin institutions, many of which were involved in vocational training, essential to the growth of Turin as a manufacturing centre.

In 1883, the Casa del Soccorso and the Casa del Deposito, the two long-standing educational organizations which had merged in the mid-1800s, became known as the Educatorio Duchessa Isabella. The Educatorio offered girls a full education from primary school to high school. Turin then had the highest literacy rates in the country. In the rest of recently unified Italy, however, the obligation to send children to primary school was often ignored, especially for girls, partly because of the lack of teachers. To meet this need, in 1899 the Educatorio started offering courses for training women as primary school teachers. These teachers took positions throughout Italy, starting a national educational system.

The Credit and Philanthropy Institute and the Bank (1932–91)
In 1932, the Fascist Government recognized San Paolo's importance to the national economy and the public interest by granting it the status of a 'public-law credit institute'. The new name, Istituto di San Paolo di Torino, Credito e Beneficenza (Credit and Philanthropy), reflected the persistence of the institution's dual mission. By now San Paolo's philanthropic and charitable activities were mostly in the form of grants, in a variety of sectors, from medical research to the arts and culture, from social assistance – where the old operating institutions were still active – to the support of universities.

Health

On the walls of Turin's largest hospitals are numerous marble plaques in memory of generous benefactors. The name San Paolo appears with particular frequency. For the Mauriziano Hospital, San Paolo disbursements became particularly intense in the post-World War Two period. For the Ospedale Maggiore, San Paolo's most important support occurred in 1925 with the bank's participation in the consortium for the construction of the hospital's new premises. San Paolo's substantial contribution to the consortium was disbursed with extreme rapidity, as the bank considered the hospital issue of 'vital and immediate importance'. San Paolo also routinely supported Turin's maternity hospital, children's hospital and Provincial Anti-Tuberculosis Consortium.

These 20th century activities had important precedents from the first half of the 19th century, when the City of Turin delegated to the Compagnia home medical assistance to the poor and the distribution of medicines. During the same period, the Compagnia also set up the Eye Hospital and the Rickets Institute.

Social commitment

In the early 20th century, San Paolo provided loans to the City of Turin and the province for infrastructure and the delivery of essential services. It also supported vocational and technical training for workers, low-cost housing and protection of workers. It financed the association for helping injured workers. It undertook an initiative to assist widows of workers with young children by building small houses in the San Paolo district to accommodate the most stricken families. In 1907, the Istituto Case Popolari was set up to build more than 8,000 rooms in various quarters of Turin and the Opere Pie di San Paolo provided a substantial grant for the initial capital. These disbursements ran parallel to San Paolo's traditional support through alms, educational grants and disbursement to nurseries, schools, charities, hospitals and homes.

After World War Two, San Paolo dropped from its name the reference to philanthropy and added instead the adjective 'bancario', thus becoming the Istituto Bancario San Paolo di Torino. This name change reflected the fact that banking operations had experienced a large-scale expansion both at a national and international level to the point that San

Paolo had become one of the most important Italian banking groups. Yet, philanthropic activities also expanded. San Paolo – still without shareholders, still a semi-public institution with a dual mission – earmarked a considerable part of its profits for philanthropy. Some representative activities are noted in the boxes below and on p61.

Culture, art and science

In 1985, the Fondazione San Paolo di Torino per la Cultura, la Scienza e Arte (San Paolo Foundation for Culture, Science and Art) was established. It was set up to coordinate and integrate the philanthropic efforts of the Istituto de San Paolo with a separate endowment. Among its most significant projects were the extensive renovations of Turin's Egyptian Museum and the Superga Basilica, a baroque masterpiece, also in Turin.

The Fondazione provided significant funding for what can be described as a full-scale salvage operation of the Abbey and Hamlet of San Fruttuoso di Camogli, in the Province of Genoa, preserving this jewel of medieval art and architecture for the enjoyment of present and future generations.

The Fondazione also organized a series of highly successful international conferences on the environment attended by scientists and researchers from all over the world with wide dissemination of their proceedings for schoolchildren and the general public.

The Fondazione financed the restoration of the Superga Basilica in Turin.

The Foundation (1991 to the present)

At the end of 1991, under new Italian legislation, San Paolo's two missions were divided. The bank became a joint-stock company. By 2007, after a series of mergers and acquisitions, it was known as Intesa Sanpaolo, one of Europe's largest banking groups. The Compagnia was reborn in the form of a private foundation to meet the new needs of civil society. In a way, the historic dualism between the Compagnia and the Monte di Pietà, owned by the brotherhood, was reintroduced. The initial sole owner of the new bank, in 1991, was the foundation. Since 1991, privatization has reduced the Compagnia's stake in the banking group to less than 10 per cent. There is now strict separation between the bank and the foundation. There are no overlapping affiliations among board or staff and the foundation plays no active role in the bank's management.

The Compagnia today

According to its General Secretary, Piero Gastaldo, the work of the Compagnia is guided by certain core values: 'subsidiarity, solidarity and social creativity, the opening of areas of freedom, promotion of live opportunity, and being aware and responsible for one's own future'.

In addition to providing financial resources, the Compagnia provides 'leadership in planning and design; it acts as a catalyst, an inter-institutional cooperation engineer, a convener of organizations and a project promoter,' he notes.

Approximately 85 per cent of the Compagnia's expenditure goes to grants. The remaining 15 per cent finances the work of the Compagnia's seven operating 'instrumental bodies', which undertake programmes consistent with and supportive of the foundation's mission and grantmaking activities. The Compagnia operates its own programmes, Gastaldo explains, in situations where it believes it can perform more effectively than grantees. He argues that the foundation can be a better grantmaker because it has operational experience from working in the field.

Because of the link between philanthropy and banking in Italy up to the 1990s, some members of the Compagnia's management team – like the management of other Italian former banking foundations – have a banking background. This connection leads to higher professionalism, argues Gastaldo: 'Banking skills are similar to the skills needed for grantmaking.'

The Compagnia spends more on European and international projects than other Italian foundations, he notes. This is based on the belief that in today's interconnected world, 'it is necessary to connect the local with the global to achieve good locally.'

Supporting scientific, economic and juridical research

The Compagnia currently finances more research than any other foundation in Italy. In the field of scientific research, funding focuses on science and technology centres of excellence and on scientific dissemination, principally involving the life sciences, nanotechnologies and microstructures, and information and communication technology.

In addition to major grants to research institutes and universities, the Compagnia's Istituto Superiore Mario Boella and Human Genetics Foundation work in this sector.

The economic and juridical research funded by the Compagnia stresses international relations, European integration, globalization, human rights, public policy, economic development, cities, territorial systems, and foundations and non-profit institutions. The Compagnia's instrumental bodies, Collegio Carlos Alberto and SiTI, contribute to these efforts.

As part of its work in international relations, the Compagnia, with other partners, recently supported two widely disseminated surveys. *Transatlantic Trends* monitors public opinion in the US and 12 European countries on issues such as global threats, foreign policy objectives, world leadership, multilateral institutions, civil liberties and the EU. The *European Elite Survey* compared the attitudes of the general public to those of MEPs and European Commission officials on such questions.

Another initiative in this area is the Compagnia's support, together with two other European foundations, of the European Foreign and Security Policy Studies (EFSPS) Research and Training Programme. According to Nicolò Russo Perez, Compagnia's Programme Officer for Economic, Juridical and Social Research, the aim of EFSPS is to 'enhance the qualifications of the next generation of European leaders' in this area. EFSPS currently provides grants to more than 90 researchers, notes Perez. It also organizes conferences and seminars and funds publications.

Active support for education

Working with its institutional bodies and through grants, the Compagnia seeks to improve the university system in Italy by promoting centres of excellence, building facilities, and supporting postgraduate training. In addition to postgraduate scholarships at the University of Turin, the Compagnia funds undergraduate scholarships for foreign students at the Turin Polytechnic. It also funds projects involving syllabus teaching, distance learning, intercultural approaches to education, and training of staff for teaching students with disabilities.

The Fondazione per la Scuola works with education institutions, national and local authorities, and others active in the school education sector to bring Italian schools closer to the highest European standards and to promote understanding of the European Union, its future prospects, and the meaning of being citizens of Europe.

Widespread support for the arts

The Compagnia's multifaceted work in the arts includes projects for the conservation of Italy's architectural, historical, artistic and environmental heritage and exhibits, events and publications. Among the most significant is the Museum Programme, a multi-year project designed to contribute to the urban, economic and social development of Turin. It involves restoration of existing museums and support for exhibits and performances.

Through its Fondazione per l'Arte, the Compagnia provides training, including advanced degrees, in restoration technology, in museum, cultural institution and heritage site management, and in Egyptology. In a creative approach to mission investing, the Fondazione per l'Arte acquires artistic masterpieces which it loans on a long-term basis to Turin area museums to enrich their collections. A major goal of the Museum Programme and related activities, notes Dario Disegni, Head of Cultural Affairs and Institutional Relations for the Compagnia, is to make Turin a major cultural tourism destination. In order to do so, according to Disegni, there is a need to assist the museums to present new exhibitions 'to keep the tourists coming back'.

Promoting culture

The Compagnia supports music, theatre and cinema through grants to the major performing arts institutions in Turin, as well as institutions in Genoa and Naples. It also funds the conservation and promotion of libraries and archives throughout Italy. Working with partners such as the European Cultural Foundation and the Network of European Foundations Cultural Cluster, the Compagnia supports international projects for research and dissemination of culture. It also supports a masters degree programme for students from developing countries devoted to cultural projects for development.

Health-related activities

The Compagnia's health-related activities focus on primary and secondary prevention, illnesses during childhood development and in elderly patients, and health and cooperation. Supported projects aim at fighting thyroid cancer, menopause complications, diabetes and depression. International programmes fund the fight against illness with major social impacts in developing countries, including projects of Médecins sans Frontières and Emergency to combat tuberculosis and develop heart surgery facilities in Guinea and Sudan.

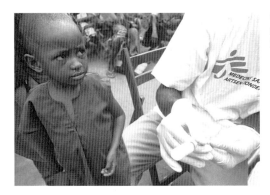

Compagnia di San Paolo supports the fight against tuberculosis in Guinea.

The Compagnia's multiyear Oncology Programme provided over €50 million in funding for the research, prevention and treatment of cancer.

A long tradition of social welfare activities
The Compagnia's long tradition of providing aid to socially deprived categories of people finds expression today in activities to support independent living, home-based care and young people. 'Social vulnerability is the cross-cutting issue today,' notes Piero Gastaldo. Funded projects seek to address difficulties in access work, housing and entitlements, focusing on social microcredit and the reintegration into society of adult former prison inmates, youths involved in the juvenile justice system and people with mental health problems.

Other supported projects promote home-based care services both to create jobs and to improve the quality of life of people needing care and others in their households.

Combating the inter-generational transmission of inequality and poverty is the aim of a number of Compagnia projects. Some seek to support single-parent families, while others foster social cohesion. One of these is the Youth Empowerment Partnership Programme, started in 2001 by the Compagnia and other European and US foundations, the Network of European Foundations and the OECD. Aimed at youth living in difficult neighbourhoods in cities in Italy, Belgium, Finland, Germany, Bosnia, Ireland and Brazil, the programme seeks to increase opportunities by creating groups of young people who can plan projects to enhance their skills and potential.

From charity to banking to philanthropy – pursuing social justice
In its present legal form, the Compagnia has existed only since the early 1990s, but it retains close connections to the brotherhood founded in Turin

in 1563 to help the poor. From that brotherhood's activities arose banking operations, initially merely as an operating arm for the charitable activities. Italian foundations of banking origin, like the Compagnia, are now 'returning to civil society'.[7]

Franco Grande Stevens, Chairman of Compagnia's Management Committee, recently articulated this vision of the role of foundations in the modern world:

> 'The role of foundations is to pursue social justice. Thus, foundations must never make decisions in homage to or out of fear of the powerful; they must defend their independence and their wealth; they must operate according to the ethics of social responsibility and not be governed by pursuit of speculative profit or power.'[8]

Italian 'former banking foundations'

Under reforms enacted in Italy during the 1990s, long historical connections between banking and charitable organizations were severed. The new laws required banks to transfer their banking operations to joint stock companies and to turn themselves into foundations to pursue public interest or socially oriented activities.[9]

The 89 former banking foundations in Italy, thus created, today have total assets in excess of €50 billion. These institutions are 'private legal non-profit entities endowed with full statutory and managerial autonomy'. They operate in a mixed way, but mostly as grantmakers, in the fields of education and research, art and culture, health and welfare, environment and economic development. These organizations have strong ties to their cities and regions, but, like Compagnia di San Paolo, are now expanding the focus of their activities.

[1] Compagnia di San Paolo Newsletter, No 13, October 2002, available at www.compagnia.torino.it.

[2] Planning Guidelines for 2005–2008, Compagnia di San Paolo, Turin, 2006, p15.

[3] Report 2006, Compagnia di San Paolo, Turin, 2007.

[4] The Risorgimento (resurgence) was the period in mid-19th century Italian history characterized by cultural nationalism and political activism leading to the unification of the Kingdom of Italy.

[5] Sandra Cavallo, Charity and Power in Early Modern Italy. Benefactors and their motives in Turin, 1541–1789, Cambridge, Cambridge University Press, 1995.

[6] See note 4, above.

[7] Profile, Compagnia di San Paolo, Turin 2002, p15.

[8] Report 2006, Compagnia di San Paolo, Turin 2007.

[9] See G Grasso, Foundation Law in Italy: Focus on banking foundations, available at http://www.efc.be/cgi-bin/articlepublisher.pl?filename=GG-SE--G-1.html

GOTTFRIED WAGNER

4 European Cultural Foundation
Promoting diversity, Europeanization and culture

**The European Cultural Foundation (ECF) is an independent
non-profit organization that promotes cultural cooperation in
Europe. Founded in Geneva in 1954 to support the cultural and
human dimensions of European integration, ECF believes that
cultural diversity is a resource. It seeks to contribute to a political
culture in Europe that is based on mutual respect and to bring
people closer together through cultural cooperation and creative
activities. The Foundation's emphasis on cultural concerns is
based on their importance in maintaining human rights and
democracy.**

How it all began – reflecting aspirations for a better future

Founded in 1954, the European Cultural Foundation (ECF) is probably the
oldest, if not the only, pan-European foundation. At the time of post-World
War Two reconciliation, when the economic and political futures of
European countries were increasingly being seen as interdependent, a
group of prominent European personalities – including philosopher Denis
de Rougemont, Robert Schuman, HRH Prince Bernhard of the Netherlands,
Hendrik Brugmans and Joseph Retinger – took the creative and prescient
step of establishing an independent foundation that would focus on
the cultural aspects of this burgeoning interdependence. Thus was the
European Cultural Foundation born in Geneva, Switzerland, the native
country of de Rougemont.

　　Its founding by a philosopher, a prince, a politician and a
businessman reflected the political and moral aspirations for a better

Robert Schuman, a Luxembourg born German-French politician and ECF's first president, is also regarded as one of the founders of the European Union.

future for the continent after World War Two. In the intervening years it has contributed to some remarkable intellectual and political debates and helped instigate real change in certain areas of policies and politics.

At the same time, the ECF has been a refuge for those who would struggle to find support elsewhere, even on a small scale. Most of the ECF's resources over the past six decades have been directed towards grassroots projects, supporting students, artists, cultural NGOs and others.

Although only one field of activity was reflected in the name of this new NGO, the declared aim was to promote and support 'cultural, scientific and educational activities on a European level'. All of its founders regarded the fledgling organization as one means of helping to further European integration. The Foundation's first president was one of the principal architects of the European Economic Community, Robert Schuman. In a decisive appointment for the Foundation's future, he was succeeded in 1955 by Prince Bernhard of the Netherlands, who remained at the helm for 22 years.

A move to Amsterdam followed in 1960. The organization's links with the Dutch royal family, which continue to this day, proved crucial in securing the ECF's future, as income from the Dutch lotteries BankGiro Lottery and The Lotto (received by agreement via the Prince Bernhard Cultural Foundation) have long been the ECF's principal source of income – though recent years have seen a marked increase in non-lottery income, from private partners such as foundations as well as public partners such

Plan Europe 2000

The ECF's Plan Europe 2000, spanning the late 1960s to mid-1970s, led to the creation of educational and cultural institutes, including the European Institute of Education and Social Policy, whose research into student mobility was vital in the setting up of education programmes such as Erasmus. The European Commission entrusted the ECF with the task of managing the educational programmes Erasmus (1987–95), Eurydice (1980–2001) and Tempus (1992–93).

as Member States and the EU. Most if not all observers would agree that the Dutch establishment link has not prevented the ECF from championing the artistic avant-garde or focusing much of its energy all across Europe, and today even beyond the borders of the enlarged EU, including the Mediterranean neighbours.

In those early days, most of the Foundation's funds were directed at developing a grants programme. This had a very modest beginning, with an annual budget in its first ten years hovering around €50,000 to €75,000 (in today's currency). Between 1960 and 1970, the average number of projects supported each year was just 17. In 1973 a new rule came into force, stipulating that 21 per cent of the gains from the Dutch General Lottery would go to cultural activities in the Netherlands. As a beneficiary, the Foundation's future suddenly looked brighter, and as the 1970s drew to a close the ECF's grants scheme became more generous and established. The range and geographical spread of supported projects has broadened considerably to 56 countries today, and the average annual spend on ECF grants is now around €1.5 million.

Responding to dramatic changes

From the early 1980s, the ECF became increasingly active in Eastern Europe, and so was well placed to react to the dramatic changes that took place in that region at the end of the decade. Cross-Mediterranean cooperation also became an ECF priority, as shown by its support for the translation of Arab authors into several European languages and its help in establishing the Roberto Cimetta Fund for cultural mobility between Europe and the region. The ECF continues to support this fund, and has recently expanded its Euro-Mediterranean activities with the setting up of a Mediterranean reflection and publication process involving cultural experts from the region, and in its role as the coordinator in the Netherlands for the Anna Lindh Euro-Mediterranean Foundation for the Dialogue between Cultures.

The new millennium saw the ECF venture into the field of cultural capacity development, especially in South-east Europe, a region severely shaken by a tragic recent history, with the Policies for Culture and Kultura Nova programmes. These programmes helped to professionalize independent cultural organizations in the region and bring artists, culture professionals and public administrators together locally to shape cultural policymaking in a spirit of collaboration. Based on these trajectories, comprising research, practice, training, democratic policy development and publishing work, the ECF's capacity development activities have recently

Projects in Central and Eastern Europe

An example of this was the East-West Parliamentary Practice Project, which allowed for the sharing of expertise between Western parliamentarians and the newly elected parliamentarians of Central and Eastern Europe (CEE). The ECF also provided much-needed support for cultural mobility in CEE, with its travel scheme APEXchanges, a precursor of its current Europe-wide travel fund STEP beyond. Another initiative, launched in Oxford in 1986 and known today as the Fund for Central and East European Book Project, supported the translation of contemporary works from a region rich in major intellectual and literary movements.

South-east Europe and the Baltic region were the geographical focus of the influential programme, Art for Social Change, which the ECF ran in partnership with the Soros Foundation Network. This aimed at getting marginalized young people active and involved in society through creative work with highly committed professional artists. The ECF's current and geographically more wide-ranging arts project, ALMOSTREAL, has expanded the notion of art for social change to 'art in context', which contributes to a contemporary artistic understanding of diversity. It works in many regions of Europe and beyond. For instance, it has supported the creation and dissemination of the work of young video artists in Lebanon.

spread their influence beyond the Balkans, for example into the Anatolian region of Turkey, Moldova, Kaliningrad and Ukraine.

The prospect of ten new Member States joining the European Union in 2004 prompted the ECF to prepare a cluster of seminars and other activities – called Enlargement of Minds – around the cultural ramifications of EU enlargement. The increasing diversity that resulted from enlargement and global migration within the European Union was one factor in the ECF's decision to focus its work on the 'experience of diversity and the power of culture', a *leitmotif* for the years to come.

Among the most notable initiatives of the past five years is the creation of LabforCulture – a knowledge-sharing and service platform dedicated to European cultural cooperation – which the ECF set up in an innovative partnership with public and private bodies. Continued investment in LabforCulture will benefit all those who create and collaborate across borders in Europe. It provides access to the most relevant information in the sector of transnational cultural collaboration, and uses the web.2 tools in a shared social networking space.

Another important initiative is 'theoneminutesjr', a partnership that facilitates the making and broadcasting of video art by young people across Europe. This initiative will culminate in 2008 in the biggest-ever festival for young video artists from diverse backgrounds. Called Stranger, the festival has been chosen as one of the flagship projects of the EU in the 2008 year of intercultural dialogue, and supported by DG Education and Culture, as by many others. Impact is achieved through a vast network with public and private broadcasters, and research conducted by Demos, the independent UK think-tank.

The ECF has changed over the years into a hybrid of a grantmaking and operating foundation. This is unsurprising when one considers that foundations have increasingly become actors in and initiators of social development. Given its original remit, it was never really on the cards that the ECF would simply be a sponsor of projects or a charity provider.

A non-political political actor

In terms of assets and budgets, the ECF is relatively small. According to some definitions it is not a foundation at all, because it has no endowment. Yet it has been disproportionately influential. Its main strength has resided in its networks of European 'believers' who have committed their time and energy to such a transnational cause, and in its leverage capacity, unlocking energies and funds for important projects in difficult geographic or thematic areas.

It could be argued that the ECF has made the seemingly impossible – European integration through culture – a bit less impossible. Everyone appears to agree that what matters finally is culture, that the glue that can unite Europeans is culture rather than markets or regulations. But Sunday sermons aside, we may well ask: 'What is Europe? And what is culture? And what or whose cultural diversity do we refer to when we "celebrate" unity in diversity?' The ECF has always sought to show concretely what it means to bring people together across borders and boundaries, and has promoted favourable conditions for 'making Europeans'.

While defending its total independence from states, political factions and denominational groups, the ECF has always affirmed a strong set of values and aspired to translate these into practice. Human rights, democracy, the rule of law, respect for cultural diversity, social responsibilities: these are, after all, the classical achievements of European enlightenment and of liberal and social movements.

Deeply motivated by the wish to overcome the catastrophes of the 20th century, the ECF's founders were among those who began the process of integrating Europe, creating the first-ever voluntary, intergovernmental and supranational experiment for intertwining interests to an extent that national divides, hatred and wars would become virtually impossible.

As a civil society organization, the ECF has always collaborated with those institutions that share the same community-building values and aspirations for the common good across traditional borders. These have included the Council of Europe and the EU institutions. Today, the ECF remains a partner of these institutions, one that is critical and independent, making the citizens' voice heard, but also a partner that is loyal to the historical adventure of creating a post-national democracy that seeks to establish peace across the globe.

Building frameworks for cooperation

Despite Jean Monnet's alleged saying (that if he were to start again he would start with culture), the post-World War Two 'Europeanization' was rightly based on the intertwining of economic interests. This resulted in a political community based on shared interests rather than cultural issues. However, visionary thinkers and doers anticipated the need to redefine the notion of a cultural 'commonwealth' against ideologies of all kinds. They can be said to have invested in cultural actors of change.

Several stages of engagement can be identified in the history of the ECF – education, media, environment, arts, the intercultural – each of them marked by an attempt to increase cooperation. The ECF's networks allowed the Foundation to advance its cultural objectives in partnership with private and public agents, by founding or supporting new institutions and initiatives as well as managing European programmes.

Having harvested the fruits of these various coalitions, the ECF moved on to the one field where European policies are still dramatically underdeveloped: providing proper frameworks and conditions for cultural and artistic cooperation, with effective cultural policies for a diverse and cohesive European Union. Despite the challenges of diversity and the 'culturalization' of difference being dramatic and obvious to all, the European Union has remained restricted to playing only a marginal role in addressing these challenges.

We had arrived at cultural policies by default, structured principally by the market; and while the pace of globalization speeds up rapidly, Europe continues to pursue national patterns of 'cultural diplomacy' rather than adopting a joint stance. This state of affairs has prompted the ECF to work simultaneously in two areas of action: providing support for cultural cooperation and for cultural policy development.

Committed to Europe and the cultural project of integration

The ECF is neither a 'national' foundation like the Fondation de France nor a company foundation; it is committed to Europe rather than a city or a region. It is not a community foundation, nor is it endowed; it is private, working for the public benefit at European level. This is surely a unique set of circumstances among the family of foundations in Europe – made even more distinctive because it is all made possible by the generosity of one EU country, the Netherlands.

Being aware of the need to strengthen civil society in Europe, and using the ECF's European mandate, previous ECF leaders played an essential role in founding coalitions, not the least among foundations in Europe. Thus, the ECF became instrumental for foundations' groupings such as the European Foundation Centre and the Network of European Foundations for Innovative Cooperation (NEF).

And how about private-public alliances? The ECF could only become a catalyst and instigator through partnerships with other actors, private and/or public actors, cultural networks, specialist institutions and Member States of the European Union. For this reason, the ECF has never been troubled by an issue that concerns other foundations – whether and to what extent a foundation should remain 'austere' or whether it should complement and partner public agencies. Nor has the ECF (which was genuinely European from the outset) had to grapple with the issue that other foundations have been pondering ever since the late 1980s: how to go beyond their remits and organize themselves at European level.

However, the challenges of such a special position cannot be overlooked. The ECF has had to depend not only on the opportunities thrown up by circumstance, but also on the strategic insight of others and their willingness and preparedness to be supportive of the ECF's goals. This situation reflects the precariousness of a transnational, trans-cultural foundation in a world that still functions according to other mechanisms.

In addition, making the case for culture and the arts is easier at local, regional or even international/cosmopolitan levels; it is still not self-evident at European level. Astonishingly, perhaps, the ECF has retained trust while remaining a 'provoker', managing to catalyse reflection and action for the cultural dimension of the European integration process in a globalizing world.

Meeting today's challenges

The ECF has always adapted its objectives and modes of working to the needs of the European environment and its own potential. The

'Europe will be cultural or it will not be' – banner on the theatre
in Freiburg, Germany.
Mascha Ihwe

ECF's mission as an independent foundation is clear and has remained
unchanged: to help achieve, through collaboration in arts and culture,
those European aspirations that are shared by Europe's citizens – a fair,
democratic, inclusive and united Europe, based on respect for diversity and
human rights.

However, the ECF's methods of achieving its objectives have varied
according to its particular strengths at particular times. Today, the ECF is
best able to contribute to the cultural commonwealth of Europe's citizens
by supporting excellence, using its unique position to act as a facilitator, a
civic convenor and a supporter of platforms for networking and connecting
the grassroots and public actors for the common good in Europe.

Europe is tremendously rich in its diverse cultures. It keeps alive and
develops its heritage. Production in the arts in Europe is at a high level and
the sharing of and participation in cultural expression has probably never
been so wide-reaching. Yet there are serious challenges and shortcomings
that affect producers, audiences and society. There is underdeveloped
potential and there are new mechanisms of exclusion.

While cultural policies do exist on the ground, and do function in
many cases, cultural policies at European level are almost wholly arrived
at by default. Cultural policies have always played a rather limited role
in liberal societies and in the EU: content is less of an issue than the
negotiation of framework conditions and allocation of resources. Even so,

European policy frameworks for culture are remarkably underdeveloped, even compared with education policies.

None the less, policies affecting art, media and culture define political interventions in a strategic context according to the agreed political culture. The contemporary challenges facing European integration are interrelated with the challenges facing the development of arts and culture in Europe. All are aspects of the emerging European citizenship.

Europe responds

Since 1989, and much more notably since 9/11 and 2004's EU enlargement, culture has become an important issue. Responding to this trend, the European Commission announced two new instruments: the designation of 2008 as the European Year of Intercultural Dialogue and the Communication on a European Agenda for Culture in a Globalising World, adopted by the European Council in December 2007. Despite the limited additional means and the somewhat symbolic approach of the 2008 initiatives, it had a mobilizing effect on the cultural sector in partnership with other sectors. The Communication – significantly the first policy document on culture and Europe since the Maastricht Treaty – points the way towards a new means of achieving joint action through the 'open method of coordination', a cooperative approach between the Commission and Member States that is both structured and flexible.

These developments are more than merely technical adjustments by the European Union in response to a developing trend. They have helped to focus minds in the cultural and foundation sectors, which can now act – and act responsibly – as genuine political players on the European stage. One flowering of this new responsibility is a cross-sector alliance co-initiated by the ECF, the Civil Society Platform for Intercultural Dialogue, supported by NEF. There has also been public and private support expressed for an artistic mobility campaign launched by civic actors including the ECF, which seeks to create a pilot mobility scheme that will hopefully become a fully-fledged programme.

Other welcome developments include the lessening of the bureaucratic burden on applicants to the new generation of the EU's culture programme, as well as the first concerted efforts towards securing a cultural dimension to its external policies. Even so vast and politically loaded a subject as a possible EU cultural foreign policy can be influenced by a small independent foundation. The ECF has been at the forefront of commissioning research and organizing high-level conferences on this subject. In addition, through its work in relation to the Balkans, the

Mediterranean and Eastern Europe, the ECF also advocates the inclusion of cultural components in the European Union's Neighbourhood Policy.

Civil society engagement is crucial

Vigilance is required. One must remain constructively critical in assessing recent EU initiatives and documents, especially when it comes to gauging the real impact of this 'mainstreaming of culture'. However, the goals are being set.

Much work will have to be done at Member State level. Some Member States are opposed to any enhanced complementary European action. Still, the very nature of culture offers realistic optimism: 'The roots of culture's ability to draw in bystanders, sceptics and even adversaries lie in [another] fundamental social difference between the arts and other activities – they trade in meanings.'[1]

Projects for the European Year of Intercultural Dialogue

The Stranger Festival

Created by the ECF, Stranger Festival has been chosen as one of the seven flagship projects for the European Year of Intercultural Dialogue 2008. This international video festival, taking place in Amsterdam in July 2008, will bring together several thousand young people to show and share their views of the world through video. Other activities include video workshops, an interactive website, DVD, travelling exhibition, Europe-wide debates, industry meetings and a video competition.

The work will be shown for its intrinsic merits and as a starting point for a debate that is critical in today's MySpace and YouTube world of instant communication with little analysis. Young people demonstrate their mastery of new media, so now is the time to talk about what is being expressed. At Stranger Festival, the debate will be led by young people themselves.

By placing individual visions in a large transnational context, Stranger Festival hopes to encourage a sense of European belonging among young people of very different cultural backgrounds.

www. rhiz.eu

Rhiz.eu was created as a bridge between the many different and diverse cultural communities across Europe. It is a space where people in arts and culture can 'discover, tell, share, play'. People can get in touch with one

Private bodies are also playing their role. There are examples too numerous to mention of foundations having learned in recent years to work alongside European public institutions for the common good – and that, naturally, includes culture.

When we consider the actual, public reality of culture's place at the European table today, we can see just how crucial is civil society's cultural engagement. For right now, cultural action depends on a meagre and under-used article (151) in the Amsterdam Treaty, as well as some EU programmes for promoting projects with an added European value – on a budget equivalent to an opera house's, but for 450 million citizens.

Europe is struggling to build a transnational community based on nation states and it is struggling to attain a respectful cosmopolitan outlook on diversity. Yet it has no means or strategy for its 'software'. We need software for the cultural commonwealth of Europe, where cultural cooperation can unlock frozen curiosity, help us encounter otherness, build

another, upload their personal stories, photos, information, have discussions online, make connections and share their experiences and projects.

It is an arts project in its own right and in its first six months, Rhiz.eu attracted more than 1,000 users. It is one of several ECF activities developed as part of its focus on diversity for the 2008 European Year of Intercultural Dialogue.

Luigi Farrauto (below) and Remixology, two members of ECF's online community Rhiz.eu.

Rebel Development Crew

up respect and change mindsets. And where art reminds us of our potential to be different ('Who am I?') and to relate to others ('Who are they?'); where cultural collaboration enables intercultural competence.

The ECF's role
Political or artistic?
Although it is small, the ECF is not a single-issue organization. Its mission and goals would be diminished if it were to choose between one or another of its two-sided nature – the political (in European terms) and the cultural/artistic. Its recent decision to choose a multi-annual focus for its work – currently cultural diversity – recognizes that the choice of focus must reflect both of these aspects, which are necessarily intertwined.

A European actor
The independent ECF can help to advance European citizenship through arts and culture. It contributes to democratic Europe's integration process to build a Europe where all citizens can feel at home and be able to participate at all levels – from the local to the European – in shaping their future on the basis of human rights, social responsibility, economic wellbeing, fairness, equal opportunities, and the promotion of cultural diversity and the arts.

This is a tall order for a small foundation. How could it even begin to achieve these aims?

The ECF contributes by supporting cultural cooperation and the arts in areas of tension, development and transition, and thematic areas of considerable friction, through projects where its European mission is best expressed and advanced. It uses the outcomes of its support activities, as well as those devoted to knowledge creation and reflection, in its role as an advocate for culture. This advocacy role, pursued from a civic perspective and in partnership with others, seeks improved framework conditions for the arts and cultural cooperation at European level. The ECF can take risks. The Foundation acts quickly and in an unbureaucratic way.

The ECF also actively promotes a climate of curiosity, understanding and mutual respect in Europe. It tries to put forward convincing cases in arts and culture for an emerging European citizenship and shared aspirations within a cosmopolitan perspective. Situated at the crossroads of the cultural sector, the public (including decision-makers and officialdom) and the media, the ECF is able to draw on its strong networks across Europe in order to connect people of different generations and from different social and ethnic groups, and to put citizens in touch with political decision-makers and vice versa.

Geographically speaking, the ECF's remit is large, taking in the wider European cultural space and the EU's neighbourhood. Its independence and its transnational, trans-cultural modes of working mean that it can critically monitor the cultural activities of national and European public institutions.

A cultural actor

The ECF is not an arts producer, nor is it an arts institution catering to specific audiences or disciplines. It promotes cultural cooperation and the arts in ways and in areas that best serve its European mission. ECF-supported projects are produced and 'consumed' locally. However, the ECF harvests the fruits of this work to make a convincing case for the benefits of contemporary 'production' and collaborative cultural processes to the wellbeing of citizens living in Europe and its neighbourhood.

The Foundation wants Europe's diverse cultural and artistic expressiveness to flourish, and it pursues excellence. It draws attention to any cultural, political and administrative shortcomings that hinder creative production, dissemination, mobility, cooperation or participation. It proposes measures for overcoming these shortcomings, offering examples of good practice as well as reflection, knowledge and instruments/tools.

A champion of diversity

In common with others in the cultural sector, the ECF has felt moved to respond to certain changes within our societies, such as the new diversity resulting from immigration and changing demographics. Multiculturalism encompasses many fears and aspirations, connects Europe with the globe and internal EU policies with external ones, and poses anew the question of European values and the notion of European citizenship. For all these reasons, the ECF has chosen to focus on 'the experience of diversity and the power of culture'. This focus is helping to define the ECF's activities more precisely. It will inevitably imply organizational change as well.

The ECF sums up its core beliefs and activities as follows: 'We believe that cultural diversity is a resource. We want to see artistic creation and cooperation turn challenging experiences into creative encounter. And we champion a political culture in a united Europe that is built on respect for diversity.'

The best advocate for the enriching power of cultural diversity is excellence. The ECF is therefore reshaping its grants programme for supporting artistic excellence and groundbreaking cultural initiatives of

Roma Pavilion

The ECF, together with the Open Society Institute and other partners, helped to make possible the first-ever Roma Pavilion at the 2007 Venice Biennale, which is historically associated with national pavilions. Presenting Roma artistic production inside a world-famous exhibition challenged the expectations of the public and the art world. It also inspired a debate about the nature of a transnational community.

The Roma Pavilion marked the arrival of Roma contemporary culture on the international stage and sent an important message: Roma have a vital role to play in the cultural and political landscape of Europe. For centuries, Roma people have been romanticized by non-Roma artists, who have conjured up images of barefoot dancers happily banging on tambourines. At the same time, works created by Roma artists have been relegated to the level of kitsch by mainstream European arbiters of culture.

The Roma Pavilion featured the premiere of Paradise Lost, an exhibition featuring the work of 16 contemporary Roma artists representing eight European countries. The ultimate goal was to destroy the exotic stereotype of the 'Gypsies' that has been prevalent in Europe since the 19th century and to put Roma artists on an equal footing in the international art world.

European relevance. At the same time, ECF's new programme will seek to ensure accessibility for creative partners from Europe's new communities, and will positively promote new talents and audiences.

Another means for creative collaboration is support for the artistic and cultural mobility of emerging talents – across Europe and across cultural boundaries. The ECF invests in it and will complement an EU pilot scheme that has the potential to become a proper EU programme.

The Foundation considers it crucial to give young people from various backgrounds a voice and to provide spaces for encounter. Beyond action, mobilization counts: the Civil Society Platform for Intercultural Dialogue seeks to create a bottom-up impact on policies.

The ECF's endeavours to research and reflect upon conditions for enhancing equality and mutuality of cultural relations are all-encompassing. However, 'reflection' is something of a misnomer, as the end results of each process are always specific actions. Such actions have a clear focus on diversity in the wider European cultural space and capacity-building programmes for the regions neighbouring the EU.

The ECF will continue its learning process regarding Europe's new diversity, communicate about it, and use its tools to allow fair access for artists from the new communities.

Sustainability – looking towards the future

Recent years have seen a dramatic increase in requests from many sides, including grassroots organizations, artists, cultural operators, networks and public partners. Today, the ECF is too small to meet all of these challenges and demands.

Issues of scale, income diversification and further Europeanization of the ECF are very much alive. These are considerations that have not only financial implications – they are about the ECF's fulfilling its role better. Members of the ECF's Board and Advisory Council, along with other experts, are currently exploring various scenarios for scaling up and the possibility of forming new partnerships with Member States, the EU, foundations, private philanthropists and corporate partners.

The ECF is a strange animal indeed. It is a foundation without an endowment, a European foundation based in – and to a great extent resourced by – an EU member country. It is a small foundation active in many partnerships with many demands placed upon it. But, for at least as long as funding for transnational activities remains the challenge, it is a very necessary animal.

[1] Francois Matarasso and Charles Landry, *Balancing act: 21 strategic dilemmas in cultural policy*, Council of Europe, 1999, p89.

DIANNA RIENSTRA

5 Fondation de France
Working together with communities for positive change

In 1969, the French Ministers of Culture and Finance – André Malraux and Michel Debré respectively – supported the creation of the Fondation de France. The Foundation became an engine for development in a barren philanthropic landscape scarred by the practices of France's Ancien Régime, under which legacies and donations were subject to royal approval. Today, the Foundation is recognized as a pioneer – a leader in its field – renowned for its independence and as an engine of philanthropic development in France.

Executive Director Francis Charhon describes Fondation de France as 'very French'. It was set up in 1969 with the mission to 'push philanthropy' in France by helping individuals and companies to carry out philanthropic, cultural, environmental or scientific projects and social activities. It serves as an umbrella or sheltering organization for other foundations and receives donations and legacies. It is also a grantmaking organization that awards scholarships, prizes and grants.

Fondation de France is fulfilling its mission. Today, this private, non-profit organization serves as an umbrella for 610 foundations (sheltered foundations), 57 of which have been created by corporations (corporate funds) and 553 by specific individual donors (donor-advised funds). There are 30 other French foundations with the capacity to shelter others, but this is a recent development and most of these 'umbrella foundations' shelter just a few funds, created by private donors.

In 2006, Fondation de France (FdF) dispersed 6,700 grants, prizes and scholarships representing €77 million. Charhon notes that all of the

André Malraux, then Minister of Culture, supported the creation of Fondation de France, along with Minister of Finance Michel Debré.
Michel Roi © S ABAM Belgium 2008

funding comes from private sources, which gives the Foundation the independence to choose its own programmes.

Born within a complex historical context
What prompted Charhon's description of Fondation de France as 'very French' was a discussion about the Foundation's beginnings. To understand its pivotal role in shaping the country's philanthropic landscape, it is important to understand the complex historical context.[1] Foundations were very active under the *Ancien Régime*,[2] but were limited by *mortmain* – laws that prohibited or limited gifts – and supervised by the church. In 1666, the Edict of Saint-Germain stipulated that all legacies and donations were subject to royal approval. The French Revolution overthrew this edict, dissolved assemblies and foundations, and confiscated church property. Foundations were allowed to exist, but were subject to government approval.[3]

Despite this, foundations continued to exist to the end of the 19th century, a period marked by the distinction between the public institution in private law and in public law, which previously had been categorized simply as officially recognized institutions. The crises of two wars that ravaged the European continent led to the disappearance of many foundations, although some have survived, including the Institut Pasteur (1887) and Fondation Thiers (1893). At the end of World War Two, their number gradually increased: 45 were created between 1945 and 1965; 60 between 1966 and 1976, and a further 30 by 1979. Today, Fondation de France is one of 541 recognized public benefit foundations.

In pursuit of a modern vision of philanthropy
Throughout history, the state has always exercised strict control over the creation and supervision of foundations. Michel Pomey, Senior Member of the Council of State in Minister of Culture André Malraux's cabinet, was intrigued by the modern vision of philanthropy evolving in Europe and across the Atlantic. Malraux, Pomey and Finance Minister Michel Debré

seized an opportunity to relax the terms and conditions surrounding foundations.

In 1965, Pomey travelled to the US to compare the American and French systems of patronage. At the end of his mission, he launched the idea of creating a large, independent private foundation that would be complementary to the state. It was intended to be a catalyst for creating other foundations to encourage a wide variety of philanthropic activity in the country.

Achieving this involved another small revolution – introducing to French law- and policy-makers the Anglo-Saxon concept of 'charitable trusts' and American-style 'community trusts'. Malraux, Pomey and Debré were supported in their endeavour by François Bloch-Lainé, President of the Caisse des Dépôts et Consignations, and later his successor Pierre Massé. Bloch-Lainé orchestrated contributions from 18 financial institutions to fund the creation of the Fondation de France, which was recognized as a public benefit foundation on 9 January 1969.

Some years later, Bloch-Lainé described the *raison d'être* of the Fondation de France: 'There was . . . the need to develop, between the state and the market, organizations of social utility that would be sustained by generosity. Our country had lagged behind considerably in this field. As a third way, about which we had other worries at the time, it was a question of encouraging new mediators to emerge between citizens and a state that was unable to fulfil the needs of the community, however great its interest.'[4]

The Foundation's statutes structured it as a private organization in accordance with the regime of public benefit foundations. A public benefit foundation is a separate legal entity that is obligated to generate enough income to pursue its objectives. It is created by decree of the Prime Minister or the Minister of the Interior and one-third of the board of governors must be representatives of the state. However, it remains politically independent.

The French philanthropic landscape still bears the scars of the rigid *Ancien Régime*. Formerly, foundations were created by royal edict. Today, they are created by decree or law, or under an agreement formalized with a sheltering structure, such as the Fondation de France. The declaratory regime of association according to a 1901 law explains the imbalance between the number of associations and foundations in the country. In 2001, there were some 880,000 associations, compared with about 1,443 foundations, of which 541 were recognized public benefit foundations.

It was only in 1987 that the word 'foundation' was introduced into law, defined as 'the act by which one or more natural persons or legal entities decide to irrevocably allocate property, rights or resources to work for the public interest and not with a for-profit objective' (Article 20 of the 23 July 1987 law). Under the new law, three types of organization could carry the label of 'foundation' – a foundation recognized as public benefit, a corporate foundation, and a foundation created under the umbrella of a public benefit foundation that is authorized to do so by the Ministry of the Interior and the Council of State. Organizations that did not meet these criteria for calling themselves 'foundations' were forced to renounce this designation by the end of 1991.

An engine of foundation development

The mission of the Fondation de France is to help organizations realize philanthropic, cultural, scientific and general interest projects. It operates within France, across Europe and, in some instances, globally. With its staff of 138, almost 500 volunteers and a network of delegations in seven regions, the Foundation is modelled after the community foundations in the UK and the US, which are typically donor-driven and pool revenues and assets donated from a variety of sources. Such foundations target action at community or neighbourhood level in a specific geographical region.

Francis Charhon notes that Fondation de France 'can create a foundation in three to six months'. Since its creation in 1969, it has created more than 800 foundations, some of which are no longer in existence, having fulfilled their mandates. Currently, the 610 sheltered foundations benefit from invaluable financial and administrative support and finance for researching and shaping projects and initiatives. Corporate funds and donor-advised funds are typically sheltered by Fondation de France.

Sheltered foundations have no legal status, nor can they engage in work outside of their declared field. However, they enjoy the same legal and fiscal status as the foundation that shelters them and have considerable financial freedom. Their accounts are established by Fondation de France and checked by an auditor. The consolidation of the accounts of all sheltered foundations is part of Fondation de France's annual report.

Fondation de France describes itself as being 'at the heart of engagement'. By running its own programmes and acting as a sheltering foundation, it is in effect a 'double organization', in the words of Charhon.

Developing philanthropy

Another of Fondation de France's missions is to develop philanthropy. Charhon points to its involvement in organizations such as the European Foundation Centre and the Network of European Foundations for Innovative

Cooperation and its founding of the Centre Français des Fondations (CFF) in 2001.

It took more than seven years to launch the CFF, Charhon recalls, to promote the role of foundations and boost their recognition. Today, it has 130 members and serves as a platform that allows foundations to exchange ideas and best practice. CFF is evolving into a network to promote collaboration and foster philanthropy across France and in Europe with the EFC.

In addition to sheltering other foundations and organizations, Fondation de France is actively engaged in communities across France by supporting projects and programmes in the areas of social cohesion, health and medical research, culture and the environment.

Social cohesion – flexible and appropriate solutions

Fondation de France promotes social cohesion in France by identifying what Francis Charhon describes as 'flexible and appropriate' solutions. It is active in the areas of housing, employment, children, prevention of violence, people with disabilities, the elderly and international solidarity.

There are dozens of projects and programmes in this area. Many empower citizens to take control of their own communities. For example, when day-care centres for pre-school children were full, parents took over. In 2002, Fondation de France started supporting the Association Parenbouge (Parenbouge alludes to 'active parents'), which has benefited more than 100 families with services such as home care and alternating shifts at day-care centres.

The Foundation has also pioneered home care for the elderly, programmes to help the disadvantaged re-enter the workforce and to foster entrepreneurship in rural France, and an initiative to help the unemployed with transportation to and from work in outlying areas poorly served by public transportation.

Fondation de France also supports projects in other European countries as well as responding to humanitarian crises around the world. It supported projects to create solidarity following European enlargement. Projects were aimed at laying the groundwork for fostering the notion of European citizenship by establishing linkages between civil society organizations in EU-15 countries and new Member States through concrete joint initiatives.

Following the tsunami that devastated South Asia in December 2004, Fondation de France raised more than €20 million to support more than 62 projects by 38 NGOs in Indonesia, Sri Lanka, India and Thailand.

Fondation de France raised more than €20 million following the
2004 tsunami in Asia. This is one of the houses built as a result.
Architectes de l'Urgence

The Foundation also helped to coordinate French aid following the disaster
by creating three information points for NGOs in Banda Aceh in Sumatra,
Colombo in Sri Lanka and Pondichery in India.

　　　Charhon notes that the media criticized the Foundation six months
following the tsunami for not having publicly accounted for all of the money
raised. 'There are many steps between collecting donations and ensuring
that the beneficiaries are the right ones to do the job,' he says. 'This is what
many people don't understand in today's fast-paced world. To do something
in a sustainable way takes time. It is just that simple.'

　　　At the same time, he concedes that despite the inherent generosity
of the French people, many are sceptical following a huge financial scandal
in 1996 that rocked one of France's largest charities, the Association for
Cancer Research (ARC), which was accused of misusing funds donated
by the public. Since then, Fondation de France has worked with other
organizations through a committee – *comité de la charte de déontologie*
– to promote good practices, and Charhon notes that the situation has
improved.

A pioneer in healthcare and medical research

Fondation de France also works in the areas of information and training, public health and medical research. It supports projects that focus on medical ethics and research, children, pain, addiction, psychological disease, palliative care, and health education for young people. Since the 1980s, the Foundation has created committees specialized in perinatal care, epidemiology, neurology, cancer, thromboses, ophthalmology and neuro-ophthalmology, leukaemia, cardiovascular disease, autism and Parkinson's disease.

In 2008, the medical research programme is focusing on five areas: cancer, cardiovascular disease, autism, Parkinson's disease, ophthalmology and neuro-ophthalmology.

Cancer is the leading cause of death in France, being responsible for about 30 per cent of all deaths. It is also the leading cause of premature death in people aged 65 or younger. Many donors have supported Fondation de France's work in this field to support research into the disease. At the same time, cardiovascular disease – another killer – has not received enough attention from private donors. For this reason, the Foundation is dedicating a portion of its resources to research in this important area.

Following extensive consultation, Fondation de France chose in 1999 to support research on autism as France had been accused of lagging behind in this area, particularly as the disease has an impact on early child development. As such, autism is at the crossroad of many disciplines, including psychiatry, neurology, paediatrics, genetics, cognitive sciences and epidemiology.

The Foundation is supporting fundamental research programmes on neuronal systems related to Parkinson's disease. Since 2004, support has been directed towards applied research and tests involving electro-stimulation of the brain. With the support of a donor, Fondation de France has created research grants in the fields of ophthalmology and neuro-ophthalmology.

This recent work carries on the Foundation's tradition of keeping one step ahead of public policy. It was the first to address palliative care issues in France, as well as the silent yet devastating condition of chronic pain and the contentious issue of autism. By bringing together all stakeholders – researchers, social workers, doctors, healthcare providers, family representatives, volunteers and others – Fondation de France designs its grantmaking from the ground up while encouraging creative, synergistic thinking that can lead to innovative public policy.

Project supported by Fondation de France that offers activities
for older people.
Francesco Acerbis

Director of Programmes and Foundations Dominique Lemaistre
explains: 'When we started addressing autism eight years ago, we were
also pioneers. Work had been done but no one was speaking to each other.
There were no statistics, no epidemiological studies. We brought together
families, scientists, doctors, neurologists and psychologists. It was not
an easy task. But eventually the stakeholders formed into teams that we
funded [through grants] on the condition they work together. This was a way
to stimulate innovation at the time.'

This is typical of how Fondation de France determines its
grantmaking strategy and defines its own programmes. Stakeholders are
brought together, a volunteer Expert Committee for each programme works
to design the programme, a call for proposals is launched, and the Expert
Committee selects which groups will receive support.

Addressing the needs of the fragile and the marginalized

Lemaistre says this 'flexible, holistic' approach typically involves the entire
community and allows Fondation de France to respond to rapidly changing
societal needs. This approach proves critical in dealing with issues such
as psychiatric care for adults who find themselves trapped within a vicious
circle that incrementally robs them of pieces of their lives.

'These adults are hospitalized only when there is a crisis. The patient is then released again into society. This cycle is repeated and each time they make this circle, they lose something – their family, their job, or housing for example. In France, the family associations fought for the status of "handicapped" so they qualify for financial assistance. But between the first crisis and the status, there are lots of circles,' she explains. It is critical to intervene with a holistic solution rather than take a band-aid, patchwork approach to such issues.

Increasingly in our society, the 'fragile are marginalized', Lemaistre adds. This includes the elderly, who have fewer rights as they become increasingly dependent. Many are shipped off to retirement homes – large, regimented facilities that are often far away from what used to be called home. Rather than continue this warehousing approach, Fondation de France introduced the concept of smaller homes within the community to accommodate a maximum of 30 people.

It also introduced the concept of creating complexes comprising two or three apartments where elderly people can remain within their communities through assisted living. In turn, this engages communities in becoming more responsive to the needs of their senior citizens by setting up new services such as delivering meals, cleaning and visiting nurses.

Lemaistre emphasizes a comprehensive, community-focused approach when thinking of strategies to meet the challenges facing society. This is because most challenges are multifaceted and complex. For example, unemployment is often linked to poor housing and transportation. Poverty is often linked to poor education, lack of opportunities or medical issues.

'Everything is connected in a community. If you lose a primary school in an area, people leave the community and its character changes,' she explains. 'One of the underlying issues we face every day is the challenge to force people to think about community and people, rather than about themselves. To move beyond thinking about the individual is something that is very easy to say, but equally difficult to do.'

A mediator between artists and society

In the area of culture, Fondation de France seeks to restore to society – in all of its diversity – the means to express its cultural aspirations and establish new relations with its artists. Within this framework, it has set up pilot programmes in which it carries out its mission as mediator between artists and society. It also helps to develop tools for training and encouraging critical analysis.

Charhon describes a unique programme whereby citizens are involved in determining art for public spaces. Usually the state decides on which art to commission for public spaces, but in the Les Nouveaux Commanditaires programme[5] (literally translated as the New Patrons) citizens are empowered to involve artists in projects they are concerned about. Since it was launched in 1993, the programme – run by seven regional mediators – has brought together 427 different public and private sector partners, including representatives from municipalities, the Ministry of Culture, regional associations, and more.

More than 130 works of contemporary art have been commissioned and installed across the country. Fondation de France regional mediators act as brokers between the community, the artist and the funders. The programme has proved so successful that is has been taken up by Belgium, Italy, the UK, Sweden and Finland.

'This programme helps to fulfil the needs of the citizens. The art commissioned isn't just for public squares, it also fulfils very specific needs. This at once brings artists closer to their communities and brings the citizens closer to their environment,' Charhon explains. 'In this way, the Foundation acts as a mediator between artists and society.'

In 2003, for example, artist Cécile Bart was commissioned to paint a children's shelter at Chassignol for 50 youngsters aged 4 to 15 from troubled families. It was the staff's idea to create a comforting, positive environment for children confronted with a very difficult period in their young lives. The result is the transformation of a sad, grey and foreboding building into La Maison Arc-en-ciel (the Rainbow House). It is a vibrant splash of colour in the landscape and uplifting to look at, promising hope and the prospect of a brighter future. The project brought together a consortium of public and private partners to commission the €224,306 transformation.

Environment – a local and collective responsibility

The tension between social and economic development and preserving the natural environment is growing within national and local boundaries, as well as internationally. Within its environment programme – Ensemble pour gérer le territoire (Working together to take care of the land) – Fondation de France has supported projects that foster rational management of natural resources, while emphasizing individual, local and collective responsibility.

Projects supported range from addressing noise pollution, polluted seashores and rivers to the CAP 2000 programme, an association created in 2001 that brings together more than 30 stakeholders to address common issues such as launching and enforcing a charter to create buffer zones

A Fondation de France programme designed to introduce
children to the world through art and artistry.
Stéphan Ménoret

between agricultural land and fragile seaside habitats. Since 1997, the
Foundation has supported more than 300 diverse projects based on local
initiatives and action in this field. It believes that social dialogue is key
to sustainable local development. When reconciling different points of
view through dialogue becomes difficult, it introduces a new expert – the
environmental mediator.

'We help our partners deal with the environment every day,' says
Charhon. 'It is a global issue and a global task, but as we do in most of our
work, we believe the work starts at the local level with a holistic approach.
For this reason, we are introducing a "green" dimension to all of our
projects, when feasible.'

Charhon explains that Fondation de France has taken its
environmental programme one step further by trying to mainstream green
technologies across its activities. All the various projects the Foundation
supports that use such technologies are given extra funding to 'go green'.
This includes, for example, constructing residences for senior citizens with
solar panels, using energy-efficient light bulbs, or encouraging project
partners to use hybrid or low-carbon emission cars when arranging
transportation for certain initiatives such as delivering meals, cleaning
services or rides to work. For example, an organization that developed a
project for people with disabilities that had already been approved by the

Foundation will receive extra funding if they want to purchase a 'green car' instead of a conventional one.

Meeting future challenges in a globalized world

The challenges ahead are manifold and daunting, particularly as globalization takes root and grows at an accelerated pace that many foundations find unmanageable. Not so for Fondation de France. Francis Charhon maintains the challenges are global but the answers are 'scattered' at local level. He believes there are no answers to be found at the global level for the work of the Foundation.

'The answer lies in local action, in communities and neighbourhoods,' he says. 'For this reason, we always look for effective and efficient local operators to work with. This is how our organization works – in many ways, we act as a broker. There are so many steps between donors and beneficiaries that we end up also serving as a bridge.'

A favourable fiscal environment

According to Francis Charhon, the French are considered a generous people. In 2006, the Foundation benefited from the generosity of 506,000 donors. The country that historically tried to thwart philanthropy and the creation of foundations has today a very favourable tax treatment that has fostered a culture of individual and corporate giving. Individual philanthropy is quite a new – but apparently growing – phenomenon in France.

Public benefit foundations, as well as the foundations they shelter, allow their founders and donors to have a good fiscal environment:
- Individuals can deduct from the tax on income 66 per cent of the amount of their donation, within the limit of 20 per cent of their taxable income.
- Companies can deduct from their tax 60 per cent of their donation, within the limit of 0.5 per cent of their turnover.

Public benefit foundations fall within a light taxation regime. They are exonerated from all transfer taxes on donations and bequests. Income from heritage and resources from the rent of buildings or from the exploitation of agricultural or forestry property, and capital income are not taxed.

This concept of 'think global, act local' is not a new one. But the Fondation de France has embraced it across all of its operations. Its philosophy and way of working is summed up by the slogan '*S'unir pour agir*' (Let's unite to act). However, as Lemaistre commented about encouraging community thinking over individualistic thinking – easier said than done.

'What we are learning every day is that even in the specialized fields we work in, there are huge cross-cutting themes,' she says. 'But the common denominator lies in identifying what causes exclusion; what are the root causes of marginalization. This is why the cultural dimension is so important. You can't just feed money into the machine and expect change. Real change happens from the bottom up. We act – and we help our partners to act – as catalysts. But at the end of the day, it is the beneficiaries who create the change.'

When considering the activities emanating from the modest four-storey office located in one of Paris's smartest districts, it begs the question: 'Would the founders be convinced that Fondation de France is fulfilling its mission and can be considered a successful endeavour?'

Francis Charhon points to the magnitude of the work done with a relatively small endowment and answers, 'yes, we have made a difference. After 40 years, there are new regulations which facilitate the development of philanthropy, the number of foundations is growing very quickly, the public has recognized foundations as important actors in social development, and at least we create the notion of service to donors in France.'

---

[1] This history is derived from a paper written by Executive Director Francis Charhon, *La Fondation de France dans l'espace public Français*, January 2008.

[2] A French term meaning Old Rule, Old Kingdom or Old Regime, which refers to the aristocratic, social and political system established in France from about the 15th century to the 18th century under the late Valois and Bourbon dynasties. The administrative and social structures were the result of centuries of nation-building, legislative acts, internal conflicts and civil wars, but they remained a confusing patchwork of local privilege and historic differences until the French Revolution brought about changes designed to end administrative incoherence.

[3] Michel Pomey, *Traité des fondations reconnues d'utilité publique*, Paris, PUF, 1980.

[4] Francis Charhon, op cit.

[5] http://pagesperso-orange.fr/eternal.network/html/etage3/nc_fdf.htm

DAVID WATKISS

6 Institusjonen Fritt Ord
Protecting and promoting freedom of expression in Norway and beyond

Painful memories of Nazi occupation and repression in Norway plus Cold War fears of communist totalitarianism were among the factors motivating the founding in Norway in 1974 of the Institusjonen Fritt Ord ('free word'), known in the English-speaking world as the Freedom of Expression Foundation. Since its founding in 1974, Fritt Ord has distributed approximately €82 million to several thousand recipients.

A public-benefit private foundation under Norwegian law, Fritt Ord is one of the few charities in Europe outside the UK devoted primarily to freedom of expression. Fritt Ord today is an independent foundation with assets of approximately €325 million and annual spending of more than €10 million. Its activities are focused in Norway, but with projects also funded in the UK, Eastern Europe, Russia and Burma. Fritt Ord's principal objective is:

'To protect and promote freedom of expression and the environment for freedom of expression in Norway, particularly by encouraging lively debate and the dauntless use of the free word.'

In addition, Fritt Ord's mandate is to support various aspects of Norwegian culture, primarily those dealing with free speech, and, in selected special cases, to promote freedom of expression internationally. Erik Rudeng, Fritt Ord's Director since 2000, and a staff of six carry out the Foundation's work from a stately townhouse in Oslo built in 1887 and located near the Norwegian Royal Palace and foreign embassies. That an organization devoted to freedom of expression, tolerance and culture should be headquartered in this structure is historically significant and somewhat ironic.

Between 1907 and 1941, this building, known as Uranienborgveien 2, housed the Russian and then Soviet embassies in Norway. During this period, one of Lenin's closest colleagues and legendary first woman to serve as ambassador, Aleksandra Kollontaj, was in residence. In 1941, after Nazi Germany's occupation of Norway and invasion of the Soviet Union, the Germans evicted the Soviets from the house and used it during World War Two as the Gestapo officers' club.

Fritt Ord headquarters building in Uranienborgveien 2.

For a short time after the liberation of Norway, the Norwegian military resistance movement (*Milorg*) occupied the house. Between 1945 and 2000, the house was the venue for cultural and artistic activities including a dance club, rock concerts and graphic design.

The acquisition of Uranienborgveien 2 by Fritt Ord in 2000 to serve as its headquarters marked a major milestone in the evolution of the Foundation from a small organization run by a part-time director and one part-time secretary and distributing the equivalent of €100,000 to €1 million per year, to one of the largest foundations in Norway with a full-time director and staff, receiving about 1,400 grant applications and funding more than 500 projects annually.

The work of Fritt Ord is overseen by a seven-member Board of Trustees, chaired since 2000 by Professor Francis Sejerstad, former member and chair of the Norwegian Nobel Committee, which awards the Nobel Peace Prize, and former Chair of the Norwegian government's Freedom of Expression Commission. The Board, with input from staff, approves all grant applications.

A Narvesen kiosk – the origins of Fritt Ord lie with the Narvesen Kiosk Company.

Fritt Ord's origins and founders

The origins of Fritt Ord lie with the Narvesen Kioskkompani (the Narvesen Kiosk Company), founded in 1894. Today, Narvesen – part of a conglomerate – is one of the largest news, magazine and fast food store chains in Norway. During World War Two and the years immediately following, Narvesen was Norway's main distribution channel for newspapers and journals through its kiosks in railway stations and other public venues.

Jens Henrik Nordlie was Narvesen's long time Managing Director. During World War Two, Nordlie worked with Jens Christian Hauge, leader of the Norwegian military resistance. Hauge would go on to become Norwegian Minister of Defence from 1945 until 1952 and Minister of Justice in 1955. Hauge was a supporter of the Norwegian Labour Party and a highly influential lawyer, businessman and politician. He was instrumental in the establishment of the Norwegian state oil company, Statoil, and the Scandinavian Airline System (SAS).

Cold War ushers in concern and fear

In the early 1970s, memories of Nazi occupation, censorship and repression were still fresh in the minds of Norwegian citizens. In addition, the Cold War created new fears among Norwegians, living in a small country bordering Russia, of a possible Soviet occupation. There was also frequent news of repression of dissent in the Soviet Union and communist Eastern Europe. At this time, it was perceived that adherents to Maoist philosophy were attempting to infiltrate Norwegian trade unions and businesses.

These concerns motivated people like Nordlie and Hauge to seek ways to protect and promote free expression, tolerance and democracy in Norway. They shared an anti-totalitarian vision and a belief that freedom of the press and freedom of expression were vital. The vehicle chosen, however, may have had something to do with Nordlie's position as Managing Director of Narvesen. In the mid-1970s, the Narvesen Kiosk Company was still wholly owned by the Narvesen family and had become a potential target for a takeover. Erik Rudeng suggests that Nordlie and Narvesen Deputy Director, Finn Skedsmo, were also looking for a way to avoid a hostile takeover.

Creating a foundation

With the assistance of Hauge, the solution they devised was to obtain the agreement of the Narvesen family to sell off their shares in Narvesen to a newly created Norwegian not-for-profit public-benefit foundation, Fritt Ord. One of the stated purposes of the Foundation was the safeguarding of the open and free distribution of publications. To make this arrangement work for the Narvesen family owners, Nordlie, Skedsmo and Hauge obtained special legislation from the Norwegian parliament allowing the Narvesen family to sell its shares to the Foundation free of capital gains tax. The company itself provided the new Foundation with the money to obtain the shares.

Fritt Ord was established in June 1974, with Nordlie, Hauge and Skedsmo listed as the official founders. The transfer of Narvesen shares to Fritt Ord occurred on 1 January 1975. On that same day, apparently as part of the deal struck in the Norwegian parliament to obtain favourable

From left to right: Fritt Ord founders Jens Henrik Nordlie, Jens Christian Hauge and Finn Skedsmo.

tax treatment, the Narvesen Kiosk Company merged with a wholly owned subsidiary of the Norwegian State Railroad (NSB), with Fritt Ord holding 59 per cent and NSB 41 per cent of the merged company, which was renamed simply Narvesen.

Nordlie chaired the Foundation from its creation until 1984. During the early years, Fritt Ord used its share of dividends from Narvesen to support the newly established Norwegian Institute of Journalism, through grants designed to stimulate exploration of issues relating to freedom of expression. It also began to fund the Freedom of Expression Prize and the Freedom of Expression Tribute.

A change of direction

In 1995, NSB sold its stake in the company to the public and Narvesen was listed on the Oslo Stock Exchange. About this time, the Trustees, who then included Erik Rudeng, began to consider whether the mission of the Foundation might better be advanced without close connections with Narvesen. By that time, Narvesen had evolved from a news distribution company to a contemporary news, beverage and fast food chain.

Freedom of Expression Prize

The prestigious Freedom of Expression Prize was and remains the Foundation's highest distinction. It is generally awarded in early May each year in connection with the commemoration of Norway's liberation from the German occupation. The prize, including a statuette and a sum of money, acknowledges individuals or institutions engaged in activities deemed especially worthwhile in the light of the Foundation's objectives.

Since its inception in 1976, prize laureates have included many Norwegian institutions and individuals – writers, journalists, human rights advocates and intellectuals, along with internationally known figures such as Lech Walesa and Andrei Sakharov.

Freedom of Expression Tribute

Established in 1979, the Freedom of Expression Tribute acknowledges people who have made remarkable efforts to promote free speech, generally in connection with current affairs. The tributes are bestowed when the Fritt Ord board deems warranted without constraints on the number of tributes given in any year. Each tribute is accompanied by a crystal vase and a sum of money.

Meanwhile, the proliferation of modern media, including the internet, had created multiple new sources of information, making the need to protect newspaper and magazine distribution outlets less pressing.

The continuing links between Fritt Ord and Narvesen also created some comic and ironic problems for the Board. As a major magazine distributor, Narvesen sold men's magazines with photos of nude women. Such publications became a major critical focus of feminists in the 1990s and, as a 51 per cent shareholder in Narvesen, Fritt Ord became the target of such criticism. During this period, Rudeng recounts, the Fritt Ord Board felt compelled 'to routinely review the men's magazines sold at Narvesen outlets'.

These considerations, together with the desire above all to increase the funds available for grants, led the Board to begin to divest the Foundation's interest in Narvesen. By 2001, Fritt Ord's remaining interest in the company was sold, thereby severing all connections.

Fritt Ord today
Committed to ethical investment
The Foundation has a diversified portfolio. For several years, it has managed to attain an annual growth of 15 per cent with annual giving of 3 per cent of the portfolio. Fritt Ord has strict ethical guidelines for its investments, consistently avoiding investments, for example, in weapons production, alcohol and tobacco. It recently sold its substantial holdings in a seafood company over concerns that the company's fish-farming activities in Canada could ruin stocks of wild salmon depended upon by native peoples and concerns over labour conditions at fish farms in Chile.

Rudeng commented: 'It's important for us to have an ethical evaluation of where our investments are placed. All companies will profit from maintaining clear ethical standards.'

Putting philosophy into practice
Fritt Ord's philosophy is that democracy cannot survive without freedom of expression and freedom of expression requires 'not only that everyone can write and say what they please, but also that contributions to the social debate actually reach the people'.[1] The Foundation focuses its activities in four main programme areas:

– **Media and democracy** seeks to explore what kinds of media structures promote democracy and freedom of expression, analysing media trends and their social consequences.

- **Information and the public debate** seeks to make information needed for public understanding and debate accessible, where the market may not guarantee accessibility, through the support of books, documentaries, small newspapers and journals, seminars and conferences.
- **Grants and training** provides support for students and educational activities to generate interest in freedom of expression and knowledge of the conditions required for it.
- **Art and culture** recognizes that important breakthroughs for freedom of expression often occur through art and general cultural debate and thus provides support for catalogues, forums for the exchange of opinion, cross-cultural dialogue about artistic expressions and debate on cultural policy.

Fritt Ord – at home and abroad

Since 1974, Fritt Ord has been funding projects dedicated to protecting and promoting freedom of expression at home and as far away as Burma. About 85 per cent of Fritt Ord's giving goes to Norwegian organizations and individuals. However, its international activities are significant and growing. A flavour of the focus and breadth of Fritt Ord's work can be gleaned from snapshots of some current projects.

Knut Hamsun Centre

The interface between art, culture, politics and expression is evidenced by Fritt Ord's participation in the creation of the Knut Hamsun Centre in Hamaroey, a small village in northern Norway above the Arctic Circle.

Knut Hamsun (1859–1952) was Norway's greatest writer of the 20th century. He received the Nobel Price for Literature in 1920. André Gide compared him favourably to Dostoevsky; Maxim Gorky, writing to Hamsun in 1927, declared, 'at this moment, you are the greatest artist in Europe; there is no one who can compare with you.' H G Wells referred to Hamsun's Nobel Prize winning novel, *Growth of the Soil*, as 'one of the very greatest novels I have ever read'. Another Nobel laureate, Isaac Bashevis Singer, called Hamsun 'the father of the modern school of literature'.[2]

Yet today there are no parks or streets commemorating Hamsun's name. He is little known or read in the English-speaking world. Hamsun is viewed with uncomfortable ambivalence in Norway. His fame in the first part of the century was stained by his highly publicized support of Nazi Germany, the result of 'misplaced nationalism rather than ideological affinity', according to one biographer.[3]

After World War Two, Hamsun, then in his eighties, was tried for treason. The Norwegian authorities hoped that his reputation could be saved by a psychiatric diagnosis of impaired mental faculties during the war years, but Hamsun rejected such attempts. In deference to his age, Hamsun was convicted, not of treason, but for the lesser crime of membership in the Norwegian Nazi Party.

Since Hamsun's death in 1952, there have been suggestions to establish a Hamsun society or centre, but these have remained controversial. In 1994, the US architect Steven Holl was commissioned to design a Knut Hamsun Centre. The design won the Progressive Architecture Award in 1996. However, continuing controversy over Hamsun's traumatizing roles as one of Norway's greatest writers and also a Nazi supporter delayed funding for nearly a decade.

Funding has now been obtained, with the Norwegian government, municipalities, local businesses and Fritt Ord participating. When completed in 2009, the Knut Hamsun Centre will support a scholar in residence programme and include exhibition areas, a library and reading room, a café and an auditorium.

'The planned exhibitions will explore the themes, ideas and aesthetics in Hamsun's work and the relationship between literature and society, and between fiction and polemics,' notes Project Director Nina Frang Hoyum.

Norwegian House of Literature (Litteraturhuset)
Initiated and supported by Fritt Ord, the House of Literature in Oslo, opened in the autumn of 2007, is dedicated to enhancing the enthusiasm of children and adults for Norwegian and international literature, both fiction and non-fiction. Fritt Ord leased a building, formerly a teachers' training college, from the Norwegian government, paid for renovations, and then assigned the lease to the Norwegian House of Literature Foundation.

Fritt Ord will be the major financial source for seven years, after which time the House of Literature Foundation will be required to find other funding.

The impressive and stately five-storey building, located near the Royal Palace, has six venues for frequently scheduled readings, debates, conferences and entertainment, often featuring internationally recognized authors. Inspired by a German literature movement in the 1980s, the Norwegian House of Literature is the largest of its kind in Europe.

On the ground level is a café with a comfortable lounge area, wireless internet and a well-stocked bookstore. The loft contains working

Opening night of the House of Literature in Oslo, 6 October 2007.

space for 50 writers who need a place to work and an apartment for visiting writers and intellectuals. One floor is devoted to activities for children and adolescents, with schools invited to bring their students for events during the day.

'The House of Literature will pay special attention to reaching out to adolescents and young adults of immigrant backgrounds,' says Executive Manager Aslak Sira Myhre. 'Helping their voice to be heard is an important task for the House of Literature.'

Democratic Voice of Burma

In spartan broadcasting studios in a warehouse in Oslo, the expatriate Burmese staff of the award-winning Democratic Voice of Burma (DVB) provides uncensored news and information about Burma (Myanmar) and the country's brutal and repressive military junta. Since 1992, DVB has broadcast radio programmes reaching millions of listeners. In 2005, DVB expanded its programming and began satellite television broadcasts via the first free and independent Burmese language television channel.

According to DVB's Deputy Executive Director, Khin Maung Win, Fritt Ord was 'among the first organizations to support our work'. This is indicative of Fritt Ord's giving philosophy, notes Erik Rudeng. Giving money 'early and fast' to worthwhile projects makes the most impact. Fritt Ord has

Radio Burma, supported by
Fritt Ord, broadcasts from a
warehouse in Oslo.

continued to support DVB with grants for programming and other needs
over the years. DVB's mission is to:

- provide accurate and unbiased news to the people of Burma;
- promote understanding and cooperation among the various ethnic
  and religious groups in Burma;
- encourage and sustain independent public opinion and enable
  social and political debate;
- impart the ideals of democracy and human rights to the people of
  Burma.

That this Burmese-run non-profit media organization is based in Oslo is
a result of contacts between Norway and Burmese expatriates made in
connection with the receipt in 1991 of the Nobel Peace Prize by Aung San
Suu Kyi, Leader of the Burmese National League for Democracy.

*Nobel Fredssenter (Nobel Peace Centre) Exhibition, Freedom of Expression –
How Free is Free?*
The recently opened Nobel Peace Centre, focusing on the lives and works
of Nobel Peace Prize laureates, seeks to help the public to explore issues
of war, peace and conflict resolution. Located in Oslo, the Centre contains
high-tech exhibition areas, a bookshop, a café and a cinema. The Centre is
supported generally by corporate sponsors.

A temporary exhibition at the Centre, Freedom of Expression – How
Free is Free, which opened in September 2007, was funded exclusively

by Fritt Ord, for a total amount of approximately €440,000. The Centre originally requested Fritt Ord to fund half of the cost of the project, with corporate sponsors funding the rest. However, the controversial nature of the exhibition caused the corporate sponsors to walk away and Fritt Ord decided to fund the entire project.

'We found it impossible to raise private money for the exhibition,' said Nobel Peace Centre Director Bente Erichsen. 'Fritt Ord played an important role in filling a gap when commercial sponsors found the project too controversial.'

The exhibit presents people pushing the boundaries of freedom of expression, including Anna Politkovskaja, Aung San Suu Kyi, Sami Al-Arian, Salman Rushdie, Theo van Gogh and more.

'Some of these have criticized regimes, other have shocked, offended or violated through their art or expression of their views,' notes Erichsen. '[The exhibition examines] how far people should be allowed to push the limits of expression.'

The connection between the exhibition, the Nobel Peace Prize and the mission of Fritt Ord is explained by Fritt Ord Chair, Francis Sejersted: 'Many Peace Prize Laureates were awarded the prize because they criticized the powers in their own countries and endured reprisals. They showed great courage. The Nobel Committee demonstrated that freedom of expression – the right to criticize those in power – is one of the most important human rights, and a prerequisite for a more peaceful world.'

Support for documentary filmmaking in Norway

'Documentary filmmaking in Norway could not survive without Fritt Ord.' So says Erling Borgen, an award-winning journalist, documentary filmmaker, author and playwright. Borgen is one of several documentary filmmakers to receive support from Fritt Ord. In 1999, after a long career as a journalist for NRK, the Norwegian public broadcast company, Borgen started his own production company to make documentaries. In 2002, he received a substantial grant from Fritt Ord to establish a TV foundation, Innsikt (Insight), to specialize in television documentaries about human rights, art and culture.

Over the years, Fritt Ord has also supported specific Borgen projects, including hard-hitting human rights exposés concerning the Norwegian industries' involvement in the Iraq War and the US confinement facilities at Guantanamo Bay ('A Little Piece of Norway'); the Norwegian state oil company's involvement with the corrupt and repressive regime in Azerbaijan ('In the Shadow of Statoil'); and the Norwegian government's dealing with granite suppliers in India that exploit and endanger their workers ('The Square of Poverty').

After 'A Little Piece of Norway' had been approved for broadcast on NRK, Borgen's former employer, some Norwegian business and government interests, apparently fearing embarrassment by the film, successfully pressured NRK management to cancel the broadcast. The station tried to justify its decision not to air the film by accusing Borgen of sloppy and inaccurate work.

Erik Rudeng publicly and vigorously defended Borgen's work and accused NRK of censorship. The result was that the film was broadcast by one of Norway's commercial stations to critical acclaim and public embarrassment for NRK. Reflecting on this episode, Borgen observed: 'Erik Rudeng is not afraid of anything. He is a bastion defending human rights and freedom of expression.'

Borgen's documentaries supported by Fritt Ord are having an impact on the behaviour of government and business. The film about Statoil's involvement with the corrupt and repressive Azeri government fuelled debate in Norway about corporate social responsibility. The film chronicling the abuses of Indian granite workers helped to instigate the inclusion of human rights and ethics clauses in Norwegian government procurement contracts.

The Index on Censorship and Article 19

For years, Fritt Ord has supported the work of two UK-based freedom of expression advocacy organizations, the Index on Censorship and Article 19. Recently, these groups sought funding from Fritt Ord to establish a facility in London, tentatively titled the Free Word Centre, in which several human rights, arts and literary groups could share office, performance and conference space.

In the summer of 2006, Ursala Owen of Index approached Rudeng with an interesting proposal: a building in central London with an auditorium, exhibition space, seminar rooms, offices and café – ideal for the Free Word Centre – was available, but only for purchase, not for rent. The consortium of nine non-profit organizations, the potential users of the facility, did not have the resources to buy it.

Owen suggested to Rudeng that Fritt Ord consider buying the building 'as a finely situated London property investment, and let [the consortium] use the building for, say, 10 years'. Rudeng was intrigued by this proposal, seeing it as a way to tie the mission of Fritt Ord to its investment strategy. Rudeng and the Fritt Ord board first consulted real estate experts and lawyers, and then engaged in protracted negations with the building's owner. An agreement for Fritt Ord to purchase the building was reached in 2007. Fritt Ord will allow the beneficiary organizations to use the building rent-free for 10 to 12 years, at which time Fritt Ord will be entitled to sell the property if it chooses.

FreeWord Centre Project Director Owen says: 'Fritt Ord's contribution to the creation of the FreeWord Centre is enormous and invaluable. By providing a highly appropriate building in Central London, it has made it possible for the FreeWord Centre to focus immediately and intensely on how to fulfil its mission. Fritt Ord's contribution is not just the building but also, through its own vision of such a centre, it has added an inspirational element.'

According to Owen, the mission of the proposed FreeWord Centre, scheduled to open in early 2009, will be to 'act as a dynamic international arena promoting and protecting the power of the written and spoken word for creative and free expression. There will be a creative synergy between free expression, literature and literacy.'

Using a foundation's investment strategy to advance its mission is not a completely new idea, but it is still relatively rare. The benefit of this approach, however, seems clear. As Rudeng notes: 'A great effect could be seen if even parts of the [Foundation's] investments were ingeniously turned towards supporting the purpose inherent in grants. That would significantly increase the capacity of the grantees.'

'Fritt Ord has been a steadfast supporter of Index's mission – the promotion and support of the idea of freedom of expression, and our activities – the publication of writing, comment and analysis on freedom of expression issues, for many years. It is no exaggeration to say that Index's existence today is due in no small part to Fritt Ord.'
Henderson Mullin, Chief Executive, Index on Censorship

Other international projects

Fritt Ord actively supports documentary photography and filmmaking. In 2007, it awarded a total of €750,000 to 38 civic-minded photographers for various projects including one that will examine the lives of people living in slums in Nairobi, Mumbai, Caracas and Jakarta. It is also supporting documentary films using human-interest stories to examine human rights situations in China, Belarus, North Korea and Burma.

Some other international projects include press prizes for recipients in Russia and Eastern Europe. In partnership with the ZEIT Foundation of Hamburg, Germany, Fritt Ord awards two monetary prizes, the Gerd Bucerius PrizeYoung for Press of Eastern Europe and the Freedom of Expression Foundation Press Prize for Russia for newspapers and journalists in Russia, Belarus, Ukraine and Georgia who work to promote a free press and liberal civil society.

The way forward

As in many countries in Europe and in Scandinavia, the state is considered the primary and dominant force in providing for social welfare. In Norway, modern charitable foundations are relatively new. Their role is evolving and not clearly understood by many politicians and large segments of the citizenry.

Combining the best of the state and the market

Writing in 2004, Fritt Ord Chair, Francis Sejersted, noted: 'There is currently a tendency to view private-benefit foundations with suspicion. Encouragement and support for setting up such funds are weak.'

One way forward, according to Rudeng, is to foster public appreciation of how foundations can combine the best aspects of both the state and the market. 'The state can engage in long-term thinking and funding irrespective of market forces, while the market is open to new ideas and can respond unbureaucratically with quick and informal action. Foundations can do both,' he says. 'Moreover, liberal societies need organizations between the state and the market to fill the gaps.'

Ensuring diversity and freedom in the public space

Sejersted agrees. Commenting on Fritt Ord's decision to provide substantial support to a prestigious but financially struggling Norwegian weekly journal, *Morgenbladet*, he explained:

'It is obvious that [Fritt Ord] has more latitude for discretion than [the Norwegian state] Arts Council . . . Based on the need for fairness, public funding will have to be spread thinly across the country, while [Fritt Ord] has more freedom to concentrate its resources on particular initiatives. The Foundation can more easily take risks by supporting interesting, but bolder projects, such as . . . *Morgenbladet*. The Foundation was criticized for having contributed to skewing the market. That is, of course, precisely the point. [Fritt Ord's] task is to skew the market, ie, to help bring to fruition worthwhile projects that could not have been brought to fruition based on market forces.

[Fritt Ord] can also be unbureaucratic, taking action in acute time-sensitive situations, such as when it saved Norway's flagship encyclopaedia *Store Norske Leksikon*, after the Ministry had rejected the publisher's application for support ... [P]rivate money can bring in broad cultural diversity, but perhaps it is most useful primarily because it can promote flexibility, freshness and unpredictability that are not easy for public money to ensure.'[4]

Fritt Ord's special responsibility, in Sejersted's view, 'is to ensure diversity and freedom in the public space'. As new threats to freedom of expression arise every day, the need for foundations like Fritt Ord will not cease. 'Eternal vigilance,' as the old adage goes, 'is the price of liberty.'

[1] Institusjonen Fritt Ord, *Annual Report 2004*, p17.

[2] Eric P Olsen, *Artist of Skepticism: Knut Hamsun, Father of the Modern School of Literature*, www.worldandi.com/newhome/public/2003/february/bkpub2.asp.

[3] Ibid.

[4] Institusjonen Fritt Ord, *Annual Report 2004*, pp9–10.

ANTÓNIO JOSÉ TEIXEIRA

7 Calouste Gulbenkian Foundation
The rich legacy of an Armenian visionary

A century ago, 'business architect' Calouste Sarkis Gulbenkian launched the oil economy. By the end of his life, the Armenian-born visionary had become one of the world's wealthiest individuals. His art acquisitions are considered one of the world's greatest private collections. Today, the Calouste Gulbenkian Foundation continues his legacy.

In 1891, Calouste Sarkis Gulbenkian had just returned from London, where he had gained a first in engineering at King's College. He needed to know more about the world before embarking on a professional career, so his father sent him on a trip around the Caucasus. And so the young man travelled around the Black Sea and the Caspian Sea. Towards the end of his trip, he visited an oil field, which was still in a very primitive state, at Baku, Azerbaijan.

Oil refining at that time was still a rudimentary affair, with kerosene used for lighting purposes. On his return to Istanbul a year later he wrote a book in French: *La Transcaucasie et la Péninsule d'Apchéron – Souvenirs de Voyage*. Besides relating his ethnographical impressions, he dedicated a few chapters to underlining the importance that oil could have as a source of energy. Two of these chapters were published in the *Revue des Deux Mondes* and caught the attention of the Ottoman government's Ministry of Mines, which sent for him.

A new era was dawning and this Armenian, who enjoyed the grace and favour of the Ottomans, had a decisive influence on it. However, his talents were not to end there. He showed himself to be an exceptional art collector and was later to endow Lisbon with one of the most important European foundations.

The making of 'Mister Five Per Cent'

Gulbenkian, an Armenian, was born on the Asian side of Istanbul on 23 March 1869. The Sultan's government asked him to compile a report on the Empire's oil deposits, especially in Mesopotamia, later known as Iraq. The report foresaw the future importance of the enormous energy reserves in the Middle East. Thereafter Gulbenkian was to become a key figure in the oil business by creating a strategic map for the industry.

In the report, he drew the Ottoman government's attention to the need to build the famous BBB (Berlin, Bosphorus, Baghdad) railway line, which would provide Germany with access to the Persian Gulf and the oil deposits of Mesopotamia. This was not a subject that aroused great concern at the time, but the young Gulbenkian's vision was to prove crucial.

He travelled between Istanbul and London, where he set up residence and married Nevarte Essayan. He acquired British nationality, but still continued to work for the Ottoman government, becoming a financial expert and a highly respected negotiator. Gulbenkian participated

Portrait of Calouste Sarkis Gulbenkian by J C Watelet, Paris, 1912.

in the creation of the Royal Dutch-Shell Group, building bridges between Americans, British, Germans, Dutch and Russians, and making a decisive contribution to the rapid growth of the oil industry in the Persian Gulf.

Two events reinforced the pioneering nature of Gulbenkian's work. In the US, Henry Ford created a popular automobile, the Ford T, a great petrol-guzzling car. In England, the First Lord of the Admiralty, Winston Churchill, proposed that the Royal Navy's vessels should stop using coal and start using oil. Oil became an essential commodity, a major boost for the industry.

Gulbenkian's business involvement stepped up after the Revolution of the Young Turks in 1908. Besides acting as an economic and financial adviser to the Ottoman embassies in London and Paris, he was a consultant to the newly created National Bank of Turkey. In 1912, he set up the Turkish Petroleum Company (TPC), which was to cover the whole of the Ottoman Empire and had four partners: Royal Dutch-Shell (25 per cent), Deutsche Bank (25 per cent), the National Bank of Turkey (35 per cent) and Calouste Gulbenkian (15 per cent).

British pressure soon led to a redistribution of shares and the Anglo-Persian Oil Company joined TPC. Gulbenkian accepted the offer of a 5 per cent share. His knack for obtaining at least 5 per cent of any deal he helped negotiate earned him the nickname of 'Mister Five Per Cent'. When World War One broke out, it led to a further reorganization of the business. Gulbenkian participated in negotiations to create the borders between Turkey and Iraq, signing an agreement between TPC and the Iraqi governor for an oil concession and bringing the French and Americans into the business.

In 1928, a new company was set up under his influence: the Iraq Petroleum Company, formed by the Anglo-Persian Oil Company (today's BP), the Royal Dutch-Shell Group, the Compagnie Française des Pétroles (Total's predecessor) and the Near East Development Corporation (a consortium of six major US oil companies and the predecessor of Exxon Mobil), as well as Gulbenkian, who still continued to hold his 5 per cent share.

This proved a very significant share considering the area covered by the concession: present-day Iraq, Bahrain, Qatar, the peninsula of Saudi Arabia except for Kuwait, plus Jordan and Syria. Drawn by Gulbenkian, this map would become known as the 'Red Line Agreement', because a thick red pencil was used to mark it out.

'These were the borders that I knew in 1914. And I ought to know them. It was within these borders that I was born, lived and served. If anyone knows any better than me, then they should say so,' he said at the time.[1]

Nobody did.

A philanthropic family tradition

Gulbenkian was born into an Armenian family of provincial bankers. His father, Sarkis Gulbenkian, was highly intelligent and gifted in doing business. Several historians maintain the Gulbenkians were Armenian nobility. Kevork Pamboukian says that over the last two centuries, 300 family members were actively involved in trade throughout the Middle East and Europe. After the Crimean War, they settled in Smyrna then moved to Constantinople. They engaged in trade and financial business, with branches in London, Manchester and Liverpool.

The family financed the building of churches and schools in Talas, in Caesarea, and made pilgrimages to Jerusalem. In March 1877, it was Calouste's turn to go, still only eight years old. The family celebrated Easter there and made donations. At the entrance to the Church of the Holy Sepulchre, they left a painting depicting the Resurrection with an inscription in Armenian: 'In memory of the Gulbenkian dynasty from Talas, 1877.'

Astrig Tchamkerten, who studied the presence of the Gulbenkians in Jerusalem, says there are several works bearing witness to the family's fondness for the Holy City. Many institutions and buildings of the Armenian Patriarchate benefited from the family's generosity and later from that of the Foundation. One of the most significant was the restoration of the Church of the Holy Sepulchre.

Calouste first studied in Calcedonia, then moved to Marseille where he improved his French at high school. His collecting instincts soon began to show. At the age of 14, his father rewarded him for his good results at school with a relatively hefty sum of 50 piastres, while, at the same time, extolling the virtues of saving. It didn't take long for the piastres to be spent at the bazaars of Istanbul, where they were exchanged for old coins. The result was a warning from his father, not that this was to have much effect – young Calouste already knew how to respect the value of his assets while cultivating his pleasures.

Taste for the arts, passion for business

This was the beginning of his taste for the arts and his passion for business, while not forgetting charitable works. Between 1920 and 1940, Gulbenkian intensified his support of Armenian communities in Turkey, Lebanon, Syria, Jordan and Iraq. He focused on education and healthcare. Many jobs were created and many churches built, particularly in Kirkuk, Bagdad and Tripoli. In 1930, he became the second president of the Armenian General Benevolent Union.

His first foundation was created some years earlier. The London-based St Sarkis Charity Trust maintained the Church of St Sarkis in the British capital dedicated to his father, the Gulbenkian Library in Jerusalem, and the Sourp Pirgiç Hospital in Istanbul.

Before he turned 40, he was already a millionaire and constantly enriching his art collection. He never ran a large company and there were few people working at his office. Gulbenkian did not like being referred to as a businessman. In one tough negotiation he was labelled in this way, but he became irritated and replied, 'I'm not a businessman, I am a business architect!'[2]

The life of this 'business architect' was divided between London and Paris. He travelled widely, through Italy, Germany, Austria, Spain, Egypt,

Calouste Gulbenkian at the
Edfu Temple, Egypt, 1930.

Palestine and Syria. He was most impressed by the beauties of nature and works of art, leaving six volumes of travel diaries that clearly reveal his aesthetic preferences. Gulbenkian's choices were eclectic: old paintings and some modern ones, sculpture, silverware, coins, Middle Eastern ceramics, Chinese porcelain, tapestry, sophisticated books, and European and Persian manuscripts. Over time, he became more demanding and fixed his attention on the great masterpieces, saying, 'Only the best is enough for me.'[3]

In a letter to a London antique dealer, he defined himself: 'I am not, by nature, a collector of periods or series, but as with paintings I like to own the best examples, whether it's an isolated object or part of a set.'[4] According to researcher António Pinto Ribeiro, he was always a 'clear-minded and determined collector, with well-defined plans for the acquisition of pieces, informed and demanding with the few (and outstanding) advisers. Gulbenkian spent his whole life refining his taste and surrounded himself with the greatest specialists in the various arts: Kenneth Clark, Howard Carter, Arthur Upham Pope, and E S G Robinson, amongst others.'

Ribeiro detected two themes running through the collection. There was his irresistible attraction for the representation of the young female figure and his propensity for acquiring works in which 'sensory pleasure and the sense of touch were crucial features'. He reminds us, in regard to this particular aspect, that Gulbenkian was an Armenian Christian, although not a practising one, who had initially been raised with the values of Islamic culture: 'He learned to establish with art objects a relationship of use, pleasure and sensual decorativism.'[5]

Collecting Soviet treasures

In the 1920s, he moved to Paris as economic adviser to the Persian Embassy. He continued to accumulate more and more pieces, which were scattered around his different homes, with antique dealers and at museums. He visited them regularly and discreetly. Gulbenkian bought a small palace on the Avenue d'Iéna, which he abandoned at the beginning of World War Two.

Between 1928 and 1930, he negotiated with the government of the Union of Soviet Socialist Republics to acquire some valuable pieces from the Hermitage Museum. The Soviets were in desperate need of foreign currency and were secretly selling off works of art. Gulbenkian signed four contracts in a highly complex negotiation process, in which, thanks to his astuteness and perseverance, he managed to outwit powerful competitors, art dealers and international millionaires.

The negotiations were like a 'fencing tournament', in the words of his son-in-law Kevork Essayan. They involved all the tricks in the book, an intense exchange of correspondence, a sophisticated logistical plan designed to guarantee the transport of the pieces, and very discreet transactions. In his letters, Gulbenkian wrote, 'You shouldn't even be selling to me and much less to others. . . . I continue to advise your representatives not to sell the pieces from your museums; but, should you sell them even so, I insist that you should give me preference, at equal prices, and I ask you to keep me fully apprised of the pieces that you wish to sell.'[6]

It was with great delight that he collected these works, which he referred to as 'his children', and kept them in his Paris home. He would observe them at length, alone. On very rare occasions, he would invite friends to his house. If any stranger asked to see his paintings, he would answer that he was an Oriental and that his habits did not include unveiling the women from his harem. This was how he referred to his works of art. 'Would you expect me to show the women in my harem to a stranger?'[7] However, he did not allow his reserved attitude to stop him from exhibiting his collections in museums.

He built up his collection between 1910 and 1940, during which time his fortune almost doubled. His acquisitions from this period include Egyptian art; Flemish, Venetian and French painting; the works of Guardi, Canaletto, Carpaccio, Ghirlandaio, Fragonard, Van Dyck, Lawrence, Manet, Monet, Degas and many others. He spent time in the company of Rodin and Lalique, from whom he bought many different works.

'No price is too high for me'

'He was a delightful, brilliant, lively and dynamic man, of medium height, who spoke perfect English,' said the American writer William Saroyan, who was also of Armenian origin.[8] Gulbenkian exuded self-confidence. When he fixed his sights on something that he liked, it seemed nothing could stop him. He sometimes confessed that his passion for art was like a disease, such was the energy and commitment that he put into possessing works. But he also felt great satisfaction with the size and quality of his collection.

The same can be said of the vision and effectiveness of his business dealings. He did, however, have other aims. In the diary of his travels through the gardens of El Retiro, in the surroundings of Malaga (Spain), he noted, 'To be a man of science and a dreamer in a garden built in my style, these are the two great aims and ambitions of my life that I have not yet managed to achieve.'

His stroll through the gardens in Malaga left him feeling 'the sadness of never having owned a similar garden'.[9] As far as science is concerned, he remembered he had wanted to study astrophysics in Paris immediately after graduating in engineering from King's College. He did not pursue this venture, so as not to upset his father, but continued to read and study books of medicine and botany.

Nine years after his visit to Spain, he succeeded in building the much-coveted garden in his own style, which he found in the region of Deauville, Normandy. In 1937, he bought an estate known as Les Enclos, to which he gradually added other plots of land, reaching a total of 34 hectares. He hired a landscape gardener, but supervised the work himself.

'The sage of Les Enclos'

'The businessman, the fighter that so many people admired for his will power and implacable tenacity, was also, at the same time, a contemplator,' commented Azeredo Perdigão, who became his lawyer and would later continue his work at the helm of the Gulbenkian Foundation.[10] The writer Saint-John Perse (Alexis Léger), winner of the Nobel Prize for Literature and Gulbenkian's friend, shared his fondness for gardens. He gave him advice and suggested different species for planting.

Saint-John Perse called Gulbenkian 'the sage of Les Enclos' and considered the park to be 'the masterpiece of all his works, because it is the most alive, the most intimate and the most sensitive, the one that is most secretly reserved for his whims'.[11]

At Les Enclos, he ordered coops and stables to be built, where he bred and reared pedigree animals. Those who knew him well said these luxury constructions proved his dedication to animals. One day, a calf was born, the offspring of a Dutch cow and a pedigree bull. When Gulbenkian saw it for the first time, the calf came up to him and licked his hand. This was enough to start a friendship of the kind that is the stuff of fables.

The calf grew, but the connection established with its owner did not extend to the steward of the estate. The steward felt obliged to confront his boss with his dilemma: either the steer was sold or he would resign. Gulbenkian appreciated the steward's work, but could not bear to abandon the animal and condemn it to the butcher's. He decided to sell the steer on condition that the new owner would promise not to let it be killed. To ensure this, the new owner would periodically have to send Gulbenkian a certificate issued by a veterinary surgeon.

The executors of his will, showing respect for the patron's presumed wishes, ensured that the animal would continue to enjoy its special privileges until its natural death. The estate of Les Enclos was given by the Foundation to the municipality of Deauville in 1973 as Parc Calouste Gulbenkian.

A 'technical enemy' protects his collections

At the palace in Avenue d'Iéna, the works of art continued to increase in number. In 1936, for safety reasons, Gulbenkian decided to entrust his Egyptian art collection to the British Museum and his best paintings to the National Gallery. When World War Two broke out, the collector maintained his diplomatic status. He was an economic adviser to the Persian embassy, which also operated from within his palace. Paris was invaded by the German troops and Gulbenkian accompanied the Persian ambassador on his move to Vichy, where the Pétain-Laval government had set itself up in direct collaboration with the German occupying forces.

This led the British authorities to declare him a 'technical enemy'. His assets, including works of art and his interests in British oil companies, were handed over to the Custodian of Enemy Property. This disgusted Gulbenkian, for he was a British passport holder who had set up oil companies that opened their doors to the British. He was so offended that he ordered part of his art collections to be shipped to the US.

Azeredo Perdigão says that Gulbenkian understood that having spent 24 years acting as an economic adviser to the Persian Embassy, 'it would not be appropriate for him to abandon his post, all the more so since, by remaining in his position, he would be better able to protect the collections that existed in the French capital, which was now occupied by German troops'.[12]

With the war now at its height, he decided to leave Vichy and go to the US, where the American government had suggested building a museum in Washington to house his collection. It was with this aim in mind that he headed for Lisbon, accompanied by a Portuguese diplomat, his idea being to later sail to the US by boat. But he never did.

The unlikelihood of Lisbon

Gulbenkian was 73 years old when he arrived in Lisbon by Rolls Royce on 10 April 1942, driven by the family chauffeur. He was accompanied by his wife, his private secretary, butler, Russian masseur and chef. He installed himself in the Hotel Aviz, which was to be his address until the end of his days. His wife stayed at the Hotel Palácio in Estoril, where the couple would meet every day at teatime. Nevarte formed a ladies' bridge group, to which Calouste gave his support and which for many years was subsidized by the

Foundation. At that time, Lisbon, as the capital of a neutral country, was the home for spies from both sides of the warring factions, exiles, traders, many diplomats, and passengers in transit to the other side of the ocean.

His apartment at the Hotel Aviz occupied almost a whole floor. He felt comfortable there surrounded by everything he liked, including cats. In a study of the life and times of Gulbenkian, Manuela Fidalgo and Maria Rosa Figueiredo write that one of the rooms was reserved for these pets – at one time he had as many as 18.

He was a most exacting gourmet. His scrambled eggs had to be turned over a specific number of times. Because of his fear of food poisoning or as a safety precaution, he was accompanied on some occasions by his private cook. Gulbenkian was greatly concerned about health and regarded sexual activity as a matter of hygiene, always acting under medical guidance.

When the war ended, Nevarte Essayan returned to the palace in Paris, but Calouste continued to reside in Lisbon. Why? Why didn't he set off either for the US or even for Paris or London? There are many explanations for this, all of them insufficient, we are told by Emilio Rui Vilar, the current president of the Gulbenkian Foundation.

There are some who say that he stayed in Lisbon because it was a quiet and peaceful city, with its hills reminding him of the Bosphorus of his native Istanbul. He appreciated the mild climate, the Portuguese countryside, and undoubtedly the hospitality, safety and low taxes. Although he did not speak Portuguese, he did find a great lawyer, Perdigão, and a great doctor, Fernando Fonseca, both of whom accompanied him until the end of his life.

The doctor, to whom Gulbenkian, a well-known hypochondriac, paid a monthly allowance – except when he was sick – went to Paris to treat his family. The lawyer helped draw up his will. To be added to all these reasons was his displeasure with Britain, which had shown such a lack of consideration when labelling him a 'technical enemy'. The declaration was revoked before the end of the war, as a result of his protests. But it was not annulled, which would have resulted in the invalidation of all its effects, something that could not happen with a simple revocation. This was a question of principle, from which he would not be shifted.

Before the war, he had discussed the possibility of creating a foundation or an institute with his name in a building to be erected next to the National Gallery in London, and the project, designed by the New York architect William Delano, was already approved. But, displeased with the English authorities, he abandoned the idea and transferred all the

View of the Gulbenkian Foundation headquarters, which are set
in their own park.

works that were in the safekeeping of the British to the National Gallery
of Art in Washington. This could have been the final destination of his
collections, but Gulbenkian did not want this to happen. The Americans
were sometimes his rivals and had not always respected him, particularly in
his oil dealings.

The improbable is not impossible . . .

What happened afterwards clearly demonstrated that 'the improbable is
not impossible' according to Rui Vilar. The improbable became possible:
'The Armenian, born an Ottoman, naturalized British, living in Paris, and
intending to travel to the US, ended up staying in Lisbon, and, despite the
extraordinary offers that he received from the US, it was to Lisbon that he
left his art collection. And his fortune.'[13] He bequeathed a trust to each of
his two children, affording them a comfortable income. This was a relatively
small part of his fortune – his annual income was roughly £4 million.

Gulbenkian made two wills. The first in 1950 was provisional and
ensured the perpetuity of a foundation with his name, headquartered in
Lisbon. Three years later, his second will confirmed that the Calouste
Gulbenkian Foundation would be a Portuguese foundation with charitable,
artistic, educational and scientific aims. He set it up in such a way that
it would be heir to most of his fortune, in which he included all his art

collections, wherever they might be found – a total of 6,440 pieces that he
had always wanted to see gathered together under the same roof.

Gulbenkian died on 20 July 1955, at the age of 86. His obituary in
The Times (London) emphasized his role as a 'negotiator' and 'organizer'
in the world of 'industrial diplomacy'. Others, such as Maurice Rheims,
emphasized his being 'one of the most prestigious art lovers that the
World of Curiosity has ever had occasion to know'. Or the man who spent
his whole life committed to maintaining his anonymity, as *Life* Magazine
recognized.[14]

The Calouste Gulbenkian Foundation is launched

There ensued an intense legal, political and diplomatic battle over setting
up the Calouste Gulbenkian Foundation, in which family members, British
interests and the will's executor, Azeredo Perdigão, acting in conjunction
with the government of Salazar, were pitted against one another. The
named trustees were his long-time friend Baron Radcliffe of Werneth,
Lisbon attorney Perdigão, and his son-in-law Kevork Loris Essayan. The
Foundation established the Calouste Gulbenkian Museum (Museu
Calouste Gulbenkian)[15] in Lisbon to display his art collection.

Perdigão was the first president and enjoyed a long period of
leadership (1956–93), in which the Gulbenkian Foundation asserted itself as
an institution that was independent from political power. According to Rui
Vilar's synthesis of the Foundation's history, its role was perfectly adapted
to a particularly complex framework of aspirations, evolving 'from its more
or less obvious function as a supplement to a retrograde state without
any resources, and a weak civil society fettered by the dictatorial regime,
to the alternative and innovative role that was required of it in view of the
profound changes occurring in Portugal – democracy and the country's full
integration into Europe – and in the world, with the fall of the Berlin Wall, the
globalization process and the new uncertainties and current threats'.[16]

Engaging in education, health, culture and science

In its first decades, the Gulbenkian Foundation played a decisive role in
combating Portugal's enormous shortcomings in the areas of education,
health, culture and science. Already in the 1950s, Gulbenkian was a
well-known benefactor, lending his support to various social welfare
centres. In its very first plan of activities, devised in 1957, the Foundation
developed a mobile library service, with as many as 160 vans, spreading
books and the reading habit across the country.

For three generations, it has distributed scholarships and research grants abroad, published low-cost editions of the classical authors, and financed both scientific research and the building of student residences.

In the area of health the Foundation's many initiatives include: a campaign to eradicate malaria, a pilot scheme to eradicate tuberculosis, the creation of cardiosurgery centres, the first intensive care units for heart patients, the introduction of ecography into Portugal, the setting up of haemodialysis units in central hospitals, liver transplants, the purchase of ambulances, and the building of nursing schools. The Foundation has spent more than €320 million on its charity and welfare initiatives alone.

In the social field, it has identified four priority areas: children at risk, the elderly, disabled and immigrants. Every year, it distributes between €5 million and €6 million for the funding of projects. The Foundation also undertakes its own initiatives in the hope that they may provide a 'demonstration effect'. In the municipality of Amadora, in the Greater Lisbon district, in an area where immigrants have been rehoused, the Foundation is lending support to the setting up of organizations that encourage children to stay at school, that help to train local leaders, or that make it possible to undertake community projects for the promotion of ethnic conviviality.

The Foundation has enabled 106 immigrant doctors and 60 immigrant nurses from outside the EU to attend a special training programme that would allow them to carry out their professions rather than working on building sites and in cafés and restaurants. Today, the Ministry of Health is keen to replicate the programme and to integrate roughly 400 doctors into the National Health Service.

Opening up new horizons

The Foundation has also created an orchestra, a dance company and a modern art centre, helping young people to discover music and supporting countless cultural initiatives. Rather than restricting itself to supplying a supplementary service to the one that is already provided by the state, the Foundation now prefers to take risks, to open up new avenues and to invest in innovation and development.

International interventions have taken place in more than 60 countries. The Foundation has a delegation in London, which awards grants and scholarships in the UK; a cultural centre in Paris located in its founder's former residence; and aid programmes for the development of Portuguese-speaking countries. It finances the recovery and restoration of the Portuguese heritage around the world, and supports Armenian

Diaspora communities, following the example of the Gulbenkian family. It is also a member of international philanthropic networks. One of its projects is centred on research and clinical activity in the area of HIV/AIDS and tropical diseases in Angola.

The Foundation's current assets, in real terms and at 1956 prices, are three-and-a-half times higher than the estate bequeathed by Calouste Gulbenkian, a fact that clearly reveals the potential of the legacy and its management over these past 50 years. Even more important is the enormous investment that the Foundation has undertaken, which has resulted in a significant enhancement of human and social capital.

In the words of sociologist António Barreto, the Gulbenkian Foundation has been 'one of the most interesting and innovative Portuguese institutions of the last century'.[17] As Barreto says, it is impossible to imagine what the country would be without the Gulbenkian Foundation.

[1] Calouste Gulbenkian quoted in *Calouste Sarkis Gulbenkian – O Homem e a sua Obra*, FCG, Lisbon, 2006.

[2] Calouste Gulbenkian quoted by Daniel Yergin in *The Prize: The epic quest for oil, money and power*, 1990.

[3] Calouste Gulbenkian quoted by José Azeredo Perdigão in *Calouste Gulbenkian Coleccionador*, FCG, Lisbon, 2006.

[4] Letter addressed to George Davey, London antique dealer, 11 April 1943.

[5] António Pinto Ribeiro, *Fundação Calouste Gulbenkian Cinquenta Anos* 1956–2006, FCG, Lisbon, 2007.

[6] Letter sent by Calouste Gulbenkian to Georges Pictakoff, governor of the USSR Central Bank, 17 July 1930.

[7] Calouste Gulbenkian quoted in *Calouste Sarkis Gulbenkian – O Homem e a sua Obra*.

[8] Ibid.

[9] Calouste Gulbenkian quoted by Manuela Fidalgo and Maria Rosa Figueiredo, *O Gosto do Coleccionador*, FCG, Lisbon, 2006.

[10] In *Calouste Gulbenkian Coleccionador*.

[11] Letter sent by Alexis Léger to Calouste Gulbenkian in *Calouste Sarkis Gulbenkian – O Homem e a sua Obra*.

[12] In *Calouste Gulbenkian Coleccionador*.

[13] Emilio Rui Vilar in 'Tertúlias do Casino', *Figueira da Foz*, 17 April 2007.

[14] Robert Coughlan, 'Mystery Multimillionaire', *Life Magazine*, 27 November 1950.

[15] See http://en.wikipedia.org/wiki/Museu_Calouste_Gulbenkian

[16] In *Fundação Calouste Gulbenkian Cinquenta Anos 1956–2006*.

[17] Ibid.

DIANNA RIENSTRA

8 Impetus Trust
Everything ventured, everything gained

Since its founding in 2003, the UK-based Impetus Trust has lived up to its slogan of 'turning around more lives'. The venture philanthropy investor fund has recorded an average increase in income of 20 per cent at the six charities that have been in its portfolio for at least 12 months. The increase is five times greater than the norm for the sector. In the last two years, a total of £6.50 has been delivered for every £1 of Impetus cash, proof that venture philanthropy is alive and thriving on this side of the Atlantic.

The numbers tell part of the story – and they are impressive. When venture capitalist Stephen Dawson decided to turn his attention to making a difference instead of making money, he ended up doing both in a very big way. The social impact of Impetus's charities measured by the number of beneficiaries served grew by more than 50 per cent a year over the course of 2007. Total funding committed to Impetus has reached £8 million, including £2.6 million in pro bono expertise and £1.5 million in co-investment. At the time of writing, Impetus Trust was working with nine charities – six of which have made remarkable transformations.

During his 20-plus years as a highly successful, leading venture capitalist, Dawson did not have a lot of confidence that money he was giving away to charity was being used and managed in the most effective and efficient way possible. After volunteering his advisory services at a small charity for a spell and experiencing the myriad challenges faced by non-profits, he decided to team up with a few trusted business colleagues and take things into his own hands.

What is venture philanthropy?

The buzz around venture philanthropy has amplified since the concept originated. Some argue it began in 1997 with a *Harvard Business Review*[1] article that argued that many grantmaking foundations did not pay enough attention to helping non-profits build efficient, sustainable structures and strengthen their capacity to deliver services. In the 11 years since that article sparked both controversy and creativity, 'venture philanthropy' has been invented and re-invented on both sides of the Atlantic.

Whatever the nomenclature, venture philanthropy – also known as 'engaged philanthropy', 'new philanthropy', 'social venture funding' or 'philanthrocapitalism'[2] – built up considerable momentum as it swept across the US like a brushfire, fanned particularly by exceptionally rich baby boomers during the dot.com frenzy. At the time, venture philanthropy earned a rather negative reputation as hugely successful internet entrepreneurs convinced themselves – and others – that their aggressive tactics could successfully be applied to the non-profit sector. Some of it turned out to be hype, some of it turned out to be real.

The European Venture Philanthropy Association (EVPA), a membership organization created in 2004, defines venture philanthropy as a 'field of philanthropic activity where private equity/venture capital models are applied in the non-profit and charitable sectors'. There are many different forms of venture philanthropy, but according to EVPA it is:

- The active partnership, or engagement, of donors, volunteers and/ or experts with charities to achieve agreed outcomes such as organizational effectiveness, capacity-building or other important change.
- The use of a variety of financing techniques in addition to grants, such as multi-year financing, loans or other financial instruments most appropriate for a charity's needs.
- The capability to provide skills and/or hands-on resources with the objective of adding value to the development of a charity.
- The desire to enable donors to maximize the social return on their investment whether that be as a financial donor or as a volunteer of time and expertise.

The first large-scale UK venture philanthropy fund was co-founded by Stephen Dawson in 2003, when he launched Impetus Trust.

Taking a donor point of view

Dawson was also determined to go beyond chequebook philanthropy and to make a difference. 'As a donor I found it difficult just writing out a cheque to one of the big brand charities and not knowing how well the money was being spent or whether it had made a difference,' he explained in 2003.[3] 'I tried to find smaller charities who might benefit more, but it was impossible, as someone with little knowledge of the sector, to find out much about them.'

At the outset of Impetus, Dawson described the frustration faced by the chief executives of small charities – the problems of long-term and core cost funding, the lack of support and, in some instances, the lack of business acumen. '[That's] what led me to venture philanthropy – thinking how you could do a better job from a donor point of view, getting the best value and providing better support for the CEO,' he says.

Dawson researched the venture philanthropy phenomenon that was sweeping across the US, but found that seemingly fearless entrepreneurs were surprisingly cautious, choosing fairly obvious beneficiaries where grantmakers were already investing. He was determined to seek out the less obvious and fund organizations that were finding it difficult to raise money.

He was also determined not to simply transplant US-style venture philanthropy to the UK. 'There was a good deal of arrogance in the venture capital turned venture philanthropy world and massive mistakes were made. People thought they could change the world in half an hour. There was a good deal of naivety about the challenges faced by the non-profit world. Some of these ventures have survived, many did not,' he says today.

Five years ago, Dawson founded Impetus Trust together with American-born Nat Sloane, whose career in management consultancy complemented Dawson's career in venture capital, specializing in buyouts, buy-ins and development capital deals worth between £5 million and £100 million. They met during a workshop on venture philanthropy in 2002. 'Nobody was doing venture philanthropy at the time, so we said, "let's do it",' he explains.

Says Sloane: 'I wanted to give money to charities not because of their brand name, but because of the impact they have.'

Since then, Impetus Trust – led by a six-member executive team and a board of trustees that includes both Dawson and Sloane as Chairman and Vice-Chair respectively and as 'Volunteer Executives' – has been living up to its slogan of turning around more lives.

Impetus Chairman Stephen Dawson with Jenny Rogers, Chief Executive of *Leap* Confronting Conflict, who describes Impetus's role as that of a 'critical friend'.

Dawson explains how it works: 'Impetus brings strategic funds and expertise to charities that turn around the lives of disadvantaged people. We support our chosen charities over a defined period of time, usually three to five years, so that they become stronger and more sustainable by the time our partnership ends. We build on our donors' funding by leveraging additional funding from co-investment and pro bono support. In return, we deliver a measurable social return on investment for our donors.'

The Impetus website says the organization provides an 'integrated venture philanthropy package', which includes translating venture capital and business frameworks for the non-profit sector. The investment approach is based on long-term funding and expertise. Hands-on support is given to management.

But the Impetus approach to venture philanthropy goes well beyond importing to the non-profit world the hard and fast business principles that underpin capital markets. Dawson and his team are hands on from the beginning. 'We bring business skills to support charities at a critical stage in their development,' he explains. Harder to measure – but equally or even more important – are the energy and passion the Impetus team brings to its work.

Ready for a step change?

Dawson points out that not all charities stand to benefit from this type of engagement. 'This isn't right for everyone. The organization has to be ready to go through a step change. If it is growing steadily or going up and down, we may not be right for them. They must need the mixture Impetus can provide – strategic funding and expertise,' he says. 'It is often difficult to judge the degree to which organizations need help. A key ingredient for us is a good chief executive and some good board members so that we feel there is a team we want to back.'

If Dawson sounds like a coach, it is because in many ways he is one – a coach looking for a good team that needs help. And, like any good coach, he brings in outside expertise when it is needed. Impetus relies on pro bono experts and corporate partners who use their skills to build capacity for organizations that have reached a key stage in their development. Such experts and partners also participate in the selection process to determine which charities Impetus takes on.

It is a two-stage decision process. First, the investment committee (grants committee) decides in principle whether the charity fits the Impetus criteria. The second stage goes deeper – a team spends a lot of time assessing the charity. This could involve several months of work as Impetus does its due diligence. 'We carefully go through every aspect of the organization in terms of its financial situation, the board or trustees, the chief executive officer, everything,' Dawson says. 'But the most important, and certainly the most valuable, aspect is analysing the market it is operating in.'

The market? Dawson admits that this is 'a foreign word' to most non-profits. But all non-profits are operating in a market, he insists, even if it is in nothing else but competing for funds. Impetus brings in London-based OC&C Strategy Consultants – a name that commands services worth £70,000 to £80,000 per project – to analyse the charity's competitive positioning in its market, examine funding trends, study government investment, and determine how best to go forward to meet both funding and organizational objectives. This gives the organization 'tremendous value' whether or not it is selected for investment, Dawson says. 'And it's free.'

Results from an independent evaluation of Impetus conducted during 2005 found that the Impetus due diligence evaluation is 'clearly valued and well respected by those who have been through it. They all learned a great deal and thought that process in itself has added value to their organization – 80 per cent of respondents felt that the application process had been of value to their organization. This feedback speaks for itself considering that fewer than 10 per cent of all applicants had been invested in.'[4]

Heavily involved from day one . . .

Once a charity is selected, it is heavy involvement, hands on from day one, according to Dawson. Monthly meetings are held with the chief executive officer, milestones are set and funding, which is contributed on a quarterly basis, is subject to achieving them. 'We work together to set priorities for capacity-building, identify gaps in the system and determine what the organization needs to achieve a step change,' he says. 'We work with them to remove obstacles to growth.'

In practical terms, this includes strengthening business skills, defining a marketing strategy, rebranding exercises, boosting earned income activity, implementing performance measurement, mentoring and management development. The 'trickiest part' is the exit strategy, although Impetus has not gone through that experience yet. In 2008, three charities will be in this phase.

'We make it clear that our involvement is three to five years max and we decide that timeframe in the beginning. There is clarity from day one about what we are trying to achieve. Funding typically increases quite rapidly and there is a burst of activity early on in the process. Both the funding and the expertise decline over time, which reduces the feeling of dependency,' Dawson explains.

An organization such as OC&C will likely be brought in at the exit phase as well. The build-up to the exit strategy includes measuring progress to date, re-evaluating the market, devising a strategy to go forward, developing a funding proposition, and identifying potential funders.

Outside expertise brings in years of experience

Impetus pro bono experts and corporate partners provide expertise on numerous strategic and operational projects. The spectrum of projects is wide, from working for a few days on a one-off project such as financial reporting to more detailed due diligence projects undertaken prior to investment in a particular charity. The experts and partners bring in years of experience with backgrounds primarily in consulting, professional services, venture capital and private equity.

What is in it for them? Often the motivation is staff development and retention, as well as extending their personal experience or their organization's experience in the non-profit sector. Dawson says they also benefit from the satisfaction of making a difference. They have certainly made a difference to the Impetus charities: from the launch of Impetus to 2007, the value of pro bono and corporate partner expertise contribution is valued at £2.6 million for services provided.

Again, such services are invaluable, but equally invaluable is the energy and passion the experts and partners bring to their engagement. They volunteer their time and experience, but it is 'brilliant for everyone', he says. 'We have learned a lot, particularly that we cannot come in and say that we know how to run things better. We choose volunteers with a healthy attitude, which means they want challenges, they want to learn, meet great people, work with beneficiaries and have some amazing experiences. It works, particularly for bright young people with a conscience.'

In October 2007, Impetus announced a partnership with ISIS Equity Partners, a private equity firm that has committed to contributing both financial support and operational expertise over a five-year period to build capacity for Impetus charities. The relationship between Impetus and ISIS demonstrates the close links between the venture philanthropy and private equity worlds. Just as Impetus takes a strategic stake with its charities, so too has ISIS in its five-year partnership with Impetus.

In addition to the financial support, it will get involved in the various stages that Impetus goes through with its charities pre and post investment. In particular ISIS will work with Impetus charity applicants in carrying out due diligence.

This is the first time ISIS has partnered with a venture philanthropy organization. The private equity firm looked at Impetus's proven ability to drive growth in the charities it backs by leveraging substantial additional funding through its network of pro bono experts, as well as its ability to demonstrate clear results – just as commercial businesses must do. The partnership with Impetus builds on ISIS's knowledge of the healthcare and social sectors and the work it does with investees.

'We are excited about our partnership with Impetus Trust. Not only is the Impetus model of funding charities very similar to the one we use in private equity, we are looking forward to helping Impetus improve lives and give something back,' says Adam Holloway, Partner, ISIS. 'By engaging with the charities that Impetus backs, we will provide support to help them grow and increase their social return.'

Other strategic partners include the British Venture Capital Association (BVCA), whose chairman, Wol Kolade, named Impetus Charity of the Year in 2007. 'The reason why Impetus stood out for me,' he said, 'was first of all because it's such a good fit with the way we work in private equity, and secondly because it has such a direct impact on the effectiveness of a whole range of other charities, and on the difference they can make in their chosen fields.'

Dawson and Impetus trustee Doug Miller were also involved in the formation of the European Venture Philanthropy Association (EVPA) in 2004. Both are still active in EVPA and Miller is currently Chair.

Impetus corporate partners and pro bono experts come from many high-profile organizations including KPMG, BBC, Worshipful Company of Management Consultants, Directorbank, O'Melveny & Myers, Debevoise & Plimpton LLP, Cavendish Corporate Finance, Worshipful Company of IT Consultants, Faegre Benson LLP and Equus Group. Individuals come from private equity firms including 3i, Advent, Bridgepoint, ECI, Phoenix and IRRFC.

Turning contributions into smart money

When Dawson and Sloane launched Impetus, they raised £2 million, primarily from other private equity colleagues intrigued by venture philanthropy's potential and Impetus's intent to turn donors' contributions into smart money. The goal is to raise £30 million by 2012, targeting £10 million each in cash, co-investment and pro bono expertise.

The Impetus website notes that individuals' or businesses' donations to Impetus enable them to 'combine the involvement and satisfaction of individual giving, with the efficiency and confidence that comes with the Impetus approach of selecting charities and involving specialist managers'. The benefits are manifold, but the ultimate satisfaction 'is knowing that you have made the biggest difference with your money'.

Co-investors are urged to support Impetus by contributing to core costs or to its investment funds, or both. Or they can get involved by introducing charities to the organization or co-funding Impetus-backed charities.

'A critical friend'

When Jennifer Rogers took on the position of Chief Executive at *Leap* Confronting Conflict in 2004, she had no idea what was ahead of her. There was no doubt that the national voluntary youth organization and registered charity was doing good work. *Leap* was providing opportunities, regionally and nationally, for young people and adults to explore creative approaches to conflicts in their lives.

During her first week, she learned *Leap* was to be subject to the gruelling four to six month process of an Ofsted audit (Ofsted is the UK Office for Standards in Education) because it had some government funding. 'This was a baptism of fire, but we came out with a glowing report. I was quickly aware of our strengths and where we needed to develop. I was assured that the quality of what *Leap* delivered was as good as we were told it was,' she says. 'But that was just the beginning.'

The Board included growing the organization in her job description. It wanted Rogers to capitalize on the back catalogue of intellectual property that *Leap* had built up – training courses, books, expert trainers developed over 16 years, but never 'milked'. The Board was also looking to expand nationally. But there was no budget to do it.

Tackling conflict is a huge area, explains Rogers. It is complex and involves an array of people – both employees and volunteers – with very different skills. Long before anyone in Britain was thinking about gangs as a problem, *Leap* had done considerable work on how young people get into conflict and why they join gangs. As early as 2003, the organization was receiving telephone calls from schools in east London, concerned about conflict and gangs forming outside of school. *Leap* was funded by the Diana, Princess of Wales Memorial Fund to research this relatively new phenomenon of gangs in the UK.

Leap initiated programmes in schools and in housing estates, working directly with young people aged 13 to 21. 'A gang is a safe wild place. You can harness that energy, companionship and loyalty and turn this into more positive activities rather than negative activities,' Rogers explains. 'We never tell young people not to get involved in gangs. We involve the entire community in finding alternatives.'

Young people from Newham in London's East End, during a
Leap 'Quarrel Shop' training session, talk about how to prevent
conflict and violence in their area.

Over the years, *Leap* had done just that and built up considerable expertise within communities, involving schools, churches, community centres and young people trained as mediators. Within six to seven years, *Leap* had developed a wide spectrum of activities and materials, and trained dozens of young people about conflict management.

Many adult practitioners have also been trained in working with challenging behaviour or youth gangs. For example, a six-month course, Quarrel Shop, is aimed at young people aged 16 to 21 from disadvantaged backgrounds and trains them to become community trainers, leaders and mediators. They then work with their peer group to help prevent violence.

But how to grow this? *Leap* was at the cutting edge with its work, but there were serious capacity issues and the organization was 'heading towards an iceberg' as government money had come to an end owing to a change in funding criteria. At this juncture, Impetus came into the picture. 'It was like listening to a completely alien language,' Rogers recalls. 'I knew we needed funding, but support to help us grow and develop? A market analysis? Growth strategy?'

Rogers knew that *Leap*'s potential was huge in many areas, particularly in the selling of its training and services. But, like some non-profits, it was suffering from a culture of dysfunction. For example, the management team comprised well-meaning, talented people who were not trained as managers.

The engagement with Impetus followed a rigorous process of due diligence by OC&C, which Rogers describes as 'a wonderful experience'. The language may have been foreign, but it was music to her ears, she says. 'The breadth of what they did was astounding. They analysed our "competitors" and tried to measure our impact, rather than our outcomes. For example, they analysed the costs of institutionalizing young people and set that against the cost of *Leap*'s programmes that can turn around young lives and prevent them from falling into the criminal justice system.'

Rogers worked closely with Dawson, a relationship she describes as 'somewhat difficult' at the beginning. They were like 'two aliens from two different planets meeting for the first time'. She was asked to create a business plan by January 2005. He declared it too 'woolly'. She became frustrated with his forensic attention to detail and went back to the drawing board. Rogers realized she had to restructure her entire management team. She had to hire an IT and systems person. She had to produce 'management information'.

By April–May 2005, she had a business plan that worked. By January 2006, she was enrolled in a social entrepreneur training course at France's prestigious INSEAD international business school. Through pro bono and Impetus support, Rogers agreed to certain milestones in year one and year two. Monthly meetings helped to keep her on track. A leadership coach helped to build her confidence by identifying target areas for personal development.

'I realized that some of it was about me as a leader and driver of change. They had confidence in me, which gave me confidence in myself to do what was necessary to grow the organization,' she says.

It was not easy. The package of just under £300,000 for three years was not going to be enough to achieve the targets set. A rule of thumb in the non-profit world is that it takes time for investment to pay off. Business people find this frustrating. But within 18 months, *Leap* 'was flying', according to Rogers. 'People were starting to take notice of us because of being branded as an Impetus charity. No more cap in hand begging for donations.'

When Impetus came in, *Leap* was stuck on a £500,000 annual turnover with income coming almost exclusively from trust and foundation funders. It was charging for adult training courses, but subsidizing the delivery. 'Now we are selling training and making a profit,' Rogers reports. 'In three years, we've doubled everything – capacity, income and output.'

Leap ended 2007 with £1.2 million. In 2004, *Leap* worked with 2,000 young people. By the end of 2007, it had worked with 4,200 young people and trained 1,400 adults, compared to 300 in previous years.

'What is needed in charities such as ours is investment in the core, in ourselves. Usually we drag ourselves along from one funding crisis to the next. Impetus set up a new model for us. They really believe in the product, the social capital,' Rogers says. But she agrees with Stephen Dawson that the process isn't for everyone, and that organizations need to be ready for a step change. 'This is the secret – you can do wonderful work, but reality is about delivery and sustainability.'

The most valuable role played by Impetus goes beyond funding. 'Helping the chief executive and managers is key. Introducing some business models for certain functions is helpful. But the critical friend role and the monthly opportunity to focus on capacity building is immeasurable,' Rogers explains. 'We don't usually have the time to think beyond the operational details long enough to do this. Working with Impetus also opened many doors and brought *Leap* to the attention of the business world and others.'

The exit strategy is playing out. Impetus is helping with *Leap*'s next funding pitch. Funding of £400,000 has come in, which was invested in higher-level managers, IT systems, staff development, regional scoping and pilot activities, marketing and recruitment and development of more specialist trainers. In a landmark development, a £3 million government grant is in the pipeline.

Reshaping the relationship between donors and beneficiaries

Dawson remains relatively modest about Impetus's achievements, but he has ambitious plans to reshape the landscape of philanthropy. The organization is committed to deepening its knowledge and expertise to

---

Flying under Impetus's wing

Six of the nine charities under the Impetus wing are flying. Since the start of the partnership, Impetus says it has helped to increase their incomes by 20 per cent a year and to help 50 per cent a year more beneficiaries. These charities include ex-offenders support group St Giles Trust, learning difficulties group Speaking Up, eating disorders charity Beat, youth charity the Keyfund Federation, *Leap*, and Naz Project London, which supports people with HIV in black and minority ethnic communities.

Impetus backed St Giles Trust to become a stronger provider of offender resettlement support and services in South-east England by helping them to define a long-term strategy. This included mobilizing the organization to focus on breaking the cycle of homelessness and offending by providing access for offenders to housing, training and jobs. An estimated 70 per cent of prisoners re-offend within two years of being released.

A series of key objectives were defined for 2004 to 2008. Since 2004, St Giles has reduced the re-offending rate by 20 per cent for its beneficiaries and its reach has increased from 2 to 20 prisons. The organization has achieved 37 per cent annual growth in income from £1.34 million in 2003–04 to £3.2 million in 2006–07. St Giles reports a 109 per cent annual growth in the total number of people helped, and 'housing obtained' numbers have risen from 160 to 1,521.

Impetus backed Speaking Up, helping them to refocus and put the stress on empowering people with learning difficulties to take control of their own lives. Key objectives set for 2004–08 were realized, with the organization reporting a 94 per cent annual growth in the number of people helped, particularly through growth in advocacy projects. The number of people who participated in a Speaking Up project increased fivefold from 500 to 2,606.

help the charities it backs to achieve higher levels of success. Impetus is also committed to sharing its knowledge and providing insight to the charity world about venture philanthropy. It publishes results, disseminates case studies, and facilitates leadership workshops between the non-profit and business worlds.

The social return has always been important to Dawson. But ultimately he wants to put something on the map that will make a difference to how charities are funded. He wants to change the way the market operates and reshape the relationship between donors and beneficiaries.

The organization has also achieved a 53 per cent annual growth in income, driven by several major advocacy contract wins during the year. With Impetus, Speaking Up has restructured consulting and training services to enable the organization to reach greater numbers of people.

Two of Impetus's nine charities, ex-offenders support group St Giles Trust and learning difficulties group Speaking Up.

'It is great to work with organizations like *Leap*, to see the changes and the successes, but this has a relatively small impact,' he says. 'If we can change the way donors and foundations look at how they fund an organization, it will make a massive difference.'

Dawson maintains that, today, resources are allocated almost randomly. Generally, funders do not have good data upon which to make judgements; they cannot influence the organizations they are funding because they do not have the instruments. 'In the business world, there are mechanisms to ensure that resources go to people who have a formula that works,' he concludes.

[1] Christine Lett, William Dyer and Allen Grossman, 'Virtuous Capital: What Foundations Can Learn from Venture Capital', *Harvard Business Review*, 1 March 1997.

[2] 'The birth of philanthropcapitalism', *The Economist*, 26 February 2006.

[3] Paul Mason, 'A Capital Idea', *Professional Fundraising*, mid-June 2003, p17.

[4] Diane Mulcahy, 'Active engagement for social impact', *Private Equity International*, June 2006, p79.

HILDY SIMMONS

9 Stavros Niarchos Foundation
Giving well – meeting a constant challenge

With more than 1,400 grants made, almost €207 million committed through 2007, and at least €300 million dedicated to the Stavros Niarchos Foundation Cultural Center in Athens, the Foundation has made a very strong start in its first decade.

Shipping magnate Stavros Niarchos understood the meaning of thinking and acting globally long before the term 'globalization' became so prominent in public policy and economics. His business operations began in Greece, yet his accomplishments were notable worldwide. He is considered one of the most successful businessmen of the 20th century.

Stavros Niarchos was born 3 July 1909 in Athens, Greece. His parents both came from small villages near Sparta in southern Greece. He studied law at the University of Athens and began working in 1929 in his family's grain business. Recognizing the substantial expense of importing wheat from Argentina and the former Soviet Union, Niarchos convinced his family that he could save money by owning the ships that provided the transportation. The first six freighters were bought during the Great Depression.

While Niarchos served in the Greek Navy during World War Two, the Allied forces leased his first vessel. He participated in the Allied operations in Normandy and was awarded the Order of the Phoenix, the Royal Order of King George I, and the Royal House Order of SS George and Constantine, among other distinguished service medals. The ship leased to the Allies was destroyed and Niarchos used the insurance funds as capital to expand his fleet after the war. He bought oil tankers, which marked the young

Stavros Niarchos.

entrepreneur's beginning as a significant player in the world of international commerce.

In 1956, less than 20 years after creating his own firm, Niarchos agreed to build and operate the Hellenic Shipyards, the first such private investment in Greece. Known as the Skaramanga Yard, it employed more than 6,000 skilled workers and rapidly became the largest Mediterranean shipyard for repairs and new construction. In 1985, the shipyard was placed under state control, but Niarchos's early and considerable commitment to Greece stands as an effective demonstration of the power of private investment for the country's economic well-being. This commitment – and investment – was to continue well after his death.

Making an impact on the world stage

Niarchos's business philosophy in shipping was to buy and build big: his super tankers set world records for size and carrying capacity. For many years, he owned the largest private fleet in the world, operating more than 80 tankers.

His personal accomplishments ranged from competitive sailing to championship horse racing. Stavros Niarchos earned recognition as an important investor in, and collector of, fine art. He worked tirelessly and expected much from those who worked for him. As master of his own success, he understood the potential of every individual.

The cover of *Time* magazine in 1956 described him as a 'shipping tycoon'. In the following 40 years before his death in 1996, his achievements and activities continued to be reported on widely in the business and popular media. While he did not necessarily seek fame, he clearly had a desire for a legacy that went beyond the sum total of his financial accomplishments.

The creation of an eponymous foundation offered just such an opportunity, with its work guided by his lifetime interests. By requiring that at least half of the funds distributed be spent in Greece, he ensured that his impact on the country of his birth would be secured in perpetuity. The Stavros Niarchos Foundation, which began operations in 1996, embodies the guiding principles Nicarchos laid out. His vision was to contribute to the well-being of Greece and to have an impact on the world philanthropically, just as he had made an impact in his many successful business ventures.

The legacy of Ancient Greece

Although the Stavros Niarchos Foundation's work in Greece and internationally has been very much in keeping with modern times, the cultural heritage of Ancient Greece is important when considering the context and underlying values of the Foundation's activities. Stavros Niarchos strongly encouraged the promotion of Hellenism as an important part of its giving programme. The cultural roots, as he no doubt understood, run deep.

The word 'philanthropy' – the love of mankind – comes from Classical Greek. It seems fitting to listen to the Ancient Greeks in reflecting on the Foundation's first decade and as the Directors and staff consider the future.

Aristotle wrote about Generosity, Extravagance and Stinginess in the *Nichomachean Ethics*. While he never tells readers what they should or should not do or give, he distinguishes excessive giving from insufficient giving and describes a mean, which he calls generosity, in an effort to help the reader understand the concept of giving well.

With growing demands on the Stavros Niachros Foundation's resources, particularly as its work becomes more widely known, the challenge to give well remains constant. It is the Directors' intent to ensure that positive change occurs as a result of the Foundation's actions.

Aristotle also wrote, 'education is the best provision for the journey to old age'. The Foundation's far-reaching interest in education, across ages and geography, is a modern-day representation of a clearly relevant message.

Socrates wrote, 'the unexamined life is not worth living' – this too speaks to the values of education, culture and well-being embodied by the Foundation's activities. Finally, the phrase, 'Give me where to stand and I will move the earth' is attributed to the mathematician Archimedes. He was offering guidance on physics, but the concept also has applications for philanthropy.

After ten years of operation, it can be said that by providing funds to create the Foundation, Stavros Niarchos's legacy was to provide a 'firm place to stand' for those charged with realizing his charitable vision. No doubt, he expected that over time the wise application of his charitable resources would help improve conditions throughout the world.

Stavros Niarchos's life and interests led those charged with executing his philanthropic vision to concentrate the distribution of funds in four main areas: arts and culture, education, health and medicine, and social welfare. In addition to the distributions in Greece, the Foundation has a strong commitment to support projects promoting Hellenism outside Greece.

Think globally and locally

In the Foundation's early years, its Directors assessed the opportunities inside and outside Greece to determine where the Foundation had the potential to add value in a significant way. With half of the Directors members of Niarchos's family and the others men who knew him well through his business activities, his thoughts and vision were ever-present in the conversations that led to the creation of the Foundation's operating strategy. Starting from scratch did not mean starting without a sense of what was important to the donor and how he might like to be remembered.

The Directors understood that the Foundation's work and the donor's philanthropic legacy were going to evolve over the long term. They were anxious to begin operations, but there was also a clear sense that much could be learned from the work of others. They deliberately took time to discuss programme strategy, to meet with representatives of US and European foundations, and to learn about opportunities within the eventual programme areas.

The most formidable operating challenge the Directors faced was how to function as an international foundation with clear European roots, but with interests in the US as well as other parts of the world. The Foundation was also committed to spending at least half of all funds in one country. Geography in the case of Greece was clearly destiny, but the mandate was to think globally, not just locally.

The new foundation was large by international standards, yet the country in which it had to distribute at least half of its funds is small in both population and geography. Added to this challenge were two other significant issues. First, the non-governmental sector in Greece was not as robust as in other Western European countries. This at once made the opportunities for effective grantmaking more compelling but also, at times, more complex. Second, the government sector as a prime service provider in many of the areas for the Foundation's prospective activities – education, health, arts and culture, and social welfare – had limited experience in working with charitable entities of this size and type.

With no formal or set payout requirement, the Directors needed to establish internal distribution parameters, ensuring that at least half of the funds distributed were spent in Greece.

Flexibility within a structure

One important result was a decision to concentrate support on activities that could be sustained over time without creating dependency on the Foundation's resources. Sir Dennis Weatherstone, the Foundation's Chairman, set the stage for the initial operations by suggesting that the Foundation embrace 'flexibility within a structure'.

While there was no rush to make distributions in Greece or internationally, a few significant grants were made in the early years to respond to some of Niarchos's interests. Four commitments outside Greece are particularly notable. The first was a contribution to the capital campaign under way at the Museum of Modern Art in New York. As a notable collector and a long-time supporter of the museum, a grant enabled a gallery to be named in honour of the Foundation.

Two gifts supported major medical institutions in the US. The Weill Cornell Medical School received support to establish research fellowships and a commitment was made to Johns Hopkins University School of Medicine to support research and treatment in ophthalmology, urology, surgery and bioethics. These gifts built on Niarchos's interest in health and medicine and offered opportunities to support new areas of investigation by both promising young scientists and more established researchers.

The largest grant during this period was made in 1999 to the Sail Training Association of the UK, now called the Tall Ships Youth Trust, to fund a new vessel. The *Stavros S Niarchos*, launched the following year, has provided challenging sailing and youth development opportunities for hundreds of young people from the UK, Greece and other countries. Everyone who knew Niarchos is confident that Tall Ships Youth Trust programmes, which combine leadership development and sailing prowess, are representative of this exceptional man.

Committed to integrity

The Foundation is committed to a high standard of integrity in all of its operations. Procedures were implemented to respond in a timely fashion and to ensure that applicants understood all operating guidelines.

Many of the early grant recipients were asked to keep the donor's name anonymous. This protected the Foundation from an early onslaught of requests that might have ensued given the visibility of the Niarchos name, particularly in Greece. The philosophy on public recognition and visibility has evolved over the years – a website was created in 2004. However, the actual amounts of individual grants are not disclosed.

To ensure responsiveness to opportunities in Greece, an Advisory Committee was formed to identify and review proposals and to make recommendations to the Directors on funding decisions. Advisory Committee members travelled throughout the country in search of opportunities. They met with and listened to people in all walks of life – government, civic and educational organizations, business and religious leaders – to better understand where the Foundation could add value.

As operations in Greece expanded, the Foundation added professional staff to meet the grantmaking challenges and realize the opportunities identified. The programme staff now reviews new requests, monitors ongoing grants and develops programmes based on research to identify areas of need. A technical staff based in Greece works with grant recipients, particularly on the implementation of capital projects, which represent a significant portion of the grants made. The members of the Greek Advisory Committee continue to provide recommendations to the Directors and guidance for the staff.

Establishing a track record at home

After establishing a track record of giving in Greece, the Directors and the Greek Advisory Committee decided to pursue a project of considerable significance. In 2007, it announced a Memorandum of Understanding with the Greek government to fully fund a major national project. The Stavros Niarchos Foundation Cultural Center will consist of a new National Library, a new National Lyric Theatre and an Educational and Cultural Park, all to be located at the Athens Faliron Delta.

The Center is expected to attract nearly 1 million visitors annually. The National Library will be a state-of-the-art facility committed to the principle of lifelong learning. In addition to extensive collections and public internet access, it will emphasize educational programmes for young children and be fully equipped to serve people with special needs. The National Lyric Theatre will be a cultural centre that can accommodate internationally produced performances.

The Educational and Cultural Park will provide much-needed green space in Athens. Through the planting of trees, the park should positively influence the area's microclimate and air quality. Importantly, this urban oasis will connect the city centre to its waterfront. The final agreement between the Foundation and the government is expected in 2008.

'[The Stavros Niarchos Foundation Cultural Center] is a unique opportunity for all involved, our foundation as the sole donor and the Greek people . . . to give life to this project. Athens, the cradle of civilization, will now have the necessary facilities to be a major and distinguished participant in the educational and cultural arena of the 21st century,' said Andreas Dracopoulos, a Director of the Foundation and the designated Board overseer of Greek grantmaking activities. 'We at the Foundation are honoured to be able to play our part in ensuring this dream can be realized.'

Promoting Hellenism

There are many things that distinguish the Foundation's work in its first decade of operations, both for the positive outcomes and for the lessons learned that will inform its future work. First is the creative implementation of Niarchos's wish to promote Hellenism.

The Directors opted for a multifaceted strategy, recognizing that there are many ways to implement this mandate. The Diaspora Greek community and the Greek Orthodox Church provided many opportunities. Grants to Greek schools have provided new facilities and educational materials. The Foundation has also provided support for social welfare programmes including Saint Michael's Home in Yonkers, New York, which provides housing and care to the elderly. Other community-based facilities are also supported, all sponsored and operated by church members for the benefit of the broader Greek community.

Support extended beyond the Greek community in 2003 to the New York Public Library and the Queens New York Public Library for a Hellenic Festival that offered a variety of exhibitions and public programmes including dance, theatre, music performances, films, workshops and lectures over the course of six months.

A more recent grant enabled the Children's Museum of Manhattan to create an exhibition on Ancient Greece that will travel to other children's museums across the US. This theme was continued through support of the Odysseus Language Project at Simon Fraser University in Vancouver, British Columbia, Canada where web-based courses are being developed with Modern Greek content for Chinese students.

An example of the implementation of this strategy is the Foundation's relationship with the Hellenic Studies Program at Yale University. After being asked to provide funding to expand Yale's offerings related to Modern Greece, the Foundation in 2001 opted for a pilot project partnership with the University to assess academic interest and to secure the University's commitment to sustain any new work over time. Funds were provided to support language instruction in Modern Greek, to offer new courses by visiting scholars, and for public outreach.

Based on the initial success of the programme and Yale's continuing commitment to the expanded offerings, a second multi-year grant was made. In 2007, the experience of six years turned into an endowment grant to establish the Stavros Niarchos Foundation Center for Hellenic Studies at Yale. The now permanent funding, when combined with the University's resources, will include support for language study and funds for library resources, research and travel to Greece, and public events.

Supporting international organizations

The positive experience of partnering with Yale over time is mirrored by relationships that developed with two international social welfare organizations. Operating support provided to the Landmine Survivors Network in 1998 proved transformative. In the case of Home-Start International, in 1999 such support helped launch a new worldwide effort, now with operations in 15 countries.

Key to the impact of these grants was the willingness of the Foundation's Directors to take some risks and to provide operating support over time. These decisions were possible because the Directors believed in the organizations' missions, trusted their leadership, and were committed to identifying projects where support could truly make a difference. This willingness to build partnerships over several years represents a second important aspect of the Foundation's activities.

Home-Start International promotes the welfare of predominantly low-income families with very young children by using trained volunteers who offer support, practical help and friendship to families under stress. An outgrowth of Home-Start UK, which was founded in the 1970s, Home-Start International was created in 1998 to respond to requests from many countries interested in adopting or adapting the model.

Believing that many families could be strengthened and sustained through crisis periods with the assistance of caring community members (many former recipients of Home-Start assistance themselves), the goal was to establish a sister organization to further the Home-Start model throughout the world. After three years, new partnerships had been created in seven countries with additional countries added in the subsequent years.

Although the Niarchos Foundation support has diminished, it was the cornerstone of the organization's funding base and led to further support from other European funders, including the European Union, for the programme's continuing expansion. Today, the Home-Start International network reaches into Africa, East and West Europe, North America, the Middle East and Australia, and the organization is well equipped to sustain its future growth.

The Landmine Survivors Network (LSN) was in its second year of operation when the Foundation first provided a three-year grant for operating support. With an operating budget of just over €680,000, LSN was seeking to expand its programmes as well as to implement a development and outreach effort. LSN's leaders understood that without a solid administrative infrastructure to support programme growth, the organization would be unable to meet the needs of those it was developed to serve.

By the end of the three-year grant cycle, LSN had developed and implemented peer support networks in six countries, offered publications that were translated into seven languages, and had a budget of more than €3.4 million thanks, in large part, to the ability to implement the development plan. A second three-year grant was made in 2002, which led to the addition of another country to the network and funding from the governments of Canada, Norway, Switzerland and the US.

As the second grant was nearing completion, LSN approached the Foundation with the idea of creating an awards programme for 'survivorship', for people who have overcome their injuries and learned to live again. LSN's goal was to recognize the important work by individuals and groups, to showcase accomplishments and to inspire others. The Foundation agreed to provide funding for the awards programme, now known as the Niarchos Prize for Survivorship. The awards have helped bring recognition to those who work in this area and have helped attract new interest in LSN's work.

Fostering collaboration

A third key component of the Foundation's operations is the value it places on collaboration, which is important given its operating methodology with offices in Athens, Monte Carlo and New York. While staff members have particular areas of assignment and geography, they are all part of the Foundation's team and work closely to ensure that Stavros Niarchos's underlying vision is implemented.

Collaboration has also been the hallmark of several of the Foundation's grants, primarily through facilitating linkages between organizations in Greece and the US or other parts of Europe. The theme also relates to the Foundation's experience and interaction with grantees.

In 2005, a conference was held in New York City that brought together representatives of many organizations that had received funding. The idea was to facilitate interaction among grantees. The discussion during the one-day event highlighted various efforts ranging from individual exchange programmes to modelling good practice on programme implementation and technology.

It also gave representatives of recipient organizations a chance to meet and discuss their respective programmes, thereby finding their own opportunities for collaboration and learning. By bringing key people together and giving them the opportunity to share lessons learned, the Foundation was able to use participation in the conference as a means to considerably expand the impact of many individual grants.

Today, there are several collaborative efforts initiated or supported by the Foundation. Some have fostered institutional collaboration and others have enabled individuals to meet and interact in new ways. Notably, even after specific grants have ended, the relationships created endure. In all of these efforts, the Foundation has sought to multiply the impact of its work and to strengthen the participating institutions individually and collectively.

For example, it provided funds to the German Marshall Fund to add Greece to the list of European countries participating in the Marshall Memorial Fellowship programme. Support to the Natural History Museum in Crete was combined with a grant to the Peabody Museum at Yale leading to a multi-year collaboration of scientists and the development of education programmes for young children in New Haven and Crete.

Foundation support enabled JSTOR – an online storage system – to be offered in Greek universities, linking the institutions and their students to a worldwide effort to provide easy access to important academic journals. Other medical exchanges have been undertaken through the Hospital for Special Surgery in New York, the Arthritis Foundation, and the US-based United Cerebral Palsy Research Foundation.

John Jay College of Criminal Justice in New York City will be offering places in its Masters programme for Greek law enforcement officials and will sponsor workshops on terrorism and conflict with representatives from the Greek National Police, as well as others from the Balkans region.

Through work initiated at the Institute of International Education, there have been new collaborations among European academics that enable the sharing of course materials and research efforts. The annual Niarchos Lecture at the Washington DC Peterson Institute for International Economics creates a forum for leaders in business and government

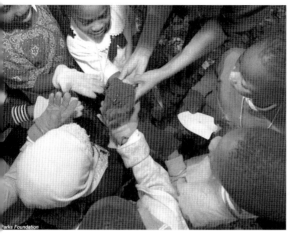

The Foundation makes grants on both sides of the Atlantic. The City Parks Foundation was created in 1989 to support the vast majority of New York City's parks that are without access to private resources. By creating arts, sports and educational programmes in over 700 public parks and by encouraging community development parks, the Foundation helps to revitalize not only parks but also the neighbourhoods that surround them.

to discuss important topics related to global economic matters. In addition, students in the US and Anatolia College in Greece are linked through the Manhattan Theatre Club's education programmes. Through videoconferencing they worked collaboratively in a playwriting project that circumnavigated the globe.

Promoting the use of technology

A fourth theme, which complements the goal of fostering collaboration, is the Foundation's commitment to promote the use of technology to provide access to information. This is deemed valuable as a means of ensuring that important resources are widely available.

Grants over the years include support to digitize materials from the collections of the New York Public Library. Grants have also supported Greekworks, a multimedia organization dedicated to providing Greek and Greek-related cultural and educational content through the internet. Early support was given to Ithaka, which is committed to the use of IT to enhance higher education globally.

In Greece, the commitment to expand access to information through technology will be represented most fully by the new National Library. In addition, the Foundation has launched a programme to provide technological and educational support to elementary schools in less advantaged areas of Greece. The goal is to properly prepare and equip students for their future academic needs and ensure that they don't fall behind their peers in metropolitan areas that have greater resources.

Another important project in Greece is the construction of a technology centre in the library of Anatolia College. In addition to offering

training and learning opportunities for the students of Anatolia and its
sister school, the American College of Thessaloniki, it is a resource for the
community. The Foundation also demonstrates its commitment to promote
the use of technology by several grants to local historical and/or cultural
organizations to preserve and digitally store folklore, music and dance
archives for future generations.

Identifying opportunities with global impact

All of these activities are consistent with the important lessons learned
from Stavros Niarchos's successful career. Just as his ships navigated
the globe carrying vital cargo from one location to another for much of the
20th century, the Foundation's support for projects that use technology to
advance knowledge is a 21st century effort to ensure that the intellectual
equivalent of that vital cargo – the power of knowledge and ideas – is also
accessible globally.

Reflecting on the Foundation's first decade, Director Spyros
Niarchos says, 'We have built our grants portfolio through actively
identifying opportunities with global impact and the recognition that we
must invest in good people. That is what truly distinguishes our first ten
years of work.'

The determination to ensure effectiveness and to continually add
value remains a cornerstone of the Foundation's activities. Now with a track
record and more visibility through the website, there is greater outside
attention to the Foundation's work.

The Directors understand clearly that the Foundation's work is more
than grantmaking. They also understand the value of using the Foundation's
convening capacity, as was done with the gathering of grantees in 2005 and
with the subsequent sponsorship of an international conference on the
future of libraries, hosted at the New York Public Library in 2006.

The Foundation also shares its intellectual capital through
the work of its Directors and staff and their ongoing interactions with
representatives of the public, private and non-profit sectors in Greece
and throughout the world. In Greece, particularly, Foundation staff offer
valuable technical assistance to recipient organizations, considerably
increasing their capacity to produce positive outcomes over time.

Partnering with governments

The Foundation's presence and contributions in Greece are also
represented by the way in which it has partnered with national and various
local governments to provide critical infrastructure assistance. Much of

this is in the form of vital equipment that public budgets cannot provide. For example, it has provided a new training centre and Super Puma helicopter for the Hellenic Fire Department and a patrol boat for the Coast Guard. The Foundation has also provided vehicles for transportation in mountainous and dangerous areas, firefighting, street and park cleaning and snow removal, as well as buses to transport handicapped children to medical and education programmes.

It has provided robotic security equipment for the Athens International Airport and funds to construct daycare centres, run programmes for children with special needs, and renovate or build housing for senior citizens. The purchase of necessary medical equipment, provision of emergency generators for remote health facilities, and upgrading of clinic facilities and ambulances have all been made possible through Foundation grants. In all cases, the ongoing maintenance and upkeep of the materials or facilities provided falls to the respective governmental or service provider.

Responding to disasters

Early on, the Directors made a commitment to respond to humanitarian and natural disasters throughout the world. The Foundation has provided assistance to the victims of the World Trade Center bombing and relief to those who suffered because of the South-east Asian tsunami.

Either through local aid organizations or international groups, it has made grants to provide relief for victims of earthquakes in Pakistan and India, the flooding in Mozambique, hurricanes in South America, and various programmes to address the health and well-being of refugees. A newly established programme mechanism allows a prompt response to such unforeseen but devastating events so that assistance can be made available as quickly as possible.

A 'wholesale' distribution of funds

Given the array in scope and geography of the opportunities for funding outside Greece and the modest number of programme staff in Monte Carlo and New York, the Foundation has looked to leverage its resources by partnering with several intermediary organizations addressing areas of mutual concern. In some measure, this reflects a 'wholesale' rather than 'retail' approach to distributing funds.

This way of working also offers a degree of assurance to the Directors as partnerships with organizations that have first-hand knowledge and expertise greatly enhance the Foundation's contributions in remote and disadvantaged areas of the world. Programmes that have been supported include the Global Fund for Women and PATH, which works on global health issues through the application of science and technology. Other beneficiaries include Leonard Cheshire International, which works globally to provide educational access for children with disabilities; Médecins Sans Frontières, which provides emergency medical care in areas of humanitarian crisis; and Mission Enfance, which provides educational programmes in developing countries.

Making a difference at local level

Support has also been given to several locally based programmes in selected economically disadvantaged areas of the world. Such efforts have included educational equipment in Chiang Mai, Thailand; homes for low-income families in Lima, Peru; water and sanitation projects in Lhasa, Tibet; and HIV/AIDS education programmes in Uganda and Rwanda.

The Foundation fully recognizes, even given its substantial size, that it can neither do everything nor be everywhere. But it has learned that even modest amounts of money can and do make a difference.

'Our work has really just begun,' says Director Andreas Dracopoulos. 'We have established what we feel is a sound track record and we continue to try to add value in Greece and internationally. In the spirit of our founder's approach to business, we look forward to the opportunities and challenges that lie ahead.'

FILIZ BIKMEN

10 Sabancı Foundation
Meeting the dynamic and changing shifts in Turkish society

This chapter paints the portrait of a place, a family, and a foundation. It attempts to tell the story of a 'traditional' foundation – one of the first established according to the new Turkish Republic laws after the Ottoman period – and how it has evolved in serving its philanthropic purpose to the greatest extent possible. Today, the Sabancı Foundation is one of the largest in Turkey, with more than €480 million in assets and an annual expenditure of €27 million.

Hacı Ömer Sabancı was a successful businessman and, with his wife Sadıka, an active philanthropist. Their six sons not only continued their legacy by building one of Turkey's largest conglomerates; they also institutionalized the charitable impulse of the family by formally establishing the Sabancı Foundation in 1974. To date, the Foundation has built and restored over 120 facilities for educational, health and cultural purposes, established a new university, provided more than 31,000 scholarships, and distributed 650 achievement awards in the areas of education, sports and culture.

Today, the Sabancı Foundation is one of the largest in Turkey – by European standards it is in the top 50 by expenditure and the top 100 in terms of assets. Looking to the future, the Foundation is strengthening institutional capacity and realigning its strategy to better meet the dynamic context and shifting mandates of Turkish society and the consequent changes in the philanthropic landscape.

The place and the person

There is a saying that you 'can take the boy from the country, but you cannot take the country from the boy'. This saying captures an important starting point in the story of Hacı Ömer Sabancı (1906–66), born in Akçakaya, Kayseri, a province in Central Anatolia. To tell the story of the person, we must also know the place from which he came.

Kayseri has an important place in Turkey's past, present and future. It has been a continuous settlement since 3000 BC and was a vital trade centre due to its location on the Great Silk Road. Ruled by various kingdoms over the years, Kayseri was captured by the Ottomans in the 15th century. Today, it is one of the main centres of industrial growth: 17 of Turkey's top 500 companies are from Kayseri. In July 2004, Kayseri applied to the *Guinness Book of Records* for the largest number of factories being constructed on a single day (139).[1]

Aside from its fascinating history, the people of Kayseri are known for the entrepreneurial merchants who have moved on to achieve great success, earning them the title of Anatolian Tigers.[2] In addition to its successful business elite, Kayseri is also the hometown of notable political leaders, such as Abdullah Gül, the current President of Turkey.

Hacı Ömer Sabancı

The Anatolian Tigers of Kayseri are equally well known for their pious and philanthropic nature. People who originate from this province are active benefactors who frequently channel their private wealth for public benefit. In one village, Hacılar, 13 out of the 15 schools have been built with private donations.[3]

This information about Kayseri sets an important context for understanding the person. Hacı Ömer Sabancı and his six sons – five of whom were born in Kayseri – undoubtedly absorbed the characteristics of their fellow *hemşehri* (townsmen) in becoming successful businessmen and active philanthropists. They realized these values in many of the communities across Turkey in which they lived and worked. The holding and foundation established by his family would later give back to Kayseri through several economic and philanthropic investments, including an important cultural centre at the Erciyes University[4] and a social and training facility for teachers.

'To give what this land has given to us back to its people . . .'
At the early age of 14, Hacı Ömer left Kayseri for Adana, a province in the Mediterranean region, where he went to work in the cotton fields and

subsequently started building his fortune. After only two years, he had saved enough to start a modest commercial venture. From there, through his many enterprising initiatives, he planted the seeds for what would later become the Sabancı Group of Companies, known today as the Sabancı Holding.

Hacı Ömer and his wife Sadıka had six sons – Ihsan, Sakıp, Hacı, Şevket, Erol, Özdemir – who took an active role within the Sabancı Group. It was their dedication and support from professional managers that helped to grow the Sabancı business after the loss of their father in 1966. The Sabancı

Sadıka Sabancı, wife of Hacı Ömer. The Foundation was established in large part with her personal assets.

Holding was formally established in 1967. Today, it is one of Turkey's most respected and successful enterprises with 70 companies in sectors such as manufacturing, technology, textiles and energy; 52,000 employees; 10 international partnerships (with Toyota and Bridgestone, to name a couple); €12 billion in sales, and €351 million in profit.

The Sabancı brothers followed in their father's footsteps in more areas than just business. Both Hacı Ömer and Sadıka were active philanthropists during their lifetime and raised their sons with a strong core value of charity and giving back. With this charitable impulse, a generous contribution from their mother, and a desire to formalize their philanthropy, the brothers formally established the Hacı Ömer Sabancı Foundation – known as the Sabancı Foundation – in 1974. The motto of the Foundation is a principle by which their father Hacı Ömer lived his life: 'To give what this land has given to us back to its people.'

The Foundation has made a constant effort to keep this philosophy alive. 'Though much has changed over the years, the spirit in which the Sabancı Foundation was established lives on today. We've made great efforts to guide our programming with Hacı Ömer Sabancı's motto and distribute our social investments as broadly as possible,' says Foundation General Manager Hüsnü Paçaçıoğlu. To date, the Foundation has made a contribution to over 78 communities in every region of the country.

Institutionalizing philanthropy – establishing the Sabancı Foundation

To ensure the growth of the Foundation's assets, some of the companies of the Sabancı group contribute between 1 and 5 per cent of their annual profit to the Sabancı Foundation, which is allocated to operational and programme activities. The Foundation's charter requires that it pays out at least 67 per cent of revenue on programmes.

To date, more than €1 billion has been spent to support the aims of the Foundation. As of November 2007, it has more than €480 million in assets and spends about €27 million annually, making it one of the largest foundations in Turkey by both assets and expenditure. The Board of Trustees has seven members, appointed by the Sabancı Holding. The current Chairperson of the Foundation is Güler Sabancı, who is also the current Chairperson of Sabancı Holding. While the governance of the Foundation comprises mainly family and corporate members, they are conscientious in including the voices and opinions of others in developing their Foundation's strategy.

The Sabancı Foundation's main aims are to support education, culture and health needs across Turkey. Its most significant programmatic investments to date have been in three areas: construction and restoration of educational, health and cultural facilities in 78 out of 81 provinces; providing more than 31,000 educational scholarships; and presenting more than 650 awards for exceptional achievement in education, culture and sports.

In addition to these investments, the Foundation has been a long-time supporter of the International Adana Film Festival and the National Folk Dance Competition. Recently, it started supporting a private theatre group that travels across the country to perform for young students, many of them from disadvantaged neighbourhoods. In addition to these programmes, the Sabancı Foundation is one of the founding members of TUSEV (Third Sector Foundation of Turkey), a network of foundations and a support organization for the third sector. It has also been a member of the European Foundation Centre and the Council on Foundations for several years.

Sabancı is clearly the leading foundation in the area of building and restoring educational institutions. A majority of the Foundation's institutions were built or restored between the mid 1980s and early 2000s, characterizing the first phase of the Foundation as one focused greatly on institutional development. As displayed on the Foundation's website, these institutions provide invaluable services to students, teachers and society as a whole in locations from the most desolate and poor areas of eastern Turkey to the most treasured parts of Istanbul. Each year, an estimated 45,000 students from pre-school to high school study and/or live in schools and dorms built or restored by the Sabancı Foundation.

A number of these institutions fill an important gap in serving the needs of disadvantaged groups. Several members of the Sabancı family as well as partners and employees of the Holding take an active part in these philanthropic endeavours. For example, following the devastating earthquake in 1999, the Sabancı Foundation, together with partners and employees of Sabancı Holding, funded the construction of a primary school in Kocaeli. The Metin Sabancı Centre for Children with Cerebral Palsy serves children with disabilities in a facility unmatched by any other private or state institution in Turkey.

One of the most significant investments of the Sabancı Foundation is the Sabancı University. The design process started in 1995 and the doors officially opened for classes in 1999. The Foundation continues to provide almost €10 million per year in support.

Primary education school in Kocaeli

Sabancı Partners and Employees Primary Education School was built with the fund established within Sabancı Foundation through the contributions of Sabancı Holding, its partners and its employees during the period following the earthquake on 17 August 1999.

The school building comprises three floors with a closed area of 5,000 square metres. Full-time education is provided for 1,500 students in 37 rooms including 29 classrooms, two science laboratories and a foreign language laboratory. There is also a 240-seat capacity auditorium, a gymnasium, cafeteria, library, and administrative sections.

Metin Sabancı Centre for Children with Cerebral Palsy

The Metin Sabancı Centre for Children with Cerebral Palsy was commissioned in 1996, with the aim to help spastic children and teenagers socialize through early education and training. It provides quality care, treatment and professional education. There are physical therapy rooms, rehabilitation units, a social analysis room, psychological research and observation rooms, hydrotherapy pool, outdoor and indoor sports facility, dorms, workshops, handicrafts exhibition section, workshops, dispensary, daycare centre and administrative buildings. There is also a conference hall for 200 people and a library with 3,500 books available for use by the people who stay and work at the facility. It also includes a grass soccer field, and volleyball and basketball fields with special floors.

Sabancı primary education school in Kocaeli.

Sabancı University

Sabancı University is a private, independent university with a state-of-the-art campus spread over 1,260,000 square metres and located 40 kilometres from Istanbul's city centre. The University aspires to develop competent and confident individuals, capable of independent and critical reflection, who possess a strong sense of social responsibility. This mission is reflected throughout the entire university, from its interdisciplinary academic programmes to its technology and infrastructure and its research and development projects in industry.

Academic activities operate within the framework of three programmes: the Faculty of Engineering and Natural Sciences, the Faculty of Arts and Social Sciences, and the Faculty of Management. The undergraduate degree programmes are built around a blend of disciplines that leverage new, scientific developments and equip students with a wide diversity of mental tools and skills needed to deal with the increasingly complex, interactive and fast-flowing environment that characterizes today's world. Graduate programmes, on the other hand, are designed to prepare students for career-specific fields and/or research.

The University is bilingual, using English as its primary language of instruction, but Turkish whenever necessary, for example for courses and readings on Turkish literature or Ottoman history. Sabancı University has fostered an environment conducive to research and has the distinction of being the first university in Turkey accepted for membership in the European Foundation for Quality Management (EFQM).

A museum was established in 2002, where recent exhibitions such as Picasso and Rodin attracted significant interest from the public.

Changes in the landscape of philanthropy usher in new opportunities

Foundations, no matter how private and independent they may be, do not act in a vacuum; or if they do, they are unlikely to maximize their fullest return to society. For years, the Foundation continued to realize its main aims of supporting education, health and culture within a paradigm of 'traditional' foundation operations, which lean heavily towards helping to address a need which is primarily the responsibility of the government and funding the construction and/or restoration of schools and hospitals. Yet this has often been the role of foundations in Turkey from the Ottoman era to the present.

However, changes in the landscape of philanthropy in Turkey have allowed foundations to take a different approach to public benefit.

Thirty-four years and €1 billion later, the Foundation leadership started to take note of the significant changes taking place in the field of philanthropy at the national and international level. They initiated a process to determine how programmes and support could be redesigned to address new needs and mandates.

The goal is to build on the original *raison d'être* of the foundation and pursue a new path. Güler Sabancı explains: 'It is time for foundations in Turkey to adapt to the rapidly changing context and take on a leadership role in promoting social transformation and sustainable development.'

Until the early 2000s, the environment and legal frameworks for civil society organizations (CSOs) and foundations were restrictive. Limited wealth and a stagnant market economy meant less philanthropic activity and a highly centralized state meant few non-state actors could do much beyond building schools and other institutions to lessen the burden of social needs and problems.

Yet, the seeds of change that would spark an important shift in these areas started bearing fruit in early 2000. While these positive developments continue through peaks and troughs, political, economic and social reforms have started to shape a more enabling environment for new ideas, actors and approaches to development in the third sector – primarily non-governmental organizations (NGOs) and other actors.

The following major shifts are most pertinent to Sabancı's decision to re-examine its philanthropic strategy:
- Third sector – legal reforms and the democratization process, much of it part of Turkey's political process and the EU accession efforts.
- Private sector – increased economic development and wealth creation.
- Public sector – shift from centralized/linear to decentralized/ integral approach of state policies and social service provisions.

One of the most important milestones in the development of civil society and foundations in Turkey is the law reform process that took on great momentum in 2001. During this period, laws governing the third sector were amended and in some cases drafted anew with an ethos of empowerment and encouragement. Most notably, the new Associations Law in 2004, and other important amendments to foundations law (although a new draft law specifically for foundations is still pending in Parliament), allowed citizen groups and CSOs to take on a more active role in service delivery and in developing local and national policy. Up to this point, foundations such as

Sabancı and others were fewer in number and thus carried more weight in addressing the social needs of the country.

This momentum, coupled with EU funding and greater pressure for the government to loosen the strings on civil society, led to the regeneration and new establishment of hundreds of CSOs and foundations. These organizations focus on 'traditional' philanthropic areas such as education, culture and health, as well as new areas such as human rights, environment, women's issues and disadvantaged groups. As a result, foundations such as Sabancı, which were once alone in their mission, now have a broader and more vibrant group of organizations to partner and cooperate with to achieve their objectives for social change.

The emergence of new wealth

In addition to the expansion of the third sector, this recent period has been one of rapid economic growth. While the seeds of privatization were planted back in the mid 1980s, the bulk of Turkey's impressive economic growth has taken place over the past six years. Indicators show that GDP per capita increased from just over €1,370 to more than €3,770 between 2001 and 2006, with an average economic growth of approximately 7 per cent per annum.[5] As a result, Turkey has also witnessed the emergence of new wealth, and thus more philanthropy and public goods.

Hüsnü Özyeğin, who made the bulk of his wealth a few years ago by selling the Finansbank enterprise, is an example of this trend. He is now transferring his private wealth for public good and ambitiously building dorms and schools across the country.[6] Now more than ever, there are 'new generation' successful business people who are keen to give to causes that the Sabancı Foundation has already contributed to most prominently: building and restoring institutions that are transferred to ministries (education, culture and health) and providing educational scholarships for needy students.

State-centred approach undergoes a paradigm shift

In the public sector, significant change is taking place in the state's approach to development. The establishment of the Turkish Republic in 1923 brought with it a very state-centred approach to modernization and development, an approach which crowded out private actors. Organizations such as the Sabancı Foundation were relegated to giving scholarships and building and restoring facilities, which would then be run under the auspices of the state.

At the same time, with the emergence of a new – and in many aspects more progressive era – the state has adopted a more integrative approach. This paradigm shift is leading to three major epiphanies:

- Increasingly challenging development mandates require more private initiative and investment.
- Private actors can add value beyond providing physical (hardware) bricks-and-mortar contributions.
- Public policy debate and development is a *sine qua non* for effective and democratic public administration systems.

This is not to say that the 'hardware' – the building of schools, dorms and hospitals – is a thing of the past. However, it is now augmented by the recognition that 'software' – education reform, protecting and promoting the rights of disadvantaged groups, and the development of a more participatory policy development/service delivery system – is essential to furthering the modernization and democratization of Turkey.

Looking towards the software of society

The influx of new CSOs in service delivery and advocacy, the increase in wealth and contributions from local industrialists and 'new' philanthropists, and the state's shift from a linear and centralized method to a more integrated approach to development, are all important factors that have led the Sabancı Foundation to reassess its role and investments in supporting the development of Turkish society. The Foundation is looking more towards the software of society and issues such as women's and human rights. As a result, the fundamental programme areas of the Foundation are currently undergoing significant changes in direction.

Taking into account global changes

All of these developments are seemingly nation-centric, happening within the borders of the country. However, it is also possible to establish linkages to the globalized nature of change in many countries today. Just as no foundation operates in a vacuum, no single country operates in a vacuum either. Thus, the development of civil society, increase in wealth and 'new' philanthropists, and the shift in role of the state are also international trends. The process of European accession has undoubtedly played a critical role in generating new perspectives in the area of social development.

In this light, the Sabancı Foundation is also taking into account the changing role of foundations in Europe and at the global level, and looking to leading organizations to benchmark its own process of change.

First things first – strengthening capacity

Prior to its strategic assessment activities, the Foundation made some essential internal changes. They moved the headquarters from Adana to Istanbul in 2006 to be closer to the Sabancı Holding headquarters, and upgraded the infrastructure of the Foundation. An intranet was developed to digitalize all documents and decisions, and compile business processes for HR, finance and legal departments as well as scholarship and facility administration. A website was created to share more information about the Foundation, as well as to increase transparency and accountability.

Today, the Sabancı Foundation is one of the only foundations in Turkey to publicly share information about its financial status.

The Foundation also took stock of what it had contributed to date by creating a detailed inventory of the more than 120 facilities and institutions built or restored since 1974. Site visits were conducted and a system developed to manage the physical infrastructure improvement process. While all facilities are officially run under the auspices of government agencies, lack of public financing for infrastructure requires that the Sabancı Foundation continue covering these costs, which amount to more than €1.3 million per year. Foundation staff also established closer relationships with the school managers, principals and teachers, and created more open lines of communication with key stakeholders.

Exploring new programme areas

While the main focus of this phase was increasing internal capacity, new programme areas were also being explored. In 2006, the Sabancı Foundation entered into a partnership with all of the United Nations (UN) agencies in Turkey and the Ministry of Interior to support a Joint Programme on the Protection and Promotion of the Human Rights of Women and Girl Children in Turkey. The Foundation also started making grants to NGOs such as the Mother Child Literacy Foundation and contributed support for the Daddy Take Me to School campaign.

The detailed strategy and programmatic design phase gathered momentum in the second phase. However, these initial efforts were important in creating a new infrastructure and direction for the Sabancı Foundation. Taken together, these changes would pave the way for developing a formal programme strategy for maximizing its contribution and value to society.

Protecting and Promoting the Human Rights of Women and Girl Children in Turkey

The UN Joint Programme (UNJP) is designed to address persistent gender inequalities by improving the national policy environment, building local government and NGO capacity, designing service models for women and girls, and raising awareness about women and girls' rights. It targets national level decision-makers as well as local governments, NGOs and the general public in six cities: Izmir, Kars, Nevşehir, Şanliurfa, Trabzon and Van. The cities were chosen according to their capacity to participate in the programme, perceived needs, and the commitment of municipalities as expressed in preliminary city visits. They were selected to demonstrate how participatory and coordinated cross-sectoral partnerships could improve services, change policy, augment resource availability and improve the lives of girls and women.

Activities include identifying the needs of women and girls through a participatory planning process involving all stakeholders. By the end of the programme, the pilot cities will be evaluated for certification as 'Women Friendly Cities'. The Sabancı Foundation is providing grants to projects developed jointly by CSOs and local governments that align with UNJP priorities. Key partners include all UN agencies in Turkey; Ministry of Interior; Sabancı Foundation; Sabancı University; mayors and governors of Izmir, Kars, Nevşehir, Şanliurfa, Trabzon and Van; and donor governments – Canada, Denmark, Finland, France, Germany, Norway, Sweden, Switzerland and the United Kingdom.

Designing a new strategy

The next steps were to start working towards a new strategic framework. This included four main actions:

- Assessing strengths, weaknesses, opportunities and threats.
- Undertaking a benchmarking process vis-à-vis Turkish and international foundations.
- Developing a new strategic framework – identifying potential programme areas and new vehicles for support such as grantmaking and fellowships.
- Organizing consultative meetings with thought leaders from different sectors to discuss the way forward.

The internal assessment revealed that the Foundation had positive name recognition in the philanthropic sector and a very strong track record in the area of education. But it also revealed that it was lacking a formal strategy. The benchmarking process exposed quite interesting results: foundations similar to Sabancı were doing more or less the same things but the Sabancı Foundation was a leader by far in the number of institutions and facilities it had helped build and/or restore in areas all over Turkey. It was also the only one to have diversified its programming by launching a formal grantmaking programme (see above).

The benchmarking with foundations in Europe and America revealed three important outcomes for the Sabancı Foundation to consider. European and American programme strategies are more clearly designed; programme areas address other 'soft' issues such as rights and empowerment; and they use more diverse types of support in achieving programmatic goals.

The outputs of the benchmarking exercise fed into a new strategic framework that included a revised mission statement to 'promote the well-being of society and encourage social awareness'. New potential programme areas were identified together with new vehicles such as grantmaking, fellowships and other mechanisms that could be used to accomplish programme objectives.

The strategic framework was then taken to the field and debated with thought leaders from academia, non-profit organizations, foundations, government and the private sector. ARAMA consulting group was commissioned to organize 'search conferences' and a 'decision conference'. The aim of these facilitated brainstorming sessions was to bring together different stakeholders and integrate suggestions and ideas for future strategies. Focus groups were conducted – Education, Social and Economic Development, and Civil Society and Social Investment. Each brought together 25–30 individuals for one day to discuss and prioritize the main issues in these fields and develop suggestions about what the Foundation should focus on.

Next, a 'decision model' was developed. The final group reviewed the general objective of the Foundation and prioritized general goals and programme areas. This was done using an algorithmic decision-making model called AHP.[7] Given Sabancı's high regard for international perspectives and thirst for diverse views, individuals from the foundation sector outside of Turkey were also invited to participate.

The Sabancı Foundation also organized a large seminar[8] with more than 200 participants. This created a forum for global perspectives in the field and opened people's minds to what could be done differently. In her opening speech, Güler Sabancı stated the importance of change for foundations and the value of developing new strategies collectively.

'Turkey is in the midst of significant economic growth and prosperity, displaying rapid integration and increased competitiveness in the global economy,' she said. 'We are facing new challenges, new mandates in the development of our society. We are now witnessing a surge of new civil society organizations and other key actors that play an increasingly important role. Sabancı Foundation is searching for a strategy with innovative and unique programmes that will support these initiatives. But the most critical part of this journey is to share different ideas and perspectives and generate a "collective wisdom".'

The benchmarking, strategic framework and stakeholder consultations provided the Sabancı Foundation leadership with a clear picture of how to move ahead. The next step is expected to be to design a detailed programme in the areas of youth, women and disadvantaged/disabled individuals, and to explore potential needs in teacher training and community development in Istanbul. These areas will be developed in the coming year and will establish a new road map for the future.

Creating a new legacy of foundations in Turkey

For centuries, foundations have been established in Turkey and have performed thousands of charitable acts and deeds, with much blessing and appreciation. Most people living in Turkey still regard the foundation sector in this way – performing simple, kind, charitable acts, focused on alleviating the immediate needs brought about by economic injustices, or, in the history of the modern Republic, addressing societal needs that the state could not.

Yet, for those closer to these issues, the reality is quite different. The story of the Sabancı Foundation reflects the evolution of this change. It began with the philanthropic impulse of Hacı Ömer and Sadıka, and continued with their sons, who translated this impulse into perpetuity with the establishment of the Foundation. This continues today in an ongoing quest to make a difference and fulfil its philanthropic obligation. This quest is likely to result in a very different approach from that of the past and will mark the beginning of yet another new phase for the Foundation.

This paradigm shift also marks an important milestone for the foundation sector in Turkey, which is likely to continue with this significant momentum of change in the coming years. This new vision will lead to an important realization that while foundations are indeed valuable legacies of Ottoman-Turkish-Islamic culture, they must not be imprisoned in their own history. Foundations must be encouraged to move into the present, be open to new possibilities and approaches, and address injustices and the root causes of social challenges.

As the title of this book suggests, foundations in Europe have a rich past and a promising future. Once new ways are unlocked to allow foundations to foster the future development of Turkish society – as Sabancı Foundation has started to do – their contributions will most certainly leave a legacy as worthy as that of their Ottoman ancestors, who are so revered today.

[1] *Islamic Calvinists. Change and conservatism in Central Anatolia*, Report by ESI, 2005. Available on www.esiweb.org

[2] A term used to refer to several provinces in Turkey which have grown economically without significant government investment, and thus are known for individuals who built businesses (mainly those which started as merchants and SMEs) which have achieved significant success. Source: 'Anatolian Tigers or Islamic Capital: Prospects and Challenges', *Middle Eastern Studies*, Volume 40, Issue 6, 2004.

[3] Ibid.

[4] Sabancı Cultural Complex at Erciyes University, Kayseri.

[5] Turkish Statistical Agency, www.tuik.gov.tr

[6] Thomas Landon, Jr, 'A New Breed of Billionaire', *New York Times*, 14 December 2007.

[7] Decision Conference® is a participatory decision-making methodology implemented by ARAMA. Analytic Hierarchy Process (AHP) is a participatory method developed based on system thinking and group dynamics theories. Decision Conference® uses AHP to add qualitative and quantitative factors to the decision-making process. AHP was developed by Thomas Saaty and is one of the most frequently used and accepted methods in the world. Decision Conference® has been used by many holdings, associations, sector organizations, public organizations and corporations in Turkey for the last 10 years.

[8] See www.sabancivakfi.org for more on the seminar and a podcast of the event.

DIANNA RIENSTRA

11 Stephan Schmidheiny
Visionary with two feet firmly on the ground

Stephan Schmidheiny has been called many things over his lifetime – environmental steward, environmentalist, business leader, visionary, champion of civil society, pioneer of sustainable development, best-selling author, entrepreneur and philanthropist. In its list of the World's Richest People, Forbes labels him the 'Green Billionaire'. In fact, he is all of these things. An overview of his accomplishments is followed by a recent interview for the purposes of this book.

The term 'visionary' has been used by many to describe this unusual man and the path he has chosen to follow. But Stephan Schmidheiny describes himself as 'a visionary with uncommon views based on common sense, with two feet firmly on the ground'. He does have uncommon views and, as his investment portfolio reveals, he has much more than common sense.

Schmidheiny is recognized internationally for his business acumen and admired for his creativity in building upon a corporate-philanthropic association that could become the model of the future for sustainable giving. The recipient of numerous awards and distinctions, he is regarded by many as a modern-day maven, a trusted expert in his field, and praised for his enlightened leadership.

'Wealth demands certain responsibilities'
He was born in St Gallen, Switzerland in 1947,[1] into a Swiss-German family who had built up an industrial fortune, started by his great-grandfather with a brick factory in Heerbruug in the eastern region of the country.

His grandfather invested in the emerging cement industry and later in asbestos, the latter of which was to spark one of the major turning points in Schmidheiny's life. His father Ernst and brother Max extended the family's investment into Wild-Leitz (microscopes and optics) and BBC Brown Boveri (a power and automation technology group), reflecting an entrepreneurial acumen that was picked up by a rather reluctant Stephan, who as a very young child harboured a desire to become a missionary.

'My forebears instilled in me the deep conviction that wealth demands certain responsibilities. This conviction has led me to seek and implement new ways of doing philanthropic work,' he writes.[2]

In his book *My Path – My Perspective*, Schmidheiny describes growing up in the Swiss countryside, surrounded by vineyards and mountains. He spent vacation time in the Mediterranean islands where he learned to dive. These experiences sparked a growing concern for the environment, which was to be a *leitmotif* throughout his adult life. Schmidheiny ended up studying law, with a view to better understanding the workings of society. He resisted following in his father's footsteps, but ended up working in one of the Group companies in South Africa. From there, he moved into the position of sales manager of Eternit AG in Niederurnen in 1974, a move that was the beginning of a stellar business career.

Stephan Schmidheiny.

Appointed CEO in 1976, he assumed his father's position as president of the holding company for the Swiss Eternit Group, a multinational asbestos-cement conglomerate, of which he become the owner in 1984 when his father divided up his estate among his children. His brother Thomas took over the Holderbank Group, later Holcim, a global cement and aggregate giant. At the young age of 29, Schmidheiny found himself responsible for overseeing a business conglomerate with plants in more than 20 countries and tens of thousands of employees.

A 'mad' decision proves prescient

When the spectre of asbestos-related illness raised its head, Schmidheiny found himself thinking with both feet on the ground. He felt that the lack of a clear scientific and technical consensus on asbestos and the unpredictability of its effects made the manufacture of asbestos-cement products both threatening to the health of employees and an unpromising business prospect. New equipment and filters were installed across Eternit's operations, and research began into how to develop asbestos-free products.

In 1981, well before the European Union imposed the ban in 1991, he made a radical decision: the Eternit Group would cease to manufacture products containing asbestos. Colleagues and plant managers called him 'mad'.

'I took the decision to get out of asbestos based on the potential human and environmental problems associated with the mineral. But it also seemed to me that in an age of increasing transparency – and increasing concerns about health risks – it would be impossible to develop and maintain a successful business based on asbestos,' he writes. 'This insight caused me to begin to ponder deeply the relationships between business and society. It was a painful period, but it was invaluable preparation for my later being thrown into a position of leadership on business and society issues.'[3]

A very private person, he suddenly found himself on the front page of the newspapers, linked to the harmful effects of asbestos. Today, he is proud of the measures he took to protect workers and glad that he remained steadfast in his decision to put an end to asbestos use, despite the uncertainty and resistance from the industry and within the company.

This painful experience was a transformative one. In a book *Changing Course: A global business perspective on development and the environment*,[4] written in 1992, during the early days of the then-Business Council on Sustainable Development, Schmidheiny wrote about the lessons learned during his struggle to get the company out of asbestos: 'Companies are meant to serve society, not the other way around; and companies that do not – and are not seen to – serve society will fail.'

In the following years, Schmidheiny diversified his investments, building his portfolio and adding enterprises related to forestry, banking and the electronic and optical equipment industries. He invested in and became a member of the boards of directors of leading companies such as ABB, Nestlé, Swatch (to the precursor of which he provided start-up funds) and UBS.

Schmidheiny describes his business model during that time: 'With few exceptions, I invested almost exclusively in distressed companies in need of basic restructuring. I consider myself fortunate to have found the right people to help me in that task. These people took over the daily management of the companies, allowing me to devote myself to long-term strategies and to my ongoing search for new business opportunities, planning new acquisitions, and evaluating new success strategies.'[5]

A first step towards philanthropy

In the mid-1980s, Schmidheiny took what he calls his 'first step towards philanthropy' in Central and Latin America, where many of the Eternit Group companies were operating. Together with the Archbishop of Panama, he set up FUNDES, an organization to promote small and medium-sized enterprises with the goals to create jobs, generate income for the underprivileged and optimize the operational parameters for those businesses. After a trial period in Panama, the programme was replicated in other Latin American countries, where FUNDES helped SMEs gain access to credit and provided them with basic administrative training.

'The more I worked with FUNDES, the more I grew convinced that helping small businesses . . . to get to know the economies of the developing world was one of the most effective ways of helping people create sustainable ways of life for themselves,' he writes.[6] Once again, he was ahead of his time. It was not until many years later that leading development agencies and banks began to embrace this vision of capacity-building through boosting SMEs. Today, the International Finance Corporation, the World Bank's credit agency, is using FUNDES' methods in its work worldwide.

From a family partnership to a main player

Schmidheiny's business empire was expanding, and his long-time interest in Latin America – where many of the Eternit Group companies were

A business solutions network

FUNDES[7] is a decentralized organization offering consulting services and business administration courses. It aims to strengthen business competitiveness through global services that combine research, training and consulting. FUNDES has developed a network of partnerships with government and municipalities at national, regional and local level, as well as with multilateral organizations and private foundations that work to promote the development of SMEs. It covers expenses by income generated by the services it offers. FUNDES calls itself a 'business solutions network'; it spans ten Central and Latin American countries, including Mexico. Headquartered in Costa Rica, the network consists of more than 20 direct collaborators and more than 400 consultants and facilitators.

In November 2007, FUNDES was rated as among the world's 85 top NGOs and was included in *The Business Guide to Partnering with NGOs and the United Nations*, published by the UN Global Compact, *Financial Times* and Dalberg Global Development Advisors. The publication is the first-ever global initiative to review and rate NGOs, UN agencies and other social actors from a business partnership perspective.

located – deepened during a vacation to Chile in 1982, where he saw the emerging forestry industry in the south of the country as an opportunity to pursue long-term business opportunities based on the sustainable planting of pine forests. If managed properly, sustainable planting allows the business's productive base to grow while at the same time increasing the quality and value of the forests.

He struck a partnership with the owners of a family-run sawmill to invest as a partner in the business. Twenty years on, the forest area planned and managed by the company has grown from 4,000 to 300,000 hectares, and the number of employees has increased from 150 to 3,200. The company processes raw material for the manufacture of solid wood pieces such as planks, moulding, doorframes and different types of pressed wood products, which are marketed internationally. The company, Terranova, has invested in forests and factories in Brazil and Venezuela. The plantations were developed on low-quality or degraded agricultural lands. In 2005, Terranova merged with Masisa, one of the world's largest producers of wood boards.

Masisa is one of the companies in Schmidheiny's industrial holding GrupoNueva, which he describes as committed both to Latin America and to sustainable development. In 1994, he sold his European-based business and focused instead in Latin America. The divisions Amanco, Masisa and Plycem are leading in the Americas in the areas of forest plantations and wood products, as well as drinking water, waste water, irrigation and piping systems infrastructure. The group, which is driven by social and environmental sustainability principles, employs about 17,600 people with net sales of some €940.8 million in 2005.

Focusing on business and the environment

Another turning point came for Schmidheiny in 1990 when a Swiss university asked him to speak on the topic of business and the environment. He also spoke at a similar meeting in Bergen, Norway, where European and North American government representatives were meeting to prepare for the upcoming United Nations Conference on Environment and Development (UNCED), known as the Rio de Janeiro Earth Summit of 1992.

Schmidheiny was then appointed as chief adviser for business and industry to then secretary general of UNCED, Maurice Strong. In the course of this work, he created a forum, bringing together business leaders from around the world to develop a business perspective on environment and development challenges. Schmidheiny's brainchild – the Business Council on Sustainable Development (BCSD) – was born. In 1995 it merged with the World Industry Council on the Environment to become the World Business Council on Sustainable Development (WBCSD). WBCSD opened its secretariat in Geneva. A second office was opened in Washington in 2007.

Today, WBCSD[8] has some 200 members in more than 35 countries and 20 major industrial sectors, involving some 1,000 business leaders globally. It also comprises a regional network of more than 55 national and regional partner organizations, primarily located in developing countries. WBCSD's strategy to 2015 concentrates on four major focus areas: energy and climate, development, the business role, and ecosystems.

During the lead-up to the Earth Summit, enthused WBCSD leaders broke into working groups to discuss issues such as energy and financial markets, and the true definition of corporate social responsibility. Their work led to the decision to write a book, *Changing Course: A global business perspective on development and the environment*. In less than a year, WBCSD organized 50 meetings in 20 countries to spread the message of sustainable development. The meetings fed into the book, which became a bestseller and was translated into 15 languages.

'The title *Changing Course* was carefully selected. Although our basic goal was to promote a long-term vision, we were also aiming at immediate action to achieve profound changes,' writes Schmidheiny. The book is aptly titled. The two years he spent working with the Rio Summit and setting up the WBCSD changed his course.

He writes: 'My "simple" assignment as a consultant to the Earth Summit turned out to be far more encompassing and long-term than I had imagined . . . In discharging the mission entrusted to me . . . I invested much of my time and several millions of my own assets. I was, however, richly rewarded for this. I enjoyed my work and gained a wide range of new insights. I was forced to think of the global challenges that are a sign of our times, and later this helped me make strategically correct decisions for companies.'[9]

Changing course . . . again

Another turning point came during the Earth Summit – both Schmidheiny's father and his brother Alexander died within a few months of each other. Alexander left him his extensive art collection, which Schmidheiny continued. He set up Daros,[10] an organization based in Zurich and specializing in art. Today, part of the Daros collection is shown publicly in different exhibitions in Zurich at a remodelled old brewery. He and his wife created the Daros-Latinamerica Collection to support artists in the region and expose them to international markets. A third collection, Daros Contemporary, focuses on collecting and promoting young art in Europe.

At this point, Schmidheiny was 45 years old. He owned three international corporations and, as he writes in *My Path – My Perspective*, he knew that 'more of the same would not be enough of a challenge' for him.[11] He moved to Costa Rica and managed GrupoNeuva from there, where he ensured that the mission of the business had an ethical and social focus. Here, Schmidheiny started thinking about making inroads into the world of philanthropy, with a view to combining the best of two worlds – foundations and business.

'It was obvious that traditional philanthropy was not the option I was looking for,' he writes. 'I needed to find a catalyst that would trigger the type of sustainable human development that all governments of the world had agreed upon at the Earth Summit.'[12]

Schmidheiny turned to an entrepreneurial solution. He heard about Ashoka, an organization that raises funds to support 'social entrepreneurs'. Qualifying entrepreneurial individuals with innovative ideas for improving society receive financial assistance for about three years to build up their organizations. The organization was successful in Mexico and Brazil, but Schmidheiny's capital and contacts helped it to expand into Latin America.

AVINA – initiatives for social change

The AVINA Foundation has an ambitious mission: 'To contribute to sustainable development in Latin America by encouraging productive alliances based on trust among social and business leaders and by brokering consensus around agendas for action.'[13]

AVINA cooperates with its partners in a spirit of commitment and joint venture. It finances activities, but also helps organizations to fundraise. It brings civil society and business leaders together to create new types of association between both sectors of society. Schmidheiny has provided the financial resources for AVINA since the Foundation was established in 1994.

AVINA has disbursed more than €224.5 million for projects and other investments on behalf of causes related to its partners and their networks. This figure includes not only AVINA's contributions to sustainable development in Latin America, but also investments made in its early years on other continents. While cash to projects continues to represent the greatest share of budget outlays (49 per cent), the proportion of funds directed to building alliances among social and business leaders is growing.

'The success of Ashoka's social entrepreneurs proved to me that heads of governments and captains of industry – those who actually should be the first responsible for improving their societies – seldom bring about significant changes. The secret lies in searching for individuals with leadership abilities, not only among the so-called elites, but in all sectors of society in order to jointly develop a network.'[14]

This insight sparked the creation of the AVINA Foundation[15] in 1994, which works with civil society and business leaders in its sustainable development initiatives in several areas: citizen participation and community organization development, the efficient administration of natural resources, and programmes in the areas of communications and formal/informal education. It also participates in projects promoting innovative economic activities, SMEs, corporate social responsibility and eco-efficiency.[16]

Closing a virtuous circle – visions and values

In yet another turning point in his life, Stephan Schmidheiny decided in 2003 to donate all of his GrupoNeuva and other stock to his new creation, the VIVA Trust, his most creative and visionary endeavour to date. (VIVA stands for 'vision and values'.) Schmidheiny says that creating VIVA is 'another step towards attaining my vision'. The GrupoNueva stock was worth about €525.2 million, and the rest brought the total gift to €656.6 million – over US$1 billion.

He writes: 'At first glance, it would seem that there are major conflicts of interest between a business and a foundation. While the former seeks to make money, the latter intends to invest it, though with no financial return. However, I began wondering if there actually exists such a deep gulf when it is the same individual's vision that gives rise to both, when both seek to add value to society, when both are based on efficiency and entrepreneurship, and when both seek to establish new modalities of partnership.'[17]

This brainchild reflects its creator's vision for the future, which he hopes could serve as a blueprint for sustainable giving. VIVA, as owner and funder, guides the strategic direction of GrupoNueva and the AVINA Foundation. It also supervises performance and efficiency. GrupoNueva defines its strategy in Latin America and supports it by meeting profitability, growth and efficiency goals, while fully assuming its social and environmental responsibilities. AVINA is expected to continue contributing to the region's social development and sustainability.

In this unique arrangement, GrupoNueva generates the resources that are then reinvested, through VIVA and AVINA, in the communities where GrupoNueva operates and in other locations. At the same time, GrupoNeuva and AVINA continue as independent organizations.

Schmidheiny hopes this new model will become a virtuous circle that will at once strengthen society's sustainable development, and encourage successful and socially responsible enterprises and civil society organizations. At the same time, it is expected to create a more extensive and stable market for the entrepreneurial group.

It is early days, but the model is working. Schmidheiny points to some concrete results. A GrupoNueva executive in Ecuador partnered with AVINA to establish a foundation to help laid-off workers set up their own businesses. A GrupoNeuva farm in Costa Rica is working with AVINA partners, helping them to restore a river basin. Businesses and foundations are cooperating in work being done with the Mapuche indigenous people in Chile and Argentina.

In 2003, following the creation of VIVA Trust, Stephan Schmidheiny retired from all of his operational tasks, including his positions in GrupoNueva and AVINA. But a man such as Schmidheiny will never truly retire. He leaves an impressive legacy through the creative organizations he has helped to set up. He is a sought-after speaker, he receives awards and distinctions, he is a role model for many. Apparently, more of the same is not enough of a challenge.

'I am not entirely satisfied. I feel that we will not attain sustainable human development until many more individuals and organizations are motivated by a vision of this sort of progress and come to value this goal. This conviction shall inspire and guide me for the rest of my life.'[18]

'Today, the important is becoming urgent ...'
An interview with Stephan Schmidheiny

In his many speeches – usually when receiving an award or distinction – Stephan Schmidheiny emphasizes the following point: today, the important is becoming urgent. Today, he is at once sad and optimistic. Sad to think of the great innovation and business opportunities we have missed because we continued with the politics of cheap fossil fuel. Optimistic because despite the desperate state of the planet's environment and the accelerated pace of change that is driving its destruction, the glass is still half full, never half empty.

This dichotomy is not unusual in a man who has so creatively combined business and philanthropy – but his analysis and vision yield plenty of food for thought. Schmidheiny shared some of his thoughts in an interview in February 2008.

You have been called many things, but how would you describe yourself?
I don't feel comfortable with clichés, but visionary comes the closest. But I am a visionary with uncommon views based on common sense. The tension that has always been in me is being a visionary with both feet on the ground. I was born with my feet on the ground, but I always had a curious mind about the world, society and how it all works. This has made me think about the future and where we are going.

When accepting your honorary doctorate at Universidad Católica Andrés
Bello in 2001, you said that in your view, 'humanity lives today in a limbo state,
burdened with a folk memory of infinite resources and lacking the wisdom to
live with limited resources'. You asked 'where is the apple of wisdom, now that
we need it?' This begs the question: Where is the apple of wisdom today?
When Adam and Eve ate of the apple of wisdom, they were expelled from
the garden into the land of scarcity and hardship. I believe we are about to
be expelled from the paradise of an abundant world. In the past, humanity
has depleted resources and created environmental disasters. We could
always move. Today, there is nowhere to move on to. We need to learn to live
with scarcity.

　　　Two phenomena – the congruence of exponential numbers and the
speed of acceleration – are leading change in our world. Countries such
as China and India are developing exponentially and their appetite for
energy is enormous. It is their right to develop, but wouldn't it be smarter
for them to learn from our mistakes and avoid creating the same wasteful
civilization that we have built up? It would be interesting if they could see
the competitive advantages inherent in consuming less energy based on
fossil fuels. These developments will push us into an era of scarcity, which
will change the rules of business and politics.

What does this mean for the future?
People historically deal with scarcity in three ways – they divide things up,
make the most efficient use of what they have (reduce consumption), or
create wars. If we don't make sufficient progress with the first two options,
option three will become the default scenario. It is already happening today
as larger economies rush to secure access to the remaining sources of oil.
Some are saying that this era has already begun with the invasion of Iraq.

You are now saying 'the important has become urgent'. Have we reached
the tipping point?
I thought that the world's nations had lost their innocence about the
state of the environment at the Earth Summit in 1992. But we ignored
the promises made and it has been business as usual. As a result, yes, in
2007 we definitely reached the tipping point in global environmental issues,
with climate change being the trigger. People are not used to distinguishing
between climate change and weather, but weather is in the news every
day and it is attributed to climate change. Public awareness about the
challenges ahead has reached the tipping point as well – and that is here
to stay.

Our key challenge today is how societies can accelerate the process of collective learning – they must or they will be forced to. We cannot afford to do the same things over the next 15 years as we have for the last; that is to go in the wrong direction.

Can we save the earth's environment?
We cannot save the environment the way it is today. It will never be the same. We have also reached the tipping point in resource consumption, including energy, food commodities and minerals. Damage prevention is no longer an option. We must change our approach to sustainability and move into mitigation and adaptation to learn how to live in a different environment. Now that we are out of paradise, there will be suffering under new constraints. An oil price of US$100 a barrel certainly changes the rules of the game. The breakthroughs in technology in the future to meet these challenges will be absolutely fascinating. Until then, it will be a very bumpy ride.

What is the role of business today?
A key point is that business will have to accept this new scenario of a world of scarcity and plan accordingly. It must participate in the public debate about how to approach solutions. It should be the role of business to think longer term, develop strategies, and find and experiment with market-based solutions that are efficiency focused. Governments will be hard pressed once scarcity settles in and will likely do the wrong things. Business needs to engage and participate to ensure that governments implement the right regulations.

Do you still view SMEs as engines of development?
Yes, that is how I started in philanthropy, with FUNDES, to support small businesses. SMEs are the foundation of an economy, especially where there are administrative obstacles to business, because they are more flexible and more dynamic. If I were to begin again today, I would fertilize the soil so that microenterprises could become SMEs. Supporting micro and small businesses should be part of any process. FUNDES resulted from an uncommon view based on common sense. I believe we were part of making this approach mainstream. Today, there are few agencies that do not include small businesses in their programmes.

In 1993, in a speech to INCAE, you listed four different types of contribution to the future that will require business initiative: competitive success, social solidarity, a commitment to the environment, and a free society. Would you add anything to this list today?

I would add education – it is key. Not general education. Business cannot do that. But business can educate their entire supply chains, their employees and their customers to think about creative ways to do things differently, for example, how to limit CO_2 in a way that will avoid the energy demand we have today. Business has the creativity we need.

How were you inspired to create the VIVA Trust? Has it been a success?

A turning point in my life was in 1992 with the Earth Summit and the passing of my father and brother. I did not feel like going back to where I had left off. I created the AVINA Foundation, which was to be a 15-year project. But I realized that societal processes are much more complex than business decisions and that people simply need time to change. I wanted to guarantee the sustainability of AVINA and to guarantee the future for the wonderful momentum the Foundation was building up. The classic solution would have been to create an endowment invested in Wall Street securities. But I disliked the idea of creating a permanent North-South cash flow. That, to me, is similar to the concept of 'aid' from rich donors.

So, I created an endowment using my business interests. Money made in Latin America funds Latin American philanthropy. This is a more interesting model to me as I can work on both sides. I grow trees, have factories, pay wages and educate people on the business side. On top of that, we make money that funds philanthropy. The structure is interesting in that it has its own checks and balances between enterprise and philanthropy. It has been a great success. We are doing very well in business and the Foundation is doing just fine. Most importantly, we have a great group of people who have absorbed the fundamental values and ideas of my vision and will keep this going the day I disappear.

A lot of your work is based on the concept of partnership between businesses and civil society. What about partnership between business and the public sector (government at local, national and regional levels)? There exists 'public-private partnership' fatigue among some critics. Do you share that view?

Partnership of all kinds is fundamental. It is AVINA's core mission to help facilitate partnerships of all kinds. Public-private partnerships work for certain things, but there is good and bad. Often they are implemented haphazardly, politicians want a photo op and business wants a good PR move. In these instances, the partnership doesn't work. If there isn't a consistent regulatory framework in place to guarantee such partnerships, they will be lost in the political noise and buried under business interests.

Is there anything you would have done differently in your business and philanthropic endeavours in the past if you could have seen the future, particularly in terms of the environment?
If I had known in 1992 what I know today, I might have tried to do more faster and bigger because I clearly underestimated today's reality. Today's reality is much worse than the worst-case scenario we feared.

Of your many accomplishments to date, which is the most important in your view? What would you like to be remembered for?
I would like to say the VIVA Trust, but really it is for coining the term 'eco-efficiency' during the time of the Earth Summit. Today, the term is used around the world, but, most important, it helped to open people and broaden their views. People used to think that caring for the environment was a conflict of interest by necessity. With eco-efficiency we opened people's minds to the notion that there is an opportunity to make money by being more environmentally efficient.

Energy is the key in this. Things are going to accelerate way beyond what we may think or imagine. My son is 28 and he will live through the end of petroleum. We don't have a clue what it means to change to a non-petroleum-based economy. But we must first and foremost remember that all life is a work in progress. In that sense, sustainability is an open-ended way of progress that will have ups and downs, failures and successes. Our most important challenge is to find ways and means to transition from a time of abundance to scarcity. And hopefully we can learn how to do this without conflict.

If you were asked to advise someone in business or working in an NGO about how to be successful, how to achieve his or her goals, what would you advise?
I would advise people to keep faithful to themselves in terms of values, living and working to their own strengths and weaknesses. You will find answers listening to your inner self. Develop leadership skills, but recognize that leadership is everything – you can't do things on your own.

[1] The background information for this chapter comes from www.stephanschmidheiny.net

[2] Stephan Schmidheiny, *My Path – My Perspective*, VIVA Trust, January 2006, p4.

[3] Ibid, p8.

[4] Stephan Schmidheiny, *Changing Course: A global business perspective on development and the environment*, World Business Council on Sustainable Development, 1992.

[5] Schmidheiny, *My Path – My Perspective*, p10.

[6] Ibid, p9.

[7] For more information, www.fundes.org/en

[8] For more information, www.wbcsd.org

[9] Schmidheiny, *My Path – My Perspective*, pp24–25.

[10] Besides works by artists representing American abstract expressionism, pop art, and minimalism, such as Pollock, Rothko, Warhol, de Kooning, Twombly, or Eva Hesse, the Daros Collection includes New York art of the 1980s and since, such as Barbara Kruger or Robert Gober, and holds important groups of works by pre-eminent German artists Joseph Beuys, Gerhard Richter and Sigmar Polke. For more information, www.daros.ch

[11] Schmidheiny, *My Path – My Perspective*, p 28.

[12] Ibid, p30.

[13] www.avina.com

[14] Schmidheiny, *My Path – My Perspective*, p31.

[15] For more information, www.avina.com

[16] Eco-efficiency – a term adopted by Schmidheiny and his WBCSD colleagues during its first year of activities, which refers to adding more value to goods and services using fewer resources and producing less waste and pollution.

[17] Schmidheiny, *My Path – My Perspective*, p38.

[18] Ibid, p41.

DIANNA RIENSTRA

12 Van Leer Foundation Group
A story of entrepreneurship, benevolence and serendipity
Portrait of an enigma

'You mustn't tell me it can't be done.' Bernard van Leer

Everyone who is interviewed about the industrialist who laid the foundation for the Bernard van Leer Foundation Group, the richest charitable organization in the Netherlands, quotes him thus. Industrialist, benefactor and circus director, Jewish-born Bernard van Leer was driven by an unstoppable entrepreneurial spirit. A workaholic, according to those close to him, who was distant from everyone, including his family. Yet benevolent. A visionary and a very rich man who took huge risks – a man who described himself as someone with a lot of luck.

In 1919, Bernard van Leer dropped out of primary school to found a packaging company that became a world leader and provided him with the means to establish in 1949 the Bernard van Leer Stiftung in Lucerne, Switzerland. The idea was to channel the revenues from his fortune to charitable causes after his death. His family agreed to be disinherited and following Van Leer's death in 1958, Oscar van Leer closed the Swiss foundation and in 1966 established the Bernard van Leer Foundation in The Hague.

Oscar van Leer took his father's vision forward and created the organizational framework for the Van Leer Group Foundation in 1971, which today is the custodian of his father's legacy. He worked on furthering his father's objectives until his death in 1996.

The Van Leer Group Foundation has been operating internationally since 1966, which sets it aside from many other family foundations such as Ford, Rockefeller and Carnegie – all philanthropists said to have influenced

Bernard van Leer.

Bernard van Leer while he was living in exile in the United States after the outbreak of World War Two.

It all started with a mysterious, sometimes contradictory man. Bernard van Leer's son Wim related: 'Father had a phrase. "If they ask you for money, give. But never get involved." He always kept far away.' Nevertheless, it often overwhelmed him. In 1956, Van Leer wrote to someone who had approached him:

'In your letter of July 10th you ask to see me and I will be pleased to receive you, providing it is not your plan to ask for money, no matter how worthy the case may be! During latter years, I have become both embarrassed and disgusted by the number of people who ask to see me and just as soon as they are in my neighbourhood they ask for money.'

But he was often swayed, especially if he found something compelling. One of his responses to the relentless stream of requests for money was: 'See what you can drum up yourselves, then I'll double it.'[1] At the same time, he gave generously to Jewish causes, for example to German Jews who had escaped from Nazi Germany.

Mysterious how he felt compelled to give back to society, yet did so anonymously. Contradictory – for this man who preferred anonymity often displayed a penchant for showmanship. For what else is a circus where the industrialist rides into the ring atop a prancing white Lipizzaner, but the ultimate venue for a showman?

The making of a tycoon

Young Bernard van Leer worked as a director of a cardboard-producing factory set up by his eldest brother. After a few takeovers, he established Van Leer's Vereenigde Fabrieken in November 1919 and went into the metal packaging business. He started making cigarette boxes for a company in Egypt, was often on the edge of bankruptcy, and was rumoured to have once cashed in his life insurance policy to meet payroll. Bernard van Leer also invented a clever closure for petrol cans, which he sold in large numbers. But in 1920s, his luck really kicked in.

Bataafse Petroleum Maatschappij – later known as Shell – gave him an enormous order for asphalt drums, and a licensing agreement with the American manufacturers of the Tri-Sure drum closure he invented allowed him to produce and sell his product around the world. In the 1930s, he set up drum factories across Western Europe, in Africa and the Caribbean. Instead of 'shipping air', as he described it, Bernard van Leer decided to follow Shell and set up manufacturing facilities close to its refineries. In 1938, he opened a rolling steel mill in the Netherlands.

By this time, Bernard van Leer was a very wealthy man. He started Kavaljos, a travelling circus with more than 20 rare Lipizzaners, Arabians and Friesians that he trained himself. Dressage was his preferred hobby. Film footage of the tycoon riding into the ring like a true showman exposes a character who was truly an enigma – mysterious and inscrutable. The small-scale circus performed in Amsterdam, Paris, Brussels and Copenhagen, with the proceeds going to good causes.

Exile in America

The tide turned during the war when the Germans occupied the Netherlands in 1940. Bernard van Leer was forced to sell his company's holdings in the Netherlands, Belgium and France. German firms took over the companies and the family was 'allowed' to leave occupied Europe. Before leaving, he made numerous donations and set up a support fund for his staff. He also left enough money to set up a foundation to subsidize Jewish musicians and cabaret artists.

The family set sail from Spain in 1941 to the US via Cuba, together with various relatives, staff, the circus violinist and 19 horses. The four-year exile was difficult, but Kavaljos did manage to perform to rave reviews at Radio City Music Hall and other venues. Staff from London ran the factories outside occupied Europe and the factory in England performed remarkably well during the war.

Bernard van Leer visited
Winston Churchill at
Chartwell in October 1946.

Rebuilding an empire

When Bernard van Leer returned to a devastated continent, he threw
himself back into work to start building what was to become an even larger
empire – the reconstruction of war-torn Europe turned into a money-spinner
as iron and steel were in demand. The Royal Packaging Industries Van
Leer became a huge international success, with 50 companies employing
5,500 people. By 1989, it had expanded to 123 establishments in 33 countries
employing about 15,000 worldwide.

But as Bernard van Leer became richer, he became even more of
an enigma – at once a bigger showman and an increasingly lonely man as
he kept the outside world at a greater distance. In 1946, he lunched with
Winston Churchill and corresponded with the British war leader for years
after offering him one of his favourite horses. He chartered a KLM aircraft
in 1947 and, with great aplomb and publicity, spent two months touring all
his factories. In the early 1950s, he travelled across Europe with a mobile
drum-making factory that delivered the product in 15 minutes. In 1957
Bernard van Leer commissioned American architect Martin Breuer to
design the company's head office in Amstelveen, the Netherlands.

Bernard van Leer with his son
Oscar.

Bernard van Leer died in 1958 at the age of 74. His family decided
he should be buried in Israel. A memorial service was held in a hangar at
Schipol Airport and his body then flown to Jerusalem.

A transgenerational philanthropic impulse at work

Bernard van Leer left behind a money-making machine and a fund that
spent the money on charities. His family had agreed to be disinherited and
he left the bulk of his holdings to the Bernard van Leer Stiftung in Lucerne,
Switzerland to be used for charitable purposes. Almost all of the donations
made went to private institutions, many of them for the disabled.

It was up to Oscar van Leer when he returned from the US in
1958 to run his father's business empire and to shape the foundation's
philanthropic goals and chart its future course. In 1963, on a trip back to
the US, he read an article by the New York developmental psychologist
Martin Deutsch, Professor of Early Childhood Studies at the University of
New York. Deutsch was researching the problems of socially and culturally
disadvantaged children. Deutsch noted that the disadvantages faced by
these children from birth resulted in the waste of vast reservoirs of talent.

Shaping the legacy – vision inspired by serendipity

Philanthropists and foundations face a common dilemma – managing change. At the same time, they need to strike a balance between maintaining the ideals of a founder or founding family and the realities of a changing world. As Oscar van Leer was shaping his father's legacy, he found a path that was to chart the Bernard van Leer Foundation's course for the future in the field of early childhood development. It was the perfect match for an international company that had made most of its fortune in developing countries.

'The original Swiss foundation was created for broad humanitarian purposes, there was no real direction. Years later, Oscar van Leer met the man who was to inspire him. It was sheer serendipity. He had found a way to give back to the communities where the company was doing business by investing in the future of their children,' explains former Van Leer Group Foundation Executive Director Rien van Gendt.

The vehicle was created before the mandate was in place. Like his father Bernard van Leer, Oscar van Leer was a visionary. But while his father was blessed with good luck, Oscar was blessed with serendipity. He laid the groundwork for the foundation's charitable work to make a real difference in the communities where the company had operations and in Israel, where the family's heart lay. Clearly, Oscar van Leer was a thinker ahead of his time, giving his successors the tools to manage change successfully while preserving the ideals of the Van Leer family.

'Thanks to a fortune made mainly by the production of oil drums and the generosity of Bernard and Oscar, thousands of children worldwide got a better chance,' adds Van Gendt. 'It's always difficult to see how things will develop, but Bernard van Leer was a man with a vision and that vision has proved productive. I think he would have been very proud if he'd lived to see this.'

When Oscar van Leer's plane landed in New York, he called Martin Deutsch and invited him out to lunch. Deutsch accepted. After their conversation, Oscar van Leer had found the path. One year later, he decided that the Bernard Van Leer Stiftung should focus on the educational challenges of environmentally disadvantaged children and youth.

'It was laid down that the [Foundation's] main aim was to enable children and youth through schoolgoing age, who are impeded by the social and cultural inadequacy of their background or environment, to achieve the greatest possible realization of their innate, intellectual potential.'[2]

In 1966, Oscar van Leer closed the Swiss foundation (the Bernard van Leer Stiftung) and established the Bernard van Leer Foundation in The Hague. A specialist in the field of early childhood development was brought in to head the Foundation, which focused on education projects for children living in countries where Van Leer companies were located.

The first project – which was also a test case for the Foundation – was the Project for Early Childhood Education, launched in Jamaica in 1966. Funds were given to the University of the West Indies to improve 1,000 Basic Schools, which were set up and run by the community. This project formed the cornerstone of the Foundation's work because it became increasingly clear that education alone was not the answer.

A more holistic approach was needed to solve the challenges faced by developing countries. The emphasis shifted towards health, hygiene, diet and child rearing, as well as education. Parents became increasingly involved and it became obvious that cooperation among school, family and community was critical. The Foundation's work expanded from 17 projects in 1968 to more than 100 in the 1980s.

A change of direction

In 1971, Oscar van Leer changed the structure that his father had set up to manage his legacy by establishing the Van Leer Group Foundation in the Netherlands, run by a board of nine members, which also oversaw the Bernard van Leer Foundation. The income for the Bernard van Leer Foundation came from the Van Leer Group Foundation, which was funded by dividends from the Van Leer Company.

Oscar van Leer's credo for the company and the foundation gives an invaluable insight into how he intended to ensure the legacy – and the spirit of the legacy – would continue. 'Do unto your predecessor what you want your successors to do unto you,' he wrote at the time. He described the seven 'building blocks' of his credo, the sixth of which explains the family's deep feeling for Israel:

'It follows that the sixth building block of the credo must be the imperative that the company and foundation should judiciously use their means and their influence, in the widest sense of these words, to advance the cause of preserving a safe, sound and just homeland for the Jewish people – even when sometimes it will hurt.'

His poetic side in describing the *leitmotif* of the credo reveals a man with deep convictions:

Always to seek and to heed
>   *the universal in specifics*
>   *the fundamental in symptoms*
>   *the invariant in changes*
>   *the necessity in chance*
>   *the pattern in randomness*
>   *the grand design in incidents*
>   *the forest in trees*
>   *the potential in beginnings*
>   *the theme in variations*

That, to me, is to have 'calibre'.
Always to
>   *practise what you preach*
>   *preach what you believe, and*
>   *believe what you practise*
>   *with conscience, not fear or conveniences, as guide and mentor*

That, to me is to have 'integrity'.
To provide
>   *An expanding and profitable corporate framework within which people*
> *can find inspiration, motivation and opportunity to realise evermore facets,*
> *and evermore of every facet, their potential, while not losing sight of the*
> *lesson to be learned from the story about the Tower of Babel, that as a general*
> *principle, the need for 'limitations upon growth' cannot be ignored with*
> *impunity. That, to me in an industrial context, is the 'proper practice of growth'.*

>   *Based upon these considerations, the seventh building block of my*
> *credo is that the future leadership of what today are our enterprise and our*
> *foundation should be irrevocably committed to 'calibre, integrity and growth',*
> *together and in the sense I have described, being and remaining the key to the*
> *conduct of all our affairs; and furthermore that, as to that same commitment*
> *in others, these future leaders should have the good sense to know it when*
> *they see it.*[3]

When he retired in 1979, Oscar van Leer left behind a unique structure
which endured until his death in 1996. Until then, the Van Leer Group
Foundation was the sole shareholder of the shares in the packaging
company Royal Packaging Industries Van Leer NV. That year, the company
was listed on the Amsterdam Stock Exchange and the Van Leer Group
Foundation sold almost 50 per cent of its shares, maintaining a majority
interest.

In 1999, the Finnish packaging company Huhtamaki bid for the shares of Royal Packaging Industries, which led to a sale of all of the shares. The Van Leer Group Foundation bought a share in the newly incorporated company, but in 2001 sold its shares in the new company.

A recognizable relationship between earning and spending

The Van Leer Group Foundation (VLGF) performs a holding function in relation to the charitable activities of the so-called Van Leer Entity, which embodies the main goal of the Van Leer family – namely a recognizable relationship between earning and spending money for charitable purposes. The Bernard van Leer Foundation, Van Leer Jerusalem Institute and Jerusalem Film Center are the charities. The general investment portfolio and Crecor BV – a for-profit venture capital company that invests in Israeli start-ups – are the sources of income.

Today, the VLGF's assets consist of a global investment portfolio of equities and fixed interest securities, which are its main source of income, with a value of more than €650 million. As a holding foundation, the VLGF takes the lead with respect to governance issues, such as the board composition and profile of members of itself and of the Bernard van Leer Foundation. Crecor BV is a fully owned company with the VLGF's Governing Council serving as its Supervisory Board.

The same eight members comprise the Governing Council of the VLGF, the Board of Trustees of the Bernard van Leer Foundation and the Supervisory Board of Crecor BV.

'This is unique in that the philanthropic impulse becomes a vital part of the business itself. The same people spend and earn. This personal union means that there are high risks involved in securing funding through an investment portfolio,' explains former Van Leer Group Foundation Executive Director Rien van Gendt. 'There is no guaranteed income to run the charitable activities. This mentality translates into also taking risks in the charitable work the Group does, which means we engage in activities that are worthwhile experimenting with.'

Living the legacy

The Van Leer Group Foundation, the holding company, functions as an umbrella to safeguard the family legacy. It has three statutory objectives:
  – To promote the optimum development of socially and economically disadvantaged children up to the age of eight, with the objective of developing their innate potential to the greatest extent possible.

- To contribute to the development and strengthening of a Jewish, democratic national home in Israel committed to a free, equitable and just society for all of its citizens; and to contribute to the pursuit of regional peace, for the benefit and betterment of social, cultural and individual lives in Israel.
- To promote and further the continuity and preservation of the identity of the Van Leer Entity.

The Bernard van Leer Foundation implements the first objective. The second objective is realized through the Van Leer Jerusalem Institute and the Jerusalem Film Center. The Van Leer Group Foundation provides a substantial part of the funding for these organizations and is represented by the Governors and the Executive Director of the Van Leer Group Foundation on the Boards of these organizations.

The third objective of the VLGF, which deals with the promotion of the Van Leer Entity, implies that the VLGF has a particular responsibility with respect to the way in which the legacy of the Van Leer family is translated into existing and new humanitarian ventures and income-generating activities.

The Bernard Van Leer Foundation – focusing on the future

True to Oscar van Leer's vision, the Bernard van Leer Foundation operates internationally, concentrating its resources on promoting the optimum development of disadvantaged children. It focuses specifically on children up to the age of eight, because research shows that interventions during this period are most effective in yielding lasting benefits to the children and the communities they live in.

The Foundation accomplishes its objectives through two interconnected strategies: a grantmaking programme aimed at developing innovative approaches to early childhood care and development; and the sharing of knowledge and know-how in the area of early childhood development with the aim of informing and influencing policy and practice.

The Foundation works in three issue areas.

- By strengthening the care environment, it aims to build the capacity of vulnerable parents, families and communities to care for their children.
- It aims to help young children make a successful transition from their home environment to daycare, preschool and school.

Projects supported by the Bernard van Leer Foundation

Roving Caregivers

A home visiting/parent support project in Jamaica that has been positively evaluated by UNICEF. It is currently working with the government and civil society organizations in four Eastern Caribbean countries – St Lucia, Grenada, Dominica and St Vincent – to replicate the approach. The objectives of the project are to improve living conditions for development and to educate a growing number of young children; to promote better parenting at the community level for child development and preparation for school; to consolidate the roving care model and document the experiences and identify new funding opportunities to take this successful project to scale.

Christian Children's Fund

This project in Samburu, Kenya, combines local knowledge and materials with solid child development principles. Aimed at enhancing early childhood development among children from birth to 8 years in the Samburu and Marsabit Districts, the project builds on the results achieved since 2002. It looks at making the community-based approach more sustainable by addressing issues such as HIV/AIDS. The 'Loipi' model developed in this project is now being implemented in Tanzania, Uganda, Ethiopia, Nigeria and Namibia.

Hand in Hand Center for Jewish-Arab Education

This project supports advances in integrated education and respect for diversity among young children from polarized communities in Israel. In the past, the Foundation has helped Hand in Hand establish a preschool in Jerusalem, a new school in Wadi Ara and an early school age unit that works with young children in both schools. Current funding is for a final phase of two years during which Hand in Hand will work to ensure the sustainability of the early childhood education it provides.

– Through social inclusion and respect for diversity, it aims to promote equal opportunities and skills to help children to live in diverse societies.

Informing and influencing policy and practice

The project work is complemented by an ongoing effort to document and analyse the projects with the objectives of learning lessons for future grantmaking and generating knowledge that can be shared. Through evidence-based advocacy and publications, the Bernard van Leer Foundation seeks to inform and influence policy and practice in the countries where it operates and beyond.

The projects are implemented by public, private or community-based partners. All focus on young children growing up in circumstances of social and economic disadvantage, but the contexts in which the projects operate are very diverse. Some are in urban slums and shantytowns, others in remote rural areas. They focus on children belonging to ethnic and cultural minorities, those growing up in multicultural societies, migrant or refugee children, children of single or teenage parents, children suffering from war or conflict or those orphaned by AIDS.

In 2007, the Foundation was supporting 150 major projects in 40 countries, both in the developing and the developed world – most are in countries where Royal Packaging Industries Van Leer NV used to operate, including Africa, Asia, Europe and the Americas, including the US. It also supports activities in Israel and a number of other countries that further the Foundation's work.

The Van Leer Jerusalem Institute – solidarity with the Jewish people
Founded in 1959, the institute and its mission are based on the Van Leer family's vision of Israel as both a homeland for the Jewish people and a democratic society, based on justice, fairness and equality for all its residents. Today, the institute's work is still shaped by the Van Leer legacy – its objective is to enhance ethnic and cultural understanding, mitigate social tensions, empower civil society players and promote democratic values.

The institute pursues its mandate by various methodologies: academic research, public policy analysis, advocacy and civil society projects. Throughout its history, the institute has initiated or participated in more than 200 different projects, which are clustered broadly under four umbrellas:

Advanced Learning
The original mission of the institute was to serve as a centre of excellence for advanced learning in the philosophy and history of science. Today, the institute is regarded as Israel's foremost centre devoted to this.

Israeli Civil Society

The institute works to implement the Van Leer family's vision by strengthening civil society through programmes that anticipate, identify and promote solutions to social crises and divisions. The methodology includes a mix of research, policy analysis and educational intervention tools. The result is new knowledge about confronting social challenges and new realities being created on the ground for Israel's most vulnerable communities.

Jewish Culture and Identity

The institute reinforces its founders' commitment to solidarity with the Jewish people and their future. The focus is on reinforcing the connection to Jewish heritage by research and other activities. Conferences, symposia and lecture series are open to the public. Issues covered by discussion and research groups include religion, society and the state, solidarity, and communities and education.

Israel, Palestinians and Mediterranean Neighbours

Recognizing that the ethnic origins of more than half of Israel's population – and the geopolitical realities of the country – are rooted in the Mediterranean, the institute aims to advance the study of regional cultures. Given that the Palestinians are Israel's closest neighbours, emphasis is placed on promoting an atmosphere of understanding and maintaining open channels of communication between Palestinians and Israelis, even during stressful times.

The Van Leer Jerusalem Institute is located in Jerusalem's Rehavia district and houses a unique, 27,000-volume library focused on the history of ideas.

The Jerusalem Film Center

In 1956, Lia van Leer and her late husband Wim van Leer founded the first film society in Israel. In 1961, they set up the Israel Film Archive, the beginning of the Jerusalem Film Center. The Israel Film Archive is the largest film archive in the Middle East and is dedicated to the collection and preservation of the art and history of film, television and video.

Today, it contains more than 30,000 prints including international cinema and all of Israeli cinema since the beginning of the 20th century. The archive also has the largest collection of Jewish and Holocaust films in the world. Founded in 1973, the Jerusalem Film Center consists of the

Projects supported by the Van Leer Jerusalem Institute

Exposing academics

The New Horizons for Religious Educators project is an academic enrichment programme that exposes principals and senior educators from orthodox religious-Zionist secondary schools (*yeshivot* and *ulpanot*) to Western thought. This highly successful year-long programme is a critical first step towards cultivating tolerance and respect. It also fosters increased participation in Israeli society and civil society by Jews of diverse ideologies.

Fostering mutual learning

The Learning the National Narratives of the Other project is funded by the Canadian government and the EU and carried out in cooperation with the Sartawi Center for Peace Studies in Al Quds University. It involves 15 Palestinian and 15 Israeli students learning relevant issues with the help of Israeli and Palestinian academics. Once the mutual learning is over, the two narratives are being published side-by-side in Hebrew-Arabic booklets, which will be introduced to the Palestinian and Israeli educational systems.

Improving coexistence

The Mutual Responsibility in the Community: Jews and Arabs in Jaffa project brought together Jewish and Arab residents of this mixed city to develop and implement projects aimed at improving coexistence. By the end of 2004, the group decided on two projects that were implemented during 2005 and concluded in 2006:
  – Saving the market in Jaffa, which was bought up by private entrepreneurs. The group raised public opinion to save this special market.
  – Monitoring the activities of the police in Jaffa. The group set up a hotline to monitor police behaviour towards the local population, with volunteer lawyers and psychologists assisting the crew.

Israel Film Archive, the Jerusalem Cinematheque and the Jerusalem International Film Festival.

The Jerusalem Cinematheque has two screening auditoriums. The Cinematheque works closely with international cultural institutions, embassies and local organizations. It has more than 8,000 members and screens five different films every day.

The Jerusalem International Film Festival attracts an audience of more than 70,000 every year. It screens more than 200 features, shorts, documentaries, experimental films and videos in categories ranging from new cinema and the avant-garde to emerging directors and films focusing on human rights and Jewish themes. For 10 days each summer, the festival is a venue for creating and stimulating dialogue and discussion for film professionals and audiences from different cultures.

The Jerusalem Jewish Film Festival has been held annually since 1999. It takes place over the Hanukah holidays and lasts for seven days. More than 50 films from Israel and all over the world are screened.

Since 1982, the Jerusalem Film Center has housed the Department for Film Education, providing more than 300 days of programming for primary, secondary and high school students and special education students. It also offers courses for adults and professionals, enabling them to develop their analytical skills and critical abilities and tapping into new creative talent.

The Ministry of Education, the Ministry of Foreign Affairs, the Ministry of Trade and Industry, the Jerusalem Municipality, the Mayor of Jerusalem, the Jerusalem Foundation, the George Ostrovsky Family Foundation, the Van Leer Group Foundation and others support the Jerusalem Film Center.

I am, you are

A series of five short films was first produced in a summer workshop in 1999. Since then, five short films are produced each year. The 'I am, you are' project involves young Arab and Jewish filmmakers from Jerusalem who write, direct and shoot their movies together. The subjects of the films reflect different issues of identity and life in Jerusalem. The Jerusalem Foundation and the Eranda Foundation in the UK support the project.

[1] Pauline Micheels, *A Legacy for humankind, The Bernard van Leer Foundation: From profits to philanthropy*, published to mark the 50th anniversary of the Bernard van Leer Foundation by the Bernard van Leer Foundation, 1999, p17.

[2] Ibid, p22.

[3] Harry Leliveld, *The Van Leer Entity 1987–2002: Preserving identity through change*, published by the Van Leer Group Foundation, 2006, p88.

DAVID WATKISS

13 The Wellcome Trust
An organization of enormous wealth and 'staggering diversity'

The Wellcome Trust's mission is 'to foster and promote research with the aim of improving human and animal health'. Created in 1936 under the terms of the will of Sir Henry S Wellcome, today the Trust is the most diverse and second largest biomedical research charity in the world.

On bustling Euston Road, near Bloomsbury and 'Medical London', stand two architecturally different but impressive structures owned by the Wellcome Trust. The Wellcome Building, constructed in 1932 under the direction of Henry Wellcome, an eight-storey Georgian neoclassical building in Portland stone, now houses Wellcome Collection, the Wellcome Library, the Wellcome Trust Centre for the History of Medicine at University College, London, a conference centre, a bookstore and a café.

Next door, in the gleaming ten-storey steel and glass Gibbs Building, opened in 2004, is the Trust's headquarters, its atrium graced by a dazzling six-storey-high glass sculpture, evoking 'falling liquid, captured and frozen in time', as described by Wellcome's literature. Its street-level windows contain colourful neon works of art inspired by medical research funded by the Trust.

Here, the Trust's Board of Governors and staff of approximately 500, assisted by strategic and funding committees whose expert members number more than 300, manage the Trust's enormous wealth and administer its multifaceted activities. The Gibbs Building is named in honour of Sir Roger Gibbs, Chair of the Trust from 1989 to 1999, who is credited with 'the transformation of the Trust from a minor national organization to one of the world's foremost biomedical research charities and who has been referred to as 'the Wizard of Wellcome'.

Through external funding and work performed by the Trust and its partners, the Wellcome Trust supports a wide range of activities, including basic and clinical research, open access to research results, technology transfer, medical and research ethics, public engagement, art and the history of medicine. With assets approaching £14 billion and annual spending of approximately £500 million, it is the second largest medical research charity in the world and the largest charity in the UK.

The Trust currently supports some 3,500 researchers in 44 countries. About 90 per cent of the Trust's funding is in the UK, with the balance supporting research and capacity-building in developing and restructuring countries. The Trust's work is multifaceted. Activities organized directly include Wellcome Collection, the Wellcome Library, Wellcome Images, conferences and courses, publications and websites.

The Trust also directly organizes policy-oriented work in such areas as education and healthcare. It owns and operates the Wellcome Trust Genome Campus at Hinxton, near Cambridge, home of the Wellcome Trust Sanger Institute; the Wellcome Trust Conference Centre; and the European Molecular Biology Laboratory's European Bioinformatics Institute.

The remarkable life of Henry Wellcome

Born in 1853 to an impoverished religious family on a farm in Wisconsin, US, young Henry Wellcome had several experiences that would shape his remarkable life. When he was eight years old, his family moved to Garden City, Minnesota, travelling for several weeks by covered wagon in a large group of settlers for protection against Indians. Soon after their arrival, there was an uprising by Sioux Indians. Wellcome helped cast bullets for the white settlers defending Garden City. He assisted his uncle, a physician who also had a pharmacy, to care for the wounded. The uprising ended in the defeat of the Indians and the hanging of tribal chiefs.

This early encounter with Native Americans instilled in Wellcome a deep interest in and concern for the conditions and plight of indigenous peoples. As a child, Wellcome observed with interest the life and culture of Native Americans, foreshadowing his passions for anthropology, archaeology and collecting. His work with his uncle fostered a fascination for medicine, pharmacy and experimentation. At 16, he began to exhibit a genius for marketing, launching and advertising his first product – homemade invisible ink – in the town newspaper.

Henry Solomon Wellcome.
Wellcome Library, London

Graduating from the Philadelphia College of Pharmacy in 1874, Wellcome took a position as a travelling salesman for a US pharmaceutical company, touring extensively, including through remote parts of South America. He was to relish travel in remote areas throughout his life. During his first trip to South America, he made a study of the preparation of cinchona bark for quinine, which was published with wide interest in pharmaceutical journals in the US and Britain. A letter written by Wellcome to his parents on his 21st birthday provides insights into the man.

'I do believe that God helps those who help themselves,' he wrote. '. . . I have always had a desire for wealth, and still have . . . but I want to live a life devoted to the true God and to mankind.'[1]

By 1879, Wellcome enjoyed a high reputation as a pharmaceutical salesman. That year, he received an invitation from another American, Silas Burroughs, a friend from Philadelphia College, to join him in business in London. Wellcome accepted, and in 1880 the two Americans established Burroughs Wellcome & Co, a pharmaceutical company, to promote a new form of compressed pill that offered major advantages over existing methods of dispensing medicines.

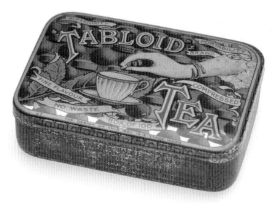

Wellcome's famous trademark 'tabloid' tin developed for the company's compressed tablet products. *Wellcome Library, London*

A leading figure in the industry

Soon thereafter, the company began its own manufacturing operations in Britain and Wellcome coined the now famous trademark 'tabloid' for the company's compressed tablet products. With Wellcome's flair for promotion, the company prospered and expanded internationally. Among other publicity devices, Wellcome created the Wellcome travelling medicine chests, which were given to famous explorers such as Henry Stanley, who provided glowing and well-publicized celebrity endorsements. Wellcome was a firm believer in aggressive marketing.

The relationship between Burroughs and Wellcome, however, was troubled and litigious. Their partnership ended in 1895 with Burroughs' unexpected death, which left Wellcome the sole owner of Burroughs Wellcome. Between Burroughs' death and the outbreak of World War One, the company experienced massive expansion and Wellcome became a leading figure in the British pharmaceutical industry.

Today, research laboratories are considered a natural and necessary adjunct to pharmaceutical manufacturing. However, in 1894 when Henry Wellcome established his first research laboratory, the idea was highly unusual. Between 1894 and 1900, Wellcome established three research laboratories, loosely connected with the pharmaceutical company. Wellcome believed in the value of scientific research as an end in itself. Commercial benefit, while important, was secondary.

A pioneer in life-saving drugs

For his laboratories, Wellcome recruited some of the best scientists of the day and gave them the freedom and means to pursue their work. During the years before World War One, the Wellcome Physiological Research Laboratories were headed by Henry Dale, who later became a Nobel Prize

Sir Henry Dale, who headed
the Wellcome Physiological
Research Laboratories before
World War One and later
became a Nobel Prize winner.
Wellcome Library, London

winner, President of the Royal Society and long-time Chair of the Wellcome
Trust from 1938 to 1960 during the challenging formative years of the Trust.

Under Dale, researchers made discoveries leading to improvements
in the production of anti-toxins for the treatment of diphtheria, tetanus
and gas-gangrene. Many of today's life-saving drugs resulted from work
at the Wellcome laboratories. During World War One, the Burroughs
Wellcome Company made major contributions, at little to no profit, to
the British war effort.

In 1901, Wellcome married Syrie Barnardo, daughter of a famous
humanitarian. Their union produced one son. After some years of
separation, the marriage ended bitterly and with public scandal in 1915,
when Syrie gave birth to a child fathered by playwright W Somerset
Maugham. Wellcome's only child suffered from learning disability,
probably dyslexia, and was deemed unsuited to run his father's business.

A passion for collecting
From his early years, Wellcome had collected objects related to human
health and medicine. His collecting activities focused on texts and items
relating to 'the preservation of [human] life and health in all ages and
cultures'. By 1905, then in his early fifties, Wellcome devoted increasing

time and substantial resources to his passion for collecting – a passion that took a toll on his marriage. Wellcome believed that studying past ways of life was vital to human progress. He had an ambition to create a Museum of Man, which he envisioned would serve two purposes: education and entertainment for the casual visitor and a resource for serious research.

To this end, over the last 30 years of his life, he travelled extensively, financed archaeological expeditions in the Sudan and Palestine, and employed a network of purchasing agents to amass a remarkably diverse and eclectic collection of artefacts, books, manuscripts and sundry objects numbering over 1.5 million items all relating broadly to medicine and health from every era and from across the globe. Wellcome also acquired thousands of books relating to the history of medicine. Most of this vast collection remained crated and uncatalogued at the time of his death in 1936.

Formal recognition of Wellcome's accomplishments as a philanthropist and patron of scientific research came relatively late in his life. Having become a British citizen in 1910, he was knighted in 1932 by King George V. That same year, he was elected as an honorary Fellow of the Royal College of Surgeons, a rare distinction for someone not holding a medical degree.

In 1924, the Burroughs Wellcome pharmaceutical company was renamed The Wellcome Foundation Ltd. In 1932, with no heir to assume the business, Wellcome made his famous will which established a Board of Trustees as shareholders of the company to provide for the continuation of the pharmaceutical business, the laboratories and the collections, and to dispose of residual income for medical research. Under the will, pharmaceutical company dividends were to be used for '... the advancement of research work bearing upon medicine, surgery, chemistry, physiology, bacteriology, therapeutics, materia medica, pharmacy and allied subjects'.[2]

The will also called for the establishment or endowment of research museums and libraries and the collection of information relating to the history of medicine. One of Wellcome's biographers observes that Wellcome's will was 'the first example in Britain of a bequest by which the profits from a great trading company are permanently dedicated to the advancement of knowledge for the benefit of mankind'.[3]

Wellcome died in 1936. In an obituary written by Henry Dale, one of Wellcome's closest colleagues in later years, Dale described Wellcome as 'curiously lonely'. 'It may be doubted whether anyone knew him with sufficient intimacy to do more than speculate as to his real feelings and motives,' Dale added.

The Trust's formative years
Legally complex and financially challenged
The legacy Henry Wellcome left to his Trustees was legally complex and financially challenging. The Trust might not have survived without the 'skill, resolution and dedication' of the Trustees and staff.[4] During the first decade of the Trust, Chairman Sir Henry Dale questioned 'whether our experience as Trustees will eventually be more suitable for record as a novel or a play'.[5]

The Wellcome Foundation Ltd was not a charitable foundation, but rather a commercial business holding the pharmaceutical company, laboratories and collections. The newly created Trust was the real charitable foundation. The Trustees were charged with distributing income solely from dividends from Wellcome shares. This curious relationship between the Trust and the businesses would continue until the Trust finally divested itself of the pharmaceutical company shares in the 1980s and 1990s.

The Trustees, as sole shareholders, had the responsibility of appointing the Directors of the Foundation and dealing with the question of ownership of the collection and library, which were assets of the business. Not until 1960 did the Trust acquire the collections from the company.

More serious problems for the Trust were created by high and unanticipated death duties owing to the British government. In addition, the will itself contained many ambiguities requiring recourse to the courts for amendment and clarification. At the same time, the pharmaceutical company had begun to lose its competitive edge. As a result, the Trustees had few dividends to use to support medical research and medical history. After paying death duties and other required bequests and expenditures, the Trust was only able to distribute a total of £1 million during its first 20 years.

Lacking funds to create the museum envisioned by Wellcome, the Trustees also struggled for years to deal with Wellcome's huge collection of artefacts, ultimately selling or giving most of it away. In the late 1970s and early 1980s, the medical core of the collection was presented to the British Science Museum in London on permanent loan.

Wellcome's biographer, Robert James, notes the critical role played by Henry Dale in the survival of the Wellcome Trust:

'Wellcome's ambitions would never have been fulfilled, and perhaps the company itself might well not have survived, had it not been for Henry Dale.

> Although others played important roles, it was above all his persistence,
> wisdom and shrewdness that gradually made some sense out of the Trustees'
> complex inheritance, and turned Wellcome's dreams into reality.'[6]

The Trust was dependent on the profitability of the pharmaceutical company.
By late 1940, the impact of World War Two, production mistakes and failure to
reinvest profits in research for new products left the company in a perilous
state. The Trustees, under Dale and his successors, decided to allow the
company to retain a majority of profits for investment in research for new
products.

A turnaround in fortune
Significant contributions were made by the American pharmaceutical
subsidiary, which recruited outstanding research talent, including two
future Nobel prizewinners – George Hitching and Trudy Elion. According to
Wellcome Trust Director Peter Williams, the two 'produced dramatic new
lines of drugs that transformed the world-wide reputation and profits of the
company, and for the first time enabled the Trustees to consider seriously
how to distribute money as set out in the will'.[7]

Several other business executives and researchers, in both the
UK and the US, contributed to the revival of the pharmaceutical company.
Between 1961 and 1970, the Trust was able to award research grants totalling
nearly £5.8 million. Returning to the original philosophy of Henry Wellcome
of investing significant sums in research for new products and aggressive
marketing, the company continued to grow. In 1981, the company introduced
Zovirax (acyclovir) – an effective treatment for herpes – its first billion-dollar
drug.

Until 1986, the pharmaceutical company had been wholly owned
by the Trust. In that year, the Trustees, under Chairman Sir David Steel,
concluded that the Trust should diversify its asset portfolio. Obtaining court
permission, the Trust sold 21 per cent of its shares. Over the next six years,
the new holding company, Wellcome plc, prospered. The Trust's funding of
medical research grew from £20 million in 1985 to £100 million in 1992.

That same year, the Trustees decided on further diversification,
selling additional shares and raising over £2.3 billion. This sale,
masterminded by Sir Roger Gibbs, enabled the Trust to dramatically
increase its funding of medical research to over £200 million in 1994. These
funds provided long-term support, short-term grants and training awards.
One British medical professor commented, 'The Wellcome Trust has saved
medical research in Britain.'[8]

In 1993, the Wellcome Trust agreed to make a $400 million gift, paid over five years, to the Burroughs Welcome Fund, a US charity established by 1955 by Henry Dale and William Creasy, Chair of the US subsidiary, in honour of Henry Wellcome's US roots. The Burroughs Welcome Fund supports medical research and other scientific and educational activities.

The final step in the separation of the Wellcome Trust from Henry Wellcome's pharmaceutical company came in 1995 when long-time competitor Glaxo purchased Wellcome plc, in a transaction that substantially enhanced the Trust's assets. By 1995 the Trust could, as stated in its 2005–10 Strategic Plan, unquestionably assert that its 'independence and size' enables it to act 'responsively and flexibly', 'to take a long-term view and to take funding risks, acting for the public good'.

A legacy of significant accomplishments

Since its creation in 1936 to the end of 2007, the Wellcome Trust has provided funding of approximately £7.3 billion for medical research, education and related activities. A few of the Trust's many major achievements are mentioned below.

Human Genome Project

As a member of the Human Genome Project, a worldwide partnership of researchers, the Wellcome Trust Sanger Institute sequenced almost one-third of the human genome, the largest single contribution to the project. Completed in 2003, the results greatly enhance the ability of medical science to study diseases afflicting humans and animals. Sir John Sulston, Founding Director of the Sanger Institute, led the UK contribution to the project and was instrumental in ensuring that the sequencing data were made freely available for the benefit of all.

Since completion of the Genome Project, the focus of the Sanger Institute's work has been on the use of genome sequence data and the development of high throughput methods to study the role of genes in health and disease. During its short history, researchers at the Wellcome Trust Sanger Institute have produced more than 800 scientific papers.

World-class malaria treatments

One of Sir Henry Wellcome's early and continuing research interests was tropical diseases and medicines. It is fitting that one of the Wellcome Trust's major achievements is in the field of treatments for malaria, a disease that kills more than 2.5 million people worldwide, most of them children under five. Led by Professor Nick White, Wellcome Trust-funded researchers in

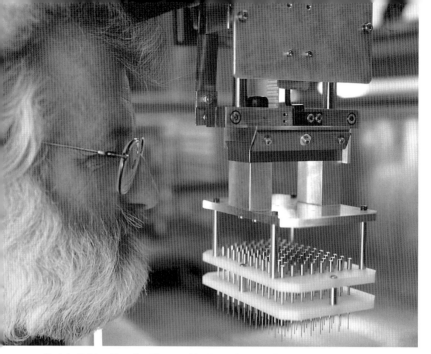

Dr John Sulston, Founding Director of the Sanger Institute, led
the UK contribution to the human genome project.
Wellcome Library, London

South-east Asia in the 1990s developed and tested an anti-malarial drug,
artemisinin, based on a Chinese herb, and have used it with enormous
success to treat malaria in Vietnam and Thailand.

In Vietnam, for example, the drug has reduced the mortality rate
from 2,500 to 100 per year. Artemisinin is now used routinely in combination
with other drugs to delay drug-resistant strains and artemisinin
combination therapy is recommended by the World Health Organization as
the best treatment for malaria.

Steroids for premature babies
With funding from the Wellcome Trust, researcher Graham Liggins
discovered that steroids given to pregnant sheep caused the lungs of
the foetus to develop faster. He later showed that steroids have a similar
effect on premature human infants. Administering steroids to women
experiencing early labour can result in premature infants being able to
breathe independently. This research has led to dramatically improved
survival rates and the technique is now standard obstetric practice.

Cognitive behaviour therapy for eating disorders
Research on cognitive behaviour therapy – which aims to help people understand and alter problematic thinking and behaviour patterns – funded by the Wellcome Trust led directly to a treatment for bulimia nervosa, a common and life-threatening eating disorder. Professor Chris Fairburn, a Wellcome Principal Research Scientist, and his colleagues have studied the origins of bulimia nervosa and developed a highly effective cognitive therapy recommended for use by the UK's National Health Service.

Science Learning Centres
The National Science Learning Centre in York, funded by the Wellcome Trust, together with nine regional centres funded by the UK Department for Education and Skills, provide teachers and technicians the opportunity to learn about new methods of teaching science and the latest scientific developments and to share experiences with colleagues. All centres offer laboratories, advanced computer equipment and innovative courses on cutting edge research and broader issues of science and society.

Part of the Wellcome Trust's educational programme, the centres seek to promote science education that equips people to live in the 21st century and to provide a stream of students with the skills and motivation for careers in science.

UK Biobank
In partnership with the UK Department of Health, the Medical Research Council and the Scottish Executive, the Wellcome Trust is funding the UK Biobank. The Biobank is a large, long-term study in the UK designed to investigate the contributions of genetic predisposition and environment – including nutrition, lifestyle, medications and so on – to the development of disease.

The study will follow approximately 500,000 volunteers aged 40–69 for 25 years. Once the data collection has been under way for several years, researchers can apply to use the database to study, for example, how genes, lifestyle and medications contribute and interact in the development of particular diseases. The aim of this research initiative is to improve the prevention, diagnosis and treatment of a wide range of serious and life-threatening diseases, including cancer, heart disease, diabetes, arthritis and forms of dementia.

Contributions to the Science Museum

The Science Museum in London has been a significant beneficiary of the Wellcome Trust. In 1976, the Trust made a permanent loan of much of Henry Wellcome's huge collection of the history of medicine. In the late 1990s, the Trust funded a new building called the Wellcome Wing at the Science Museum. Opened in 2000 by Her Majesty Queen Elizabeth II, the Wellcome Wing houses exhibitions of present and future science and technology.

Wellcome Collection – a world first

Housed in the newly renovated building that once served as Henry Wellcome's corporate headquarters, Wellcome Collection is a remarkable venue and, according to Dr Mark Walport, Director of the Wellcome Trust since 2003, 'a powerful means for engaging with the public'. Opened in June 2007, Wellcome Collection is a world first.

It combines three contemporary galleries, the famous Wellcome Library, a public events forum, café, bookshop, conference centre and members' club. Its aim is to provide visitors 'with radical insight into the human condition'. During its first six months, Wellcome Collection had more than 100,000 visitors, Walport reports.

The collection contains more than 1,300 exhibits over three galleries combining art, science and history, from the bizarre to the beautiful, the ancient to the futurist. The exhibits include works by artists such as Leonardo da Vinci, Marc Quinn, Antony Gormley and Andy Warhol. The objects range from Aztec sacrificial knives, used guillotine blades, 19th century sex aids, amputation saws and a lock of King George III's hair containing arsenic traces (an 18th century cure for madness) to Admiral Lord Nelson's razor.

One gallery hosts temporary exhibitions featuring newly commissioned works and shows on topics of medical, cultural and ethical significance. A second gallery contains Medicine Man, an exhibition of more than 500 strange and wonderful artefacts from Henry Wellcome's original collection. In the third gallery, Medicine Now, medical topics – such as Genomes, The Body, Malaria, Obesity and The Experience of Medicine – are explored through the eyes of scientists, artists and popular culture in a contemporary, interactive environment. Public events expand on exhibition themes.

The Wellcome Library, now part of Wellcome Collection, contains more than 750,000 books, 70,000 rare books (published before 1850), some 250,000 paintings, prints and photographs, and a film and audio collection of 2,500 titles. The public areas of the library cover two floors and include a

Aims of the Wellcome Trust's 2005–2010 Strategic Plan
- Advancing knowledge: to support research to increase understanding of health and disease, and its societal context.
- Using knowledge: to support the development and use of knowledge to create health benefit.
- Engaging society: to engage with society to foster an informed climate within which biomedical research can flourish.
- Developing people: to foster a research community and individual researchers who can contribute to the advancement and use of knowledge.
- Facilitating research: to promote the best conditions for research and the use of knowledge.
- Developing our organization: to use our resources efficiently and effectively.

stately two-level reading room, originally built as a Hall of Statuary by Henry Wellcome in 1932. A touch-screen installation, Uncover, allows visitors to view some of the Library's most prized and interesting works.

The online resource, Wellcome Images, a selection of 200,000 images from the library's collection depicting medical and social history, healthcare and biomedical science, can be downloaded for non-commercial use.

The Wellcome Trust – today and tomorrow
In 2003, Dr Mark Walport, a specialist in immunology and the genetics of rheumatic diseases, became Director of the Wellcome Trust, after having served on the Board of Governors for a number of years. Under his direction, the Trust developed its current *Strategic Plan 2005–2010: Making a Difference*. The Plan identifies six aims of the organization.

Walport describes the new plan as 'evolutionary, not revolutionary', but notes that in the past the Trust's funding had been 'process-driven, rather than science-led'. Under the new plan, 'science itself [is] at the heart of everything we do', Walport explains. 'Science streams will take pre-eminence, with the mechanisms of funding providing the tools by which the Trust's mission can be achieved.'

Under the Strategic Plan, the Wellcome Trust's funding activities are structured around six thematic funding streams defined broadly to encompass essentially all fields of biomedical research. These include: Immunology and Infectious Diseases, Population and Public Health,

Neuroscience and Mental Health, Physiological Sciences, Molecules, Genes and Cells, and Medical Humanities.

A Strategic Committee of experts oversees each of the streams and advises on the best ways to develop research and training in that particular field. Each stream also has one or more Funding Committees responsible for awarding grants. In addition, there are two Strategic Committees to advise on the cross-cutting activities of Technology Transfer and Public Engagement.

Priorities under the Strategic Plan include ensuring that most of the Trust's funding is used to support 'basic, curiosity-driven, investigator-led research and career initiatives', using about 10 per cent of the annual spend to respond to new and unanticipated opportunities, increasing support for clinical research, increasing support for the use of knowledge flowing from biomedical research for health benefit, and increasing international funding to address disease in developing countries.

Among other initiatives, the Wellcome Trust is actively advancing the use of knowledge in two significant ways. First, through its Technology Transfer funding, it facilitates the development of early-stage health technologies to the point where the market can further develop them. Second, the Trust has been in the forefront of the open access movement. Open access seeks to overcome the problem that many scientific research papers are not easily and freely available to other researchers and the public.

To address this problem, the Wellcome Trust in 2006 modified its grant conditions to require that all papers funded in whole or part by the Trust must be made freely accessible on online websites within six months of publication. The Trust includes in its research grants funding to cover the costs of page proofing and peer-review. Working with other UK research funders, the Wellcome Trust is also supporting the establishment of a UK website to provide a permanent, freely accessible online archive of full-text, peer-reviewed research publications.

According to Walport, two significant challenges facing the Trust are 'making the best grants' and ensuring the long-term financial stability and growth of the Trust's assets so that the Trust's funding can continue. To address the first challenge, the Trust looks for partnership opportunities with governments, research and academic institutions, and other funding institutions.

Echoing Henry Wellcome's philosophy when hiring researchers for his laboratories in the early decades of the 20th century, making effective grants also demands 'choosing the brightest people'. Walport continues:

'Through supporting the best people with the best ideas and providing flexible funding, we hope to support the generation of new knowledge to underpin future discoveries and their subsequent application.'

To ensure the stability and growth of its assets, the Trust has a highly diversified investment portfolio managed by more than 300 fund managers, which includes approximately £6 billion in alternative investments such as private equity buyout funds, private equity venture funds and hedge funds. The Trust recently became the first charity in the UK to sell a public bond, using its triple A credit ratings to raise approximately £550 million at an attractively low rate, thus increasing the Trust's funding power and flexibility.

As a young man, Henry Wellcome aspired to wealth for the service of mankind. Through his original vision – aided mightily by the brilliance, perseverance and dedication of subsequent generations of Trustees and staff – those aspirations are being fulfilled. The staggering diversity of the Trust's activities – science, technology transfer, history, ethics, public engagement and art – is, according to Walport, 'a tremendous strength'.

'Looking at medical research in the context of society gives one a much greater understanding of the opportunities and implications. And it makes the Trust an absolutely fascinating place to work,' Walport concludes.

[1] R H James, *Henry Wellcome*, Hodder and Stoughton, 1994, p59.

[2] Helen Turner, *Henry Wellcome: The man, his collection and his legacy*, The Wellcome Trust, 1980, p28.

[3] Ibid, p28.

[4] James, op cit, p382.

[5] A R Hall and B A Bembridge, *Physic and philanthropy: a history of the Wellcome Trust 1936–1986*, Cambridge University Press, 1986, Foreword.

[6] James, op cit, p376.

[7] James, op cit, p378.

[8] James, op cit, p383.

Essays
The diverse roles played by European foundations

FILIZ BIKMEN

14 The rich history of philanthropy in Turkey
A paradox of tradition and modernity

There is a common saying about the extent to which foundations (*vakif*, in Turkish) in the Ottoman Era affected people's lives – it was possible for a person to be born in a *vakif* hospital, study in a *vakif* school, work in a *vakif* institution, and be buried in a *vakif* graveyard. Given that more 35,000 foundations were functioning during this period, it is quite likely the saying held true for many.

The history of Ottoman foundations is full of richness in both assets and activities and considered a very important part of Turkish (not just Islamic) culture and tradition. Although foundations have continued to play some role in society, they are still more commonly known through their rich legacy.

Foundations reached their peak in the 18th century, ranging from Anatolia to the present-day Balkans and Thrace, and reaching into Syria and Egypt. With significant assets in the form of land and, later, cash, foundations constructed caravansaries, schools, hospitals and roads, serving many of the same functions of basic service provision performed by today's modern welfare state. Yet the role of foundations was significantly curtailed, starting in the late Ottoman period, and this continued throughout the beginning of the new Turkish Republic – from the mid-to-late 19th century to the early 20th century.

The foundation sector was weakened greatly by both external forces and internal politics, yet the philanthropic impulse of Turkish people remained. While fewer incentives and strict state controls made foundations less appealing for many, this did not prevent a small but powerful segment of society from continuing this tradition, and allocating private wealth for public good – and today, reaching beyond that to supporting positive social change. Currently there are more than 3,000 privately established foundations in Turkey.

The view of Turkey as a 'paradox of tradition and modernity' or a 'bridge between east and west' can also be applied to the foundation sector. Today, many foundations – characterized as 'traditional' – in Turkey bear a striking resemblance to their ancestors of the Ottoman period. Their most common characteristic is the practice of building institutions such as schools, hospitals and museums. There is also a 'modern' generation of foundations that have gone beyond building institutions to undertaking policy analysis, advocacy and innovative programmes aimed at social change, taking an active role in creating a democratic and civil society. In this sense, foundations are beginning to search within and across borders for new ways to serve – perhaps even redefine – the public good, in a society undergoing a remarkable political, economic, social and cultural transformation.

A great deal of this momentum for change is owed to the EU accession process, yet the effects of changes in the greater global context are also felt within Turkey's borders. Some call this momentum a 'silent revolution',[1] indeed its effects may not be seen or heard immediately. Yet these changes are slowly carving out a more prominent role for modern foundations, parallel to Turkey's political and economic development.

As the title of this book suggests, philanthropy in Europe has a rich past and a promising future. And as one of the oldest institutional forms of philanthropic endowments, the Ottoman *vakif* is the basis of Turkey's very rich past; while Turkish foundations are a testament to both its present and its future. This chapter attempts to describe the foundation sector in Turkey in just this way, with highlights from its rich past, assessments of its present, and a number of opportunities for realizing its promising future – many of which may be pursued in cooperation with European foundations.

A rich past

What is commonly known in the West as a 'foundation' is in its most basic form very similar to the institution known as *waqf* in Arabic (or *vakif*, in Turkish[2]). At their very core, *vakifs* and foundations share the following main characteristics:

   – There is an endowment of private wealth for a specified activity of public benefit.

  – Objectives, purpose and detailed directives on how revenue from
    the endowment is to be managed and allocated are stated in a
    founding document.

Philanthropic endowments have a history considerably older than Islam,
and are likely to have been influenced by earlier civilizations including
ancient Mesopotamia, Greece, Rome and pre-Islamic Arabs. It is still
unresolved to what extent Islamic *waqfs* were influenced by these
traditions; however, it is likely that Muslims adopted this practice from
earlier civilizations. Some scholars suggest that medieval Europe may
have learned of these institutions through the *vakif* system. Some go as
far as to suggest that it was not Roman or Germanic law but Islamic *waqfs*
that greatly influenced the development of the trust law of England and
throughout the Christian Mediterranean.[3]

　　　Despite the lack of agreement on the various factors that may have
influenced its emergence, the institution of *vakif* become known after
the death of the Prophet Mohammed and its legal structure was firmly
established during the second half of the second century.[4] According to the
Foundations Directorate of Turkey,[5] the earliest documentation of a *vakif* in
Anatolia dates back to 1048. Yet this was probably just one of many, as there
were an estimated 2,773 foundations active in year 986.[6]

The role of *vakifs* in Ottoman society

Vakifs are often referred to in an Islamic context, leading many to think
that they are actually part of the religious text and practice. They were
established within the framework of Islamic law, which was in practice
during the period when *vakifs* emerged. However, what fascinates scholars
about the emergence of the *vakif* as an institutional form is that it is not
referred to specifically in the Koran, but it was – and continues to be –
widely used as a vehicle through which pious Muslims could realize, in
perpetuity, their religious obligations. Such obligations include charitable
deeds, which are described in great detail in the Holy Book.[7] While many
foundations during this period did adopt religious observation as a central
objective, their role was much broader in serving public benefit. And, as
described in this chapter, this would change significantly in the era of the
modern Turkish Republic where foundations now play a very limited role in
promoting religious practice.

　　　Although foundations were active for many centuries, it was during
the Ottoman Era[8] that these institutions reached their peak in terms of
numbers, acquisition of assets, services to the public and institutional

development. It was, in fact, a vibrant sector. In the absence of government or centralized regulation – which came at a later point – common procedures and frameworks were developed that practitioners today would consider self-regulatory.

One of the most important reasons for this exponential growth was the major role foundations played in delivering basic services to society. The responsibility of the Ottoman state to its people was solely to provide justice, safety, freedom of religion and the possibility of individual self-development. As such, there was no budget or system for the provision of all other basic services. In the absence of this, foundations became the sole providers of basic services, from municipal services (the water system in Istanbul was entirely developed by foundations) to education, health, culture and religion.[9]

Foundations also developed sophisticated tools for economic generation, offering services similar to microfinance and modern banks, at times providing major injections of capital into the economy. Funds endowed were lent to borrowers without the borrowing rate charge and gains with interest were put back into the foundation, with revenues spent on social and pious purposes.[10]

The rise and fall of the *vakif*

There are many gaps in figures and statistics, mainly due to the lack of centralized registries for many centuries. Yet scholars estimate more than 35,000 foundations were established and operational throughout the Ottoman Era. During the 16th century, there were approximately 2,860 foundations in Istanbul alone and 485 in Aleppo. Foundations were established not only by elite segments of society, but also by middle-income individuals and families. Even more fascinating is that women established almost 40 per cent of these foundations.[11] Although no statistics are available, this number is likely far smaller today.

Given the vast scope and sophistication of foundation services, their financial assets constituted a significant portion of the Ottoman State budget. Foundations had two major forms of 'corpus' or endowed assets: cash (movable) or property (immovable). By the 16th century, most foundations were cash foundations,[12] giving them greater liquidity. It is estimated that foundation assets comprised approximately 12 per cent of the state budget in the 16th century, slightly higher at 18 per cent in the 17th century, and peaking at 27 per cent in the 18th century.[13]

Until the early part of the 19th century, foundations enjoyed a relatively *laissez-faire* relationship with the state and were granted full autonomy. However, this was to change dramatically in the 19th century due to internal politics and economic challenges, as well as external pressures from guarantors in Europe on the Ottoman state following the Crimean War, which mandated the weakening of the *vakif* system. As a result, the revenue base of foundations was cut almost in half[14] and a majority of their assets were centralized through many state operations.

Yet their wealth was of such great proportions that, regardless of these conditions, foundation revenues continued to be a vital source for funding of basic public services in the first ten years of the establishment of the Republic in 1923.[15]

The turn of the 20th century brought a new paradigm of state administration, and with it a school of thought influenced greatly by the French, which at one point discouraged the emergence of intermediary actors such as foundations serving public needs and services to citizens. The ethos of the Turkish Republic reflected this position,[16] and it was not until after the new Civil Code of 1926 that a new legal framework for foundations was created.

A portrait of the present

Even today, the revenues and assets of Ottoman foundations are of massive proportions and continue to play a significant role in modern Turkish society. There are currently more than 65,000 movable and immovable assets of Ottoman foundations (commonly referred to as *eski vakiflar* or simply 'old foundations'), which are managed directly by the Foundations Directorate, the central regulatory authority.

Most are property and land; the buildings, including mosques, *medreses* (Islamic theological elementary schools), libraries, bridges and schools, are considered historical artefacts. The Foundations Directorate ensures they are preserved according to cultural heritage regulations and, if possible, used as public spaces and/or museums. Their revenues continue to provide charitable support to the poor and needy in the form of food, assistance and scholarships. Valuable properties are now being rented and sold for real estate development projects, and revenues being re-invested in foundation endowments to serve their original charitable purposes. In this way, 'old' foundations are revalued within the system of Turkey's vibrant market economy.

The 4,449 foundations established since the new Civil Code in 1926 are referred to as 'Civil Code' or 'new' foundations; these are also regulated by the Foundations Directorate. Though governed by a new set of laws, the *vakif* has retained its main institutional characteristics as inherited from the Ottoman period – an endowment, a specific purpose and a founding document outlining management details. Yet, as times have changed, so has the way in which foundations realize their charitable purposes.

A majority of new foundations – almost 1,900 of the 4,449 – were established between 1967 and 1985, with a major growth surge between 1995 and 1997, with a peak of 439 in 1996. This growth surge was primarily a result of the Habitat II Conference organized in Istanbul, which gave a huge boost to the development of civil society. There is still a lack of centralized data collected and made available to the public.[17] However, what we do know about new foundations – excluding the 1,200 government-established foundations – is based on a recent study commissioned by TUSEV.[18]

Most of the data reveals that, as in most countries, the majority of the assets in the sector are in the hands of a few foundations. A rough estimate suggests that only the top five foundations have a collective sum of several billion euros. However, a majority tend to rely more on donations, which account for 57 per cent of income. This also suggests that a greater number of foundations are established with smaller assets and thus have little endowment income to rely on.

Tradition and modernity

Looking more closely at their purposes and programmes, private foundations can be categorized as either traditional or modern. Traditional foundations resemble Ottoman foundations in many ways; they have significant assets, most of which are endowed by wealthy industrialists of the modern Turkish Republic era. They do not operate programmes, nor do they make grants per se. They provide scholarships and build dormitories, schools, hospitals, teachers' centres and other key institutions, which are then transferred by protocol to respective state ministries and run under their auspices. The first of these foundations emerged in the 1960s. The founder of the Vehbi Koç Foundation, Vehbi Koç, is considered to be one of the main architects of the post-Ottoman foundation sector in Turkey.

Traditional foundations have played a prominent role in the development of sophisticated higher education institutions, having funded and established approximately one-third of the country's universities. The first was Bilkent, founded in 1984 by Ihsan Dogramaci Foundation, and many thereafter, including the Koç University (Vehbi Koç Foundation) and the Sabancı University (Sabancı Foundation). Many of Turkey's best hospitals and prestigious museums are also foundation investments.

New roles for traditional foundations

Ottoman foundations were very likely important role models for some of these traditional foundations, given their role in institution building. However, this practice also bears a great resemblance to the foundation practices in much of Europe, and the early days of the major US foundations, both of which were quite important influences on the development of foundations in Republican era Turkey. These foundations continue to allocate the bulk of their funds to institutions; however, they are also leaning towards new initiatives. For example, the Education Reform Initiative (ERI)[19] – a watchdog and think-tank for education reform in Turkey and part of the Istanbul Policy Centre at the Sabancı University – has been able to attract support from traditional foundations such as the Koç Foundation. ERI's objective is to reach foundations supporting education mainly by building schools and getting the foundations more involved in addressing what happens inside the schools they help to build.

Some foundations are taking their work a step further. For example, the Aydin Doğan Foundation has engaged in a partnership with the UN Development Programme to address pressing concerns of sustainable development and to develop an organic farming system in the Black Sea region. The Sabancı Foundation is the first to undertake a substantial effort to develop a new programme strategy beyond institution building. This effort included an internal and external assessment, exploring new programmes and tools (grants, fellowships, research) and the development of the foundation's capacity (see Sabancı profile, p157). Yet for the most part, the traditional model is still a very popular one, even among new philanthropists such as Hüsnü Özyeğin,[20] who is committed to building more than 100 dormitories for schools across Anatolia in the next five years.

Institution building and scholarship provision remain an important contribution of many foundations today. Indeed, the need for this form of support remains significant, although it is officially a function of government. At the same time, changes in the broader context, primarily democratization reforms and a more legally enabling environment, economic growth and state policies that favour greater partnership in social policy and service provision, have created the space and opportunity for the modern foundation to emerge. They share the same legal framework as traditional foundations, but modern foundations have some distinct characteristics in terms of founders, objectives and funds. For example, modern foundations tend to be established by a group of individuals – most of them social visionaries from a broad range of sectors and backgrounds.

Their objectives are not the buildings and 'hardware' of institutions, but the programmes or 'software' of social change.

The emergence of the modern foundation

The number of modern foundations increased dramatically in the 1990s. This was due primarily to the restrictive association law enacted in 1980, which greatly limited freedom of association. As such, foundations became a more attractive and feasible structure for collective efforts for social services and change.

Modern foundations tend to focus on issues such as poverty, economic development, human rights and democracy. Their programmes combine service delivery with a research and policy change agenda. Because a modern foundation operates extensive programmes, they tend to have professional staff with expertise, and their national and international linkages are more extensive. They use a broader array of tools, including publications, training and policy analysis, and spend considerable amounts of time convening with other organizations, policy-makers and beneficiaries. In the absence of large endowments, modern foundations rely mainly on funds raised from donors. The bulk of their funding comes primarily from funding institutions such as the EU and international foundations, as well as some individuals committed to their particular mission.

Today, these foundations – which resemble the 'operating yet fundraising' foundations or large-scale NGOs in Europe and the US – take on a critical role both in service delivery and in setting and shaping the policy agenda. The Mother Child Education Foundation (ACEV) incubated early childhood education and maternal literacy programmes, which are now being incorporated in government programmes. The leading environmental organization, TEMA, is the driver of policies and government practices to ensure greater environmental sustainability. The leading think-tank TESEV feeds the policy-making process with critical analysis and recommendations regarding issues such as migration, poverty and governance. The TOG (Community Volunteers Foundation) mobilizes thousands of young people in universities to take a more active part in community development.

TUSEV (Third Sector Foundation of Turkey) was established in 1993 as part of this wave of new foundations. Formed as an advocacy platform for foundations, it was established with the foresight that the foundation sector needed an organization that would conduct research, promote networking, and amplify the voice of the foundation sector. The European Foundation Centre (EFC) was an important model for TUSEV, which was EFC's first

Turkish member. Celebrating its fifteenth year in 2008, TUSEV brings together traditional and 'modern' foundations in one network. Programmes are focused on promoting the sector, working for policy changes, promoting international partnerships, and introducing new concepts and practices to the foundation sector in Turkey, such as grantmaking and community foundations.

Foundations and the EU accession process

The recent surge of activities among the modern foundations is closely linked with developments in the broader context. The main agenda for social change is about bridging economic, ethnic and religious divides within Turkey and between Turkey and EU nation states. Reforms of the fundamental frameworks of the state establishment – rule of law, individual freedoms and rights, gender equity and improvement of basic services – are all essential for Turkey's future prosperity. Although there is significant internal political will for reforms in pursuit of a 'better Turkey', it is well accepted that the EU process is the strong wind at their backs. And for all involved, there is no doubt that this process – perhaps better defined as a journey – will be quite complex and lengthy.

One of the most vital aspects of this journey of development and democratization is the inclusion of a civil society. This is not, by any means, unique to Turkey. In almost every corner of the globe, the presence of a civil society is at the forefront of development agendas. In writing about comparative perspectives of foundations in Europe, author and researcher Helmut Anheier[21] claims that the political climate in the EU has led to a reduced role for the government and a greater space and responsibility for private actors. It seems there has been a similar effect in Turkey.

This may explain why the EU is spending more than ever – some €21.5 million – in funding the Civil Society Dialogue Programme in Turkey. This includes addressing areas such as youth, towns and municipalities, strengthening professional organizations, universities, and culture, as well as providing funds for NGOs to participate in events in the EU, and developing joint projects and addressing critical social issues of disadvantaged populations.[22] This is also a testament to the goals put forth by the EU in creating more space for the voluntary sector and foundations.[23]

Comparatively speaking, €21.5 million pales in comparison to the hundreds of millions of euros traditional Turkish foundations spend in building and operating state-of-the-art educational, health and cultural institutions in Turkey. Yet the strict focus on software means EU funds are helping to both spark and support programmes that are critical to development beyond foundation funds, which have been limited mainly to funding the 'hardware' of physical institution development. Yet this is precisely where the future opportunities lie for traditional foundations, and an area that they can support with funds, convening power and leverage.

Foundations today – insurmountable opportunities

A wise man once said: 'We are confronted with insurmountable opportunities.'[24] The challenges of Turkey's present are also full of opportunities that can sometimes seem difficult to transform into tangible actions. What are these opportunities and what are some specific ways foundations can take advantage of them? Is there a role for European foundations in the process?

One important opportunity for foundations is the promise of a more enabling legal framework and greater political support from the government. Just as the new associations law of 2004 helped bring a new level of dynamism to the NGO sector, the new foundations law of 2008 (pending Parliamentary approval) is likely to have similar effects on the foundation sector. In addition, changes in attitudes of policy-makers and the bureaucracy will also help shed a new light on the added value of foundations rather than them being perceived as a threat.

A more enabling environment has also created more opportunities in the sector. With greater numbers of NGO actors working to address critical challenges facing Turkey, from both a service delivery and a policy change perspective, there are more actors and potential partners for foundations to work with. Adding new approaches such as grantmaking, partnerships and fellowships will allow foundations to carve out a new role in helping the third sector be a stronger player for reform and development. In adopting new ways of working, foundations will also be forced to think more strategically about designing initiatives and using these tools and their leverage to push change forward.

Although the 'partnership mantra' has been a frequent subject of debate in the global foundation sector, the topic is still rather new to Turkish foundations – and another significant opportunity to tap into, especially vis-à-vis European foundations. Existing networks such as TUSEV and the EFC offer fertile ground for coming together to discuss common interests and develop relationships. In this light, the EFC Annual General Assembly in Istanbul (May 2008), hosted by TUSEV, is taking place at the most opportune moment. Organized under the theme of Fostering Creativity, this conference will be a real tipping point for further developments in Turkish-European foundation cooperation.

This is not to say that there is no history of cooperation to date – recent projects related to migration, research on Turks in Belgium, and mother-child education supported by the King Baudouin Foundation, and initiatives of Körber Stiftung and Bosch Stiftung related to Turkish-German relations are some examples of this budding potential.

In the cultural arena, the European Cultural Foundation has been increasingly active in supporting media and culture projects with a particular focus on Turkey. The Gulbenkian collection at the Sabancı Museum, the Aydın Doğan Foundation political cartoon exhibition in Brussels, and Istanbul's election as the 2010 European Capital of Culture are also important examples of how cultural exchange has been an important starting point for Turkish-European foundation cooperation.

Given the due course of EU-Turkey relations and the important role of foundations in fostering 'parallel diplomacy', such partnerships are likely to increase. Organizations such as NEF (Network of European Foundations for Innovative Cooperation) will be even more valuable in their role of connecting foundations on specific projects on issues such as migration, youth and education – all subjects which are of mutual interest to both Turkish and European foundations. Turkish foundations can be valuable counterparts in design and implementation of programmes both in Turkey and with Turkish communities in Europe – quite significant with an estimated 3 million Turks living in Germany alone. European foundations have much to offer Turkish foundations in terms of sharing the know-how of strategic programme management and delivery.

A promising future

Turkey's rich legacy of foundations tells a fascinating story – albeit still lacking many details as a result of limited research of our past and present. While we must certainly invest more in learning about where we have come from and where we are, we must not miss the opportunity that the current political, economic and social conjuncture in Turkey offers: an opportunity to take a more proactive role in discussing the future role of foundations.

There are many issues to discuss in this light, as this chapter attempts to touch briefly upon – internal management, strategy, programmes, tools and relationships with other foundations and stakeholders – to name a few. Yet a particularly important opportunity is to nurture relationships with European foundations, which are at minimum neighbours in the region, and possibly in the future partners in an enlarged EU.

[1] *Turkey in Europe: More than a Promise?* Report of the Independent Commission on Turkey, September 2004 www.independent commissiononturkey.org

[2] The author uses '*vakif*' and 'foundation' interchangeably.

[3] Monica Gaudiosi, 'The influence of the Islamic law of Waqf on the Development of the Trust in England: The Case of Merton College', *University of Pennsylvania Law Review*, Vol 136, No 4, 1988, pp231–61.

[4] Fuat Köprüllü, *Vakif Müessesesinin Hukuki Mahiyeti ve Tarihi Tekamülü*, Vakiflar Dergisi, sayi II, 1942.

[5] www.vakiflar.gov.tr

[6] Tahsin Özcan, *Osmanli Devleti'nde Eğitimin Finansmani*, Osmanli Araştirma Vakfii www.osmanli.org.tr

[7] Murat Çizakça, *A History of Philanthropic Foundations: The Islamic world from the seventh century to the present*, Bosphorus University Press, 2000.

[8] Ottoman foundations are discussed inclusive of the Selcuks, Beyliks and Ottoman periods.

[9] Nazif Öztürk, *Sosyal Siyaset Açisindan Osmanli Dönemi Vakiflari* www.sosyalsiyatset.com

[10] Çizakça, op cit.

[11] Ibid.

[12] Ibid.

[13] Öztürk, op cit.

[14] Çizakça, op cit.

[15] Davut Aydin, *Foundations in the Republican Era*, in *Philanthropy in Turkey: Citizens, foundations and the pursuit of social justice*, TUSEV Publications, 2006.

[16] Çizakça, op cit.

[17] Foundations' financial records are not considered public information and are not required to be published as such.

[18] Filiz Bikmen, *The Landscape of Philanthropy and Civil Society in Turkey: Key Findings, Reflections and Recommendations*, TUSEV Publications, 2006.

[19] See www.sabanciuniv.edu/erg

[20] Thomas Landon Jr, 'A New Breed of Billionaire', *New York Times*, 14 December 2007.

[21] Helmut Anheier, 'Foundations in Europe: A Comparative Perspective', in *Foundations in Europe: Strategy Management and Law*, Bertelsmann, 2001.

[22] European Commission, *Communication from the Commission to the Council, the European Parliament, the European Economic and Social Committee and the Committee of the Regions: Civil Society Dialogue between the EU and Candidate Countries*, COM(2005) 290 final, Brussels, 2005.

[23] European Commission, *Communication from the Commission on Promoting the Role of Voluntary Organizations and Foundations in Europe*, COM 97/241 Luxembourg, Office for Official Publications of the European Communities, 1997.

[24] Walt Kelly, American cartoonist, 1913–73.

WILHELM KRULL

15 Encouraging change
European foundations funding
research

Change and talking about change and the challenges that go with it are
as old as European thinking. The Greek philosopher Heraklitos once said:
'Change is the only thing in the world which is unchanging.' And yet, when
we look back at the fundamentally new developments of the past 10 to 15
years, we cannot help but recognize that the speed as well as the impact of
change has increased quite dramatically.

This applies not only to the European political landscape and its
restructuring since 1990, but also to the public and private infrastructures
that have such a deep impact on our daily lives. We live in a highly complex,
largely science- and technology-driven world and it seems that the
enormous changes we have been witnessing since then are merely a
foretaste of the challenges ahead.

A changing economic paradigm
During the next 20 years, Europe's economic paradigm will
change fundamentally. While the manufacturing base will shrink
continuously, future growth and social welfare will rely increasingly on
knowledge-intensive products and services. We can also observe that,
particularly with our demographic development in Germany and more or
less in the whole of Europe, we are faced with a completely new challenge of
how an ageing society can actually innovate. In this respect – as well as with
respect to the overall financial situation – priority setting will become even
more important in the future.

As a consequence of this crucial development, the European Union
(EU) has vowed to develop into a knowledge-driven society and to create

a European Research Area (ERA) following the Lisbon European Council in March 2000, which set out a daring strategic goal for the EU to become the most competitive and dynamic knowledge-based economy in the world by 2010. Declarations and agreements named after cities such as Bologna (1999), Lisbon (2001) and Barcelona (2003) are publicly acknowledged signposts of new policies and approaches in the higher education and research landscape of Europe that more or less simultaneously affect institutions at various levels of decision-making within the EU.[1]

Creating European Higher Education and Research Areas (EHEAs, ERAs) is by no means a straightforward endeavour. Indeed, it forces us to thoroughly rethink and subsequently realign our hitherto quite stable institutional concepts and approaches, particularly when it comes to meeting the requirements of up-to-date and sustainable undergraduate and graduate education, but also in creating a stimulating and inspiring environment for achieving breakthroughs in research and technological development. Ultimately, each institution has to live up to the challenges of increasing global competition and establishing its own culture of creativity.

Encouraging fresh ideas and new ways of thinking

Against this background, it has become more and more imperative for relevant actors in Europe and across the globe to go further in encouraging fresh ideas and new ways of thinking, particularly in the areas of research, innovation and higher education. A forward-looking and proactive approach towards the challenges ahead is needed. Even under rapidly changing circumstances, it still holds true that the best way of approaching future challenges is to get involved in actively confronting and shaping them continuously.

Foundations and philanthropic organizations can play a leading role in supporting these efforts. To do so, foundations – in particular those active in research, innovation and higher education – will have to make more efficient and effective use of their competitive advantages. However, foundations are a very heterogeneous pool of institutions whose defining characteristics often depend on local factors and the regulatory environment. In comparison to the US, foundations in Europe have played a less prominent role until now.[2]

There have nevertheless been important developments within the European landscape of foundations over the last few years, which are radically changing the old picture. One vehicle for foundations' increased involvement in research and innovation is the European Forum on Philanthropy and Research Funding, which was launched in the summer of 2007. The Forum is led by the European Foundation Centre (EFC) with support from the European Commission and individual funders. It aims to help underpin philanthropic funding for research through the exchange of experiences and best practices, the development of cooperation on research funding, and the promotion of a favourable environment for foundation and private philanthropy undertakings.

At the European level, it makes sense for foundations to engage in this kind of common effort to launch more cooperative programmes, and to strengthen public and private investment in R & D. For the EFC and its members, it will be an opportunity and a challenge to take the lead in this endeavour by convening foundations committed to research funding, by supporting frontier research, and by engaging in collaborative actions with universities, research organizations, governments and businesses.

The European Forum on Philanthropy and Research Funding will help to develop philanthropic potential in Europe by supporting initiatives that pave the way for a new environment for philanthropy in research. An environment that would see:

- effective philanthropic support for research through improved legal and fiscal environments;
- documented and better understanding of the added value of foundations' contribution to research;
- increased awareness and visibility of the role of philanthropy in supporting research;
- philanthropic investment in research as a complement to, but not a substitute for, public funding.

Effective facilitators of change

Given the billions of euros spent by public authorities and businesses, one might ask what impact comparatively small-scale foundations can achieve in this area. It is indeed not the overall amount of money spent but rather the approach taken by foundations that makes the difference. Their autonomy, alertness and flexibility enable them to operate effectively as facilitators of change, to establish islands of success, and thereby to achieve considerable impact on policymakers and decision-makers.

By fostering risky projects, encouraging networking across disciplinary, institutional and national borders, and helping some of the most creative researchers to break new ground, foundations are able to prove that even on a European scale, small things matter.[3] Let me illustrate this point by providing three examples.

Institutes of Advanced Study

The first one has to do with encouraging new ways of independent thinking in Central and Eastern Europe by setting up new Institutes of Advanced Study. The first such institute, the Collegium Budapest, was established in 1991. It was soon to be followed by others, such as the New Europe College in Bucharest, established in 1994 as a private foundation under Romanian law, and the Sofia Nexus Institute of Advanced Study in Bulgaria.

In view of the 'wounded sensibility of small cultures',[4] it was particularly important that in each case the initiative was taken by local researchers, and then in an inter-culturally sensitive manner picked up by the heads of the Wissenschaftskolleg in Berlin, as well as a closely cooperating network of grantmakers. When the respective national governments were still reluctant – and some are hesitant even today – to support such apparently luxurious places of freethinking and intellectual debate, primarily Swedish, Swiss and German foundations stepped in to facilitate the process of setting them up. These foundations have stayed committed to supporting these institutes ever since. Thus, they have secured the institutes' successful attempts at reaching the necessary levels of deep thinking, sophistication and creativity.

However, this does not imply that these institutes are in danger of becoming the new ivory towers in an otherwise still-suffering research environment. On the contrary, the pause for thought provided by them is often used by their fellows to rethink and reconfigure their own priorities and ultimately engage in social and political practice.

Central European University

Another breeding ground for future leaders is the Central European University (CEU) in Budapest, where several former students have become ministers, or chief executive officers of large companies in their home countries. Thanks to the generosity of the Hungarian-born American philanthropist George Soros, Budapest can be congratulated for hosting the first foundation-based, fully endowed private university in Europe, able to run its core operations on the basis of its own regular income resulting from the investments of some €420 million.

Compared to our large publicly financed universities with tens of thousands of students, the CEU is still a relatively small institution with about 100 professors and some 1,500 students. Yet to establish such a stronghold of independent teaching and research provides many challenges, not only to the Rector and the members of the Central European

University but to us all – not least because of the lessons we, and in particular our public universities, will have to learn.

Due to the fact that almost everywhere in Europe citizens are used to carrying a high tax load, we still expect governments to fully cover the costs of our universities and research institutes. All too often, this coincides with tight regulatory regimes of managerial accountability and quite disproportionate government control. Let me say clearly that this will have to come to an end. The global competition for the most talented young people can be won only if we change paradigms quickly.

No doubt, our universities must become more efficient, but to achieve this they must be given real autonomy and the freedom to establish optimal structures for the institution as such and also for their staff. The latter really calls for opening up new opportunities to develop independent career paths early on in academic life. With it goes, at each level of decision-making, the readiness to personally take on the responsibility for the choices made. In full agreement with Yehuda Elkana, the Rector of CEU, who has emphasized this on many occasions, I would like to stress that we have to reinforce the need to exercise informed and independent judgement in our universities. In addition, university leadership will have to see to it that more private resources are tapped in order to adequately water the new seeds in hopefully fertile grounds.

European Foreign and Security Policy Studies

My third example does not focus on any specific institution but rather on individuals and the need for intellectual networking across Europe. It is a joint funding initiative of the Compagnia di San Paolo, the Riksbankens Jubileumsfond and the VolkswagenStiftung on European Foreign and Security Policy Studies. The participating foundations are convinced that the national views that dominate academic and practical approaches towards a Common Foreign and Security Policy (CFSP) should recede in favour of a transnational perspective.

The envisioned research and training programme aims at developing such a perspective by young researchers and practitioners in their further qualification. The programme also aims at mobility across borders and between the academic and practical spheres. The candidates can work at academic institutions of their own choice and appropriate European organizations engaged in CFSP. Each participant in the programme will be funded for up to two years. At least half of the time should be spent abroad in an academic or practice organization. Individual activities should be combined with active participation in conferences and summer schools involving the other researchers funded in this initiative. Events should be held every six months. Joint publications and internet presentations could serve as further instruments for supranational networking.

Candidates for funding were young researchers and practitioners aiming at postgraduate or postdoctoral research in the field of CFSP. They were selected according to personal qualification and the expected quality of the proposed piece of research. Particular disciplines or nationality, or belonging to an EU Member State, were not prioritized. The about 100 candidates who have passed, or are currently engaged in the research and training programme, should be able to work as university teachers, analysts for institutes or think-tanks, or in the media, the civil service, or policy-oriented NGOs.

It is a crucial task not only for research and research funding institutions to open up these career perspectives to young researchers. Above all, innovation is created by brilliant minds and their ideas. A well set up innovation process, on the other hand, will result in the creation of ideas and, subsequently, of bright minds who pursue these ideas. Foundations should be striving to be part of such a 'self-sustaining' innovation process – because we need these ideas to further develop our work.

Foundations act more freely, flexibly and quickly

Foundations can act autonomously in supporting the first experiments in new areas, in taking risks when it comes to exploring hitherto unknown territories, and in substantially encouraging frontrunners in institutional reform. Unlike publicly financed agencies, which are dependent on political decisions and have to provide equal opportunities for all, private foundations do not have to wait for political consensus. They can act much more freely, flexibly and quickly. For them, the objectives to be achieved are always more important than bureaucratic rules and regulations.

Foundations can therefore add value to higher education reform and research efforts in a variety of ways, for example by:
- stimulating private means and initiatives to the long-term benefit of the public at large;
- identifying relevant topics or infrastructural demands for priority-setting processes;
- encouraging new developments and creating role models for an effective change of institutional strategies or structures as well as common practices;
- assisting in implementing topical or structural innovation on a wider scale;

   – contributing to the creation of a research-friendly society.

For foundations, leading institutional change is, therefore, similar to encouraging and supporting institutions and its leaders to engage in change processes towards achieving research- and innovation-friendly structures. In some of his recent publications, Rogers Hollingsworth has found medium-scale research organizations to be the most probable environment for achieving major breakthroughs in research and innovation. His studies on research institutions in the field of biomedicine revealed two basic concepts that seem to be institutional conditions *sine qua non* for groundbreaking research: first, an interdisciplinary organizational structure and, second, strong leadership connected with very high quality standards.[5]

   For these reasons, foundations are vitally interested in research-friendly, flexible structures at universities and do help them concerning their decision-making and administration, for example by helping them to create the structures and processes to make their governance and administration more efficient. All of this serves the need to create a research-friendly environment in which minds and ideas can develop. Thanks to private foundations, which respect an individual university's right to summon its strengths and pull itself out of difficulties, more than 20 of the 85 universities in Germany have been supported in reconfiguring their capacity to manage their affairs more effectively.

Fostering creativity

Europe can be successful in establishing and maintaining a globally competitive knowledge-based society only if it continuously strives to enhance the quality of its research base, to strengthen the structural dynamics of the various research and innovation systems, and to support frontier research in carefully selected areas. Each institution will have to review its own processes of quality assurance. Each must also respond to the question whether it provides a stimulating training and research environment that encourages risk-taking and enables its members to break new ground.

   Achieving and maintaining such a culture of creativity is not at all straightforward. On the contrary, it is full of paradoxes and contradictions. Every institution, not least for securing its own survival, has to insist that its members adhere to its rules, quality standards, and so on. However, the creation of new ideas is ultimately about breaking the rules and about being tolerant of errors made. Epistemologically speaking, radically new ideas can often not be phrased in terms of the initial question, and the openness for 'fresh thinking' is required not only by those who produce new ideas but also by those who are expected to pick them up. The readiness to listen to independent voices inside and outside of one's own institutional network, to encourage risk-taking in off-the-beaten-track areas, and to foster a climate of mutual learning, are prerequisites for successfully establishing a true culture of creativity. They have to be complemented by an innovation-friendly human resource policy.

In view of the increasing complexity of knowledge production, many universities and research institutions have tried to expand in size and diversity, and subsequently created an increase in hierarchical structures and bureaucracy. It has become more and more clear that such increases in size and diversity have negatively affected performance, and produced a great deal of unproductive heterogeneity and a decrease in interdisciplinary interaction, or trans-disciplinary integration, and ultimately led to great losses in innovation-friendly experimentation and flexibility.

Encouraging change and contributing to fostering cultures of creativity are two musts when it comes to tackling challenges through promoting higher education, research and innovation. Although these concepts are two sides of the same coin, it is by no means a straightforward process to establish them. When it comes to establishing a true culture of creativity, there are at least seven aspects which have to be considered:

Competence
The first precondition of a culture of creativity is to provide the best training for the future generation of academics and to enable researchers in general to develop their skills as freely as possible.

Courage
Not only researchers, but also the institutional leadership and funders must be both courageous and adventurous. Only if you are prepared to share the risks can you encourage people to enter new fields and leave the beaten track. The readiness to take risks must be complemented by a high degree of tolerance of errors.

Communication
Thought-provoking discussions are essential for achieving progress in research, particularly cross-disciplinary and transcultural exchanges, but also interactions with the outside world.

Diversity

Also in academia, monocultures do not provide an adequate breeding ground for exceptional thought. New knowledge is usually formed at the boundaries of established fields, so the interfaces between these areas of expertise must be activated. To be successful, it is essential to provide ample opportunities for all the researchers to interact intensively so that new paths can be developed and breakthroughs achieved.

Innovativeness

The fifth precondition of success in achieving breakthroughs is to foster innovativeness. We have to make sure that we identify and encourage those researchers who are prepared to take a risk with unconventional approaches. Academic leaders as well as heads of foundations must appreciate unconventional approaches and encourage risk-taking by providing incentives such as additional funding and long-term commitments.

Persistence and perseverance

To forge new paths in a barely known territory often takes longer than two or three years, the usual length of project funding. Mistakes must be allowed as well as changes of direction.

Serendipity

It is impossible to plan the precise moment at which a radically new idea emerges or a major scientific discovery occurs. But there are numerous examples in the history of research which prove that it is possible to establish a particularly stimulating environment more conducive to scientific breakthroughs than others. Although there is no one-size-fits-all recipe we can apply, it is certainly worthwhile to try and try again.

Tackling the challenges of change

The rapidly evolving global political and economic architecture creates numerous challenges for international cooperation in higher education and research. They call for greater flexibility and, among other things, intercultural sensitivity. Coping with change and challenges of such a huge dimension requires not only flexibility and spiritedness but also creativity. Ultimately, it is only the ability to see beyond one's own horizon, and to collaborate effectively beyond borders – be they national ones, or those set by academic disciplines or generational differences – that will result in the creation of new knowledge.

Due to the perpetuity of their funds, foundations are reliable partners, willing to foster risky projects and to help researchers to break new ground. They can help their partners in universities and other research institutions to act, not only to react, in the respective innovation processes, in the development of scholarship, and in selected areas of basic and strategic research. Foundations can help higher education and research institutions as well as individuals to tackle the challenges of change. Many of these can be met only if we take a long view. We Europeans must be prepared to exercise judgement, to take risks, and to make long-term commitments, while maintaining the flexibility to respond to new challenges.

[1] Wilhelm Krull, 'A Fresh Start for European Science. The scientific community must take up the challenges set by the EU objectives', *Nature* 419, 19 September 2002, pp249–50.

[2] Helmut K Anheier, 'Foundations in Europe: a comparative perspective', in Andreas Schlüter, Volker Then and Peter Walkenhorst (eds), *Foundations in Europe*, London, 2001.

[3] Wilhelm Krull, 'Encouraging Change, The role of private foundations in innovation processes', in Sönke Albers (ed), *Cross-functional Innovation Management. Perspectives from different disciplines*, Wiesbaden, 2004, pp407–20.

[4] Emil Cioran, Romanian philosopher and essayist, 1911–95.

[5] J Rogers Hollingsworth et al, *Fostering Scientific Excellence: Organizations, institutions, and major discoveries in biomedical science*, New York, 2003.

CAROLINE HARTNELL

16 European foundations' support for civil society
A means to an end or an end in itself?

'The primary mission of philanthropy is the nurturing and support of the institutions of civil society.' Barry D Gaberman

'The levers of meaningful change do not rest in the hands of one particular group.' Luc Tayart de Borms

Speaking at the European Foundation Centre (EFC) conference in Madrid in June 2007, Barry Gaberman, until recently Senior Vice President of the Ford Foundation, described 'the nurturing and support of the institutions of civil society' as 'the primary mission of philanthropy'. 'I want to be very clear here,' he insisted, 'I make this point not only because of the instrumental tasks that the institutions of civil society perform – such as providing needed services, educating us throughout our lives, helping to develop public policy, conducting advocacy, and strengthening our identity through artistic and cultural expression – but also because this layer of institutions performs an important generic function.' He went on to describe civil society as 'a fifth estate that helps to guard against the abuse of power'.

In an earlier article for *Alliance*,[1] he suggests that 'a vibrant civil society and the social capital it builds' may offer the best protection against regression to 'more authoritarian regimes' from 'the more open and participatory systems' that have been established in Latin America, Eastern Europe, Africa and Asia over the last few decades.

Gaberman sees the connection between foundations and civil society organizations (CSOs) as natural, unbreakable. He speaks of civil society with affection – and the same attitude can be sensed in many other prominent Americans in the philanthropy sector.

Different models of civil society
Luc Tayart de Borms of the King Baudouin Foundation, in his book *Foundations: Creating impact in a globalized world*,[2] has dubbed this view of civil society as the 'Anglo-Saxon model'. 'In these societies,' he says, 'civil

society organizations are viewed as being a counterweight to government and the state. In an ideal situation, they fulfil a complementarity function in fostering pluralism and cast themselves in the roles of critics of the state and advocates of reform.'

By contrast, he describes a variety of continental European models, which have in common that they do not accept this view of civil society as 'adversarial' to the state, seeing rather a collegiate, cooperative relationship (except perhaps in Latin countries). In Belgium, Germany and the Netherlands (the Rhine model), there are strong CSOs 'that are institution-like and often receive contracts from the state; it is a form of societal corporatism.' In Scandinavian countries, too, 'the state traditionally plays a strong role, but because of their Protestant roots, personal initiative is viewed as a positive.' CSOs 'thrive and fill a complementary role to bridge the gaps in the system', with CSOs often identifying a need that is later filled by government.

In the 'Latin/Mediterranean model', however, politics rule supreme and CSOs 'face a challenge in being accepted as independent and autonomous. There is a persistence to control organizations and associations politically, either through representations on the boards or by legal measures.'

How do these differing perspectives on civil society affect European foundations' relations with CSOs? Does civil society hold for them the special place it clearly holds for Barry Gaberman? Another way of putting this is to ask if European foundations see support for civil society as a means to an end or an end in itself.

A survey of EFC members

A brief survey of EFC members gives some indication of the extent to which European foundations implement their programmes through CSOs and to what extent through other types of entity. Just over three-quarters (33) of those that responded[3] said that they make grants to CSOs, while 36 said they make grants to other entities. Out of these, most specifically mentioned universities as grant recipients, and this was so across the geographic spread. Other entities supported are government, municipalities, museums, health-related organizations and think-tanks. Just two foundations currently support for-profit organizations, the Norwegian Fritt Ord (Freedom of Expression Foundation) and the German Deutsche Bundesstiftung Umwelt (German Federal Foundation for the Environment). In post-communist countries, respondents tended to adopt a wide definition of civil society. The Trust for Civil Society in Central and

Eastern Europe mentions 'formal and informal organizations, groups, coalitions, movements, individuals, representatives of the media and academia'.

In all, 31 foundations make grants both to CSOs and to non-CSOs. Generally speaking, most do so because they feel that they can best achieve their aims by not limiting their support to one particular type of organization. The attitudes behind these decisions will be explored at greater length later in this essay.

The survey also sought to establish if European foundations see strengthening civil society as part of their role, either as a way of strengthening their grantees or with the aim of strengthening the civil society sector more widely. The vast majority (36) said that they do see strengthening civil society as part of their role, with only five feeling that their purpose is solely to strengthen their grantees. Fifteen said that their aim is to strengthen the sector at large, and an equal number said that their purpose is to strengthen both. Many consider that they fulfil this role not only by grantmaking or direct programme activities but also, among other things, by acting as convenors – facilitating communication within the civil society sector and between the sector and others.

Finally, those who said they support the civil society sector more widely were asked if they see this as an end in itself because of what civil society is – a space in which citizens can associate, a repository of values, the political domain where deliberation takes place – or as a way of strengthening CSOs as valuable deliverers of foundation programmes. Most said that they support civil society because of what it is *per se*, with only a handful feeling that CSOs should be supported because they are a useful means for carrying out foundation programmes. Some felt that the real answer lies in a blend of the two.

These answers suggest a greater level of support for CSOs, and for the idea of civil society, than Luc Tayart's models might lead us to expect, certainly among continental European foundations. However, a quick search of the EFC database reveals that only 38 members out of over 200 mention civil society in their profiles – though 70 mention 'non-profit organizations'. This suggests that some of this apparent enthusiasm for civil society might have been prompted by the actual words used in the survey questions. A series of brief follow-up interviews suggest that most foundations, in continental Europe and in the UK, do fund organizations that are part of 'civil society' but relatively few think of themselves as doing so. It would be interesting to know whether smaller US foundations in general think in terms of civil society.

Foundation attitudes in the UK

Out of 14 interviews, a disproportionate number come from the UK because the UK is really the test case. As the supposed home of the Anglo-Saxon model, an identity-threatened island halfway between the US and Europe, the UK should be the one place in Europe where we will find that affection for civil society shown by American foundation leaders. Is it there? Or is the UK really more like continental Europe?

According to David Emerson of the Association of Charitable Foundations, UK foundations usually don't conceptualize civil society as such. They support what they generally refer to as 'voluntary organizations' because that's what trusts and foundations think they do. They're there to help charities try to change things. 'They don't mostly think, shall we fund a research organization or a government entity or a charity, they just assume, we're going to fund a charity, in the arts or something else. I think in their hearts what they're doing is supporting civil society but I don't know that that is how they see it explicitly.'

But conceptualizing or not conceptualizing is not just a matter of personal style; it leads inevitably to differences in behaviour. If I don't think of CSOs as forming a sector, I won't see any need to support that sector. I might recognize the benefits of strengthening a particular group within the sector, say organizations working with blind people if my trust works with blind people, but that is a long way from seeing the sector as a good thing *per se* and deciding to support it. In the UK, only a few do this to any great extent.

Stuart Etherington of the UK's National Council for Voluntary Organizations (NCVO) agrees with Emerson's assessment. With the exception of 'a few far-sighted foundations', he says, 'in general I think foundations in the UK have a much more instrumentalist view of civil society. They are interested in aspects of what charities and CSOs do but they're not particularly interested in the health of civil society generally.'

In fact, NCVO itself has only just begun to make the transition in vocabulary. Their new strapline 'Giving voice and support to civil society' replaced the former 'Giving voice and support to the voluntary and community sector' only at the end of 2007. What this will mean in practice remains to be seen.

Lenka Setkova, currently coordinating the Carnegie UK Trust's 'Inquiry into the future of civil society in the UK and Ireland', corroborates the views expressed by David Emerson and Stuart Etherington. 'People in the UK probably think of civil society in terms of the voluntary and community sector and as deliverers of their programmes rather than civil society more broadly,' she says.

For me, all this raises the question of who does support 'civil society more broadly'? Or do we simply have different foundations, with different aims, all supporting some of the organizations that have been grouped together under the banner of 'civil society'?

So how different is Europe?

In the US there's only one model, says Gerry Salole of the European Foundation Centre. 'You make grants to activist organizations or to NGOs or to people in the field and that's how you further the work. In Europe you can choose alternatives – you can give money to local government or to NGOs; you can create entities that are your agents, there is more variety.' As he sees it, this is a positive thing rather than a negative, 'but it does mean that you downplay the importance of civil society'. Summing up, he says that Europe offers 'a plethora of choice and a dilution of focus'.

The way many European foundations responded to the survey question asking why they support both CSOs and non-CSOs reflects this plethora of choice, with CSOs seen as just one option among many for foundation support. Here is a small selection of the responses:

- 'Our purpose is to invest in causes that benefit the general public. We do not limit ourselves to certain organizations.' (Sparebankstiftelsen DnB NOR, Norway)
- 'We focus on the projects and the ideas, not the organizations behind them.' (Egmont Foundation, Denmark)
- 'We do not favour one over the other. We look for organizations that have good ideas and can deliver.' (Nuffield Foundation, UK)
- 'We receive a broad range of proposals and accept those who best fit our criterias.' (Pro Victimis Foundation, Switzerland)
- 'Different partners are appropriate for different projects at different times. Our attitude is to seek like-minded people.' (Evens Foundation, Belgium)

Charlie McConnell recently ushered in a change of policy at Carnegie UK Trust. 'When I came to Carnegie in 2003,' he explains, 'the voluntary and community sector was seen as *the* vehicle for change. You see a hundred flowers blooming and hope for change. We want to have an impact on issues like climate change, sustainable development, strengthening democracy and rural development, and civil society is one of the players, not the only one. You also need to work with government and the private sector.' He also advocates working with faith-based organizations, trade unions and informal associations rather than the narrowly defined part of civil society, the voluntary and community sector, that UK trusts have traditionally worked with.

Robert Dufton of the UK-based Paul Hamlyn Foundation describes himself as 'neutral and balanced' between funding CSOs and non-CSOs where there is a choice, for example in their Free With Words programme, which aims to catalyse those running prisons to do a better job of providing education opportunities for prisoners. The choice will depend on their effectiveness in each particular case. While funding a CSO that is working in partnership with non-CSOs 'is often thought to be the starting point for foundations', he feels it can be just as effective to fund the non-CSO direct. And he finds the same variation in effectiveness in CSOs and in government entities.

Andrea Silvestri of the Italian Fondazione Cassa di Risparmio di Cuneo also says they make grants to a very wide range of different entities, depending on the field of activity. Social welfare, arts and culture, public health and local development initiatives are just some of the areas they work in. But he doesn't see CSOs and non-CSOs as likely to be equally effective. Given a choice between making a grant to government or to a CSO, all other things being equal, his preference is not for the CSO but for government. 'In most cases,' he says, 'it's safer to provide grants to public entities like local governments and municipalities. They will have a complete system of control over the activities they carry out. When we receive a proposal from a CSO, we look at their balance sheet and their recent history to be sure it's a reliable organization that we can trust and the project will be carried out.'

When it comes to supporting civil society, which Silvestri does see as the role of his foundation, it is to help them increase their competence, for example to help them become more viable recipients of research grants by 'bringing them to work in a more structured way and to adopt a more scientific approach to their activities'. He also tries to help CSOs to cooperate with each other. 'One problem we see with CSOs is that often they don't cooperate with each other. This means they don't have enough resources to continue their activities or carry out new projects even if other CSOs are working on very similar projects.'

What about funding businesses?

As we have seen, only two of the foundations that responded to the survey said that they are willing to support businesses. One is the Norwegian Fritt Ord. 'It doesn't really matter what type of organization we fund, it's our aims that matter and the quality of the project itself and the relevance to our guidelines. Our main aim is to strengthen the freedom of speech,' says Elin Lutnes. And this extends to companies, in this case publishing companies, for example if they want to publish a book 'about a certain debate', and to newspapers 'as they are essential to freedom of expression'.

Are they worried about the possibility of a grant leading to a profit being made? 'We tend to support books that won't be very successful economically,' Lutnes explains. 'Some of them wouldn't be published at all without the grant. If one is unexpectedly successful, that would be OK.' In fact, it would surely be a bonus.

The German Deutsche Bundesstiftung Umwelt also funds for-profit groups, in their case small to medium enterprises (SMEs), as Ulrich Witte explains. 'We have several big areas where we are funding. One is technique, and you find the SMEs who are coming up with innovations in areas like renewable energy, energy reduction, energy efficiency. Another is environmental communications – awareness-building, information provision and so on. Here 70 per cent of groups are associations, usually with no money.' This is clearly not a matter of case-by-case decision-making, more a sophisticated view of which type of entity is suited to which type of activity.

I suspect that the limited number of foundations making grants to businesses is a result of foundation attitudes rather than their constitution. Robert Dufton admits that he can't think of any reason why Paul Hamlyn Foundation shouldn't give a restricted grant to encourage better practice in a privately run prison in the same way as they have done with state-run prisons. Their constitution allows PHF to fund 'charitable activity' not charitable entities. It's just something they haven't done.

Foundations and social justice

How different are attitudes to civil society when it comes to a foundation like the UK's Joseph Rowntree Charitable Trust (JRCT), which is committed to working for greater equity and social justice? 'Traditionally, we've always worked with civil society,' says Stephen Pittam. 'Our focus was how to achieve change and the vehicle was CSOs.'

But this does not extend to civil society as a whole. 'I don't think we'd say we have a deep concern for developing capacity or infrastructure,' says Pittam. 'We're not interested in CSOs existing *per se*; we don't put money into NCVO, for example. In those areas where we fund, we feel an interest and responsibility to ensure the core costs of organizations that are important and effective are covered. Support for civil society is focused around supporting specific groups that carry out policy and advocacy work for change.' JRCT also supports these groups by means such as bringing together organizations working in a specific area, both their grantees and other key organizations.

Broadly speaking, JRCT's attitude to civil society doesn't seem to me to be very different from those of most other foundations: they fund those CSOs that are best suited to achieving their aims as a funder. This is something that surprised me as I had somehow assumed that a social justice funder like JRCT would be committed to 'civil society' as such. This brings us back to the Anglo-Saxon model and the idea of civil society as a counterpoint to the state and a guardian against abuses of power. It is undoubtedly true that the groups JRCT supports would mostly see themselves in this sort of way – and that is why JRCT chooses to support them. But that doesn't mean JRCT has an interest in supporting civil society as an end in itself.

I do, however, see a real difference between JRCT's attitude to the CSOs it funds and that of many other funders to their grantees. This relates to the question of who sets the agenda, and this relates in turn to the issue of legitimacy. 'Whose agenda are we working to?' asks Pittam. 'Because people have money, should they be setting the agenda?' As Lenka Setkova of Carnegie UK Trust also points out, 'It can seem contradictory for foundations to see CSOs as a vehicle for change and then themselves define the change they want them to achieve.' For JRCT civil society is still a means to an end, but that end will be best achieved if CSOs themselves come up with the ideas and set their own agenda within the broad framework established by JRCT. In this way a social justice funder seems to give more value to the organizations it funds.

'There's a legitimacy about people coming to us and persuading us that they know what should be done,' says Pittam, 'if they are people who are committed and have fire in the belly and want to work on that issue.' He admits to feeling 'emotionally and intellectually very supportive when American foundation leaders like Barry Gaberman and Mark Rosenman make this point'.

Nicholas Borsinger of Switzerland's Pro Victimis Foundation also brings up the question of who sets the agenda. In fact, he 'doesn't see a huge divide between supporting CSOs to do the work of the foundation and supporting CSOs "in themselves" because we don't support CSOs as an outlet for our own ideas. It's *their* ideas that sit within what is *our* focus. It's not such a divide because the ideas really come from them.'

However, it is not a policy of Pro Victimis 'to support CSOs so as to allow people to be more vocal about their own rights'. Nor do they make grants specifically to strengthen civil society in a particular country. 'We may be getting there but we haven't got there quite yet. We have probably a bit of an exaggerated terror of funding organizations that help other people to organize themselves,' Borsinger admits. 'Are we funding the salaries of people who are running talkshops but don't really reach out as they should do? At the same time we are realizing more and more that there is a need out there.'

Civil society as a space for deliberation

Supporting a specific group of CSOs to carry out advocacy and policy work is clearly very different from supporting civil society *per se*. Civil society can be used for many ends, as demonstrated by the widely acknowledged success of the US right-wing funders in supporting grassroots groups to promote their own values.

The potential dangers of supporting civil society have been pointed out by various writers, including Luc Tayart in a recent article for *Alliance* where he questions the assumption that foundations should necessarily support civil society.[4] 'Civil society organizations are not always a bridge over troubled waters,' he points out. 'By their very nature, many reinforce exclusiveness; their efforts towards building an inclusive society may be skewed towards serving their own interests at the expense of others.'

The view that civil society is a conduit for creating a foundation for stronger democracies Tayart dismisses as 'both simplistic and somewhat naive'. If civil society holds true to its commonly held definition, he says, 'it is composed of a patchwork of special interest groups, each armed with its own agenda, each advocating its specific cause, and each representing diverse constituencies.' Put very simply, if we support civil society as a space in which citizens may deliberate, we may not like all the groups that come to deliberate in it.

Open grants programmes

One foundation that has recently moved more in the direction of supporting civil society *per se* is the Esmee Fairbairn Foundation, one of the UK's largest foundations. In January 2008, they moved to a more reactive open grants programmes, similar to one that has long been run by the Tudor Trust. Why have they done this? According to Dawn Austwick, it stems both from their view about where change will come from and from what they perceive as 'the gap'. 'We looked at the funding marketplace,' Austwick explains, 'and asked what other funders were doing. One of the messages that we got quite clearly is that a lot of funding is getting more programmatic and more constrained, and that can be difficult for those who are seeking funding.'

But it's not just a matter of responding to changes in the foundation sector. In Austwick's view, funding civil society is a particular role of foundations. 'Other sectors have their own sources of funding,' she says. 'And that brings us back to the question, what's the role of foundations? What can we uniquely do? Every time we look at an application, we should be asking, "Is this something that only we can support or are there others who could do it?"'

Here we seem to have echoes of Barry Gaberman's views on the essential relationship between foundations and civil society, and this comes through in Austwick's view of civil society too. 'I think civil society can be the guardian of the interests of the people,' she says. 'There are strong forces operating at the level of government and the private sector. Civil society provides a counterpoint to that, looking at equity, looking at the needs of people.' This is true – to an extent. But isn't government also the 'guardian of the interests of the people', in fact the most obvious one – though it doesn't always do its job as well as it should? Equally, not all CSOs are guardians of the interests of the people. Many perfectly benign but self-serving organizations are looking to the interests of very small groups of people while others, less benign, represent the aims of groups that Esmee Fairbairn would certainly not want to support. When it comes down to it, I don't imagine that any foundation anywhere really supports civil society *per se*. Civil society by its nature encompasses the full spectrum of values, and a foundation's choice of which CSOs to support will inevitably reflect its own values and priorities.

Civil society as counterpoint to government?

As we have seen, Luc Tayart sees the view of civil society as counterpoint to government as typically Anglo-Saxon (though it seems to be in short supply even in the UK), and definitely not prevalent in the rest of Europe. In Northern Europe and Scandinavia, government provides core funding to many CSOs. In addition, CSOs on the whole see government as doing a good job. 'International NGOs are often surprised that continental European foundations don't support human rights organizations or reproductive health organizations,' he says. 'We have the feeling that our governments are doing this all right, by funding CSOs themselves and by taking positions that are credible and good.' There are some NGOs, for example, that are pushing government on the environment, but these are mostly funded by individuals. 'There is more a collaborative feeling between foundations and the government.'

The one example he gives of an occasion when there was a general feeling that government had failed is very much the exception that proves the rule as the King Baudouin Foundation was asked by the Belgian Government to step in. 'We had a crisis involving missing children about ten years ago,' Tayart explains. 'There was a feeling among the population that the government hadn't done their job well enough. So we were asked by the PM to see if it would be possible to create something like a Centre for Missing Children in Belgium. From the start it was a kind of private-public partnership.'

In Latin countries, where the primacy of politics mean that government often wants to control NGOs by having representatives on boards and so on, he admits that 'there is perhaps more of a need for a critical role of independent NGOs, but I don't see a lot of foundations doing that.' Andrea Silvestri of Fondazione Cassa di Risparmio di Cuneo doesn't seem to welcome this sort of role. Asked whether CSOs should be a counterweight to government, he replied, 'Yes they can monitor government activities, but I prefer to see them as complementary.'

Neville Kluk of the Belgium-based Evens Foundation sees the relationship between government and foundations as a collaborative one. 'We think the foundation's role is often the risk role, the pilot role. If you're trying to affect something like the way migrants, or women, are treated in society, in the long term, after the initial impetus of the foundation, sustainability is normally the responsibility of a public authority or local government or the mayor.' Several writers have been sounding the death knell of this model of foundation-funded pilot schemes being taken up and replicated by government, yet Kluk insists that it's a viable approach as long as you work with the relevant agencies from the beginning. 'So often people go out and design programmes but have no hope of authorities adopting them because no one has bothered to find out what programmes they want to see in place. Then they drop their programme because it doesn't work.' Luc Tayart's 'Scandinavian model' for civil society also refers to CSOs often identifying a need that is later filled by government.

Ulrich Witte of Deutsche Bundesstiftung Umwelt is the only continental European interviewed who sees something like an adversarial role for civil society. 'In the field of environmental communications, small groups have an important role,' he says. 'They talk about the problems, future challenges and so on, which politicians aren't doing. We need them, otherwise we don't get necessary developments.'

But we need to go back to Anglo-Saxon territory, in this case to Northern Ireland, to find a pure articulation of the role of civil society as counterpoint to the state – not that Northern Ireland, with its long history of conflict, is typical of either the UK or the US. 'Politics is sometimes seen as being solely about control of management of the state by elected politicians,' writes Avila Kilmurray of the Community Foundation for Northern Ireland (CFNI).[5] 'One of the benefits of civil society networks and organizations is that they can counterbalance centralizing power tendencies, but this requires the active participation of citizens. . . . In a period of fear, when the common wisdom was that "whatever you say, say nothing", community groups and NGOs created small niches within society where people felt safe to exchange views and to share their anger, hopes and aspirations. The other critical role undertaken by some CSOs was to speak out against periodic atrocities and abuses of human rights.' But CFNI would undoubtedly support only a very small segment of CSOs.

:::

Should the relationship between foundations and civil society be seen as a love match or a marriage of convenience? In continental Europe, at least, the answer seems clear-cut: the relationship is barely a marriage of convenience, more that of a dating couple when they feel inclined. For foundations, this is a good arrangement because it enables them to work with different types of organization on different occasions, always depending on what will be most effective in achieving their goals. And for many CSOs, it may also be fine because they have their more regular date – government.

In the UK, the situation is less straightforward, as one would expect in our 'identity-threatened island'. While some such as the Nuffield Foundation and the Paul Hamlyn Foundation select their grantees from a range of different types of entity, most foundations probably support CSOs unreflectively but faithfully under the rubric of 'charities' or 'voluntary organizations'. As a matter of common sense, they will choose to support the organizations that seem most likely to achieve the foundation's goals, and social justice funders like JRCT and the Community Foundation for Northern Ireland are no different in this respect. Finally, there are a few that support civil society more explicitly and for its own sake, but even they will in practice be highly discriminating about which organizations they support. Even in the UK, home of the Anglo-Saxon model, there is little sign of that affection for civil society shown by American foundation leaders.

The potential loser in this overall picture is civil society infrastructure. For continental Europeans, Gerry Salole points out, civil society is not indispensable. And if foundations have other options and can manage without civil society, why support the infrastructure? In the UK, civil society is probably slightly more necessary but also not much thought about. The difficulties experienced by philanthropy associations like the EFC and the Association of Charitable Foundations in persuading their members to support them adequately are well known – though last year's decision by EFC members to increase membership fees marks a real step forward.

If European foundations have historically been reluctant to support their own infrastructure, how much more likely that the infrastructure of such a little supported or understood 'sector' as 'civil society' will fall through the net? The danger being that other less ambitiously conceived but more understood groups such as 'NGOs', 'non-profit organizations', 'charities' and 'voluntary organizations' may fall through the net in the resulting confusion. The adoption of a European foundation statute, strongly advocated by Gerry Salole in his essay in this book, would be a good first step in clarifying some of the confusion over terminology.

[1] Barry D Gaberman, 'Associations of grantmakers: why should we care about them?' *Alliance*, vol 6, no 1, March 2001.

[2] Luc Tayart de Borms (2005) *Foundations: Creating impact in a globalized world*, John Wiley, pp41–45.

[3] The survey was carried out in December 2007. Forty-four out of 210 responded, a 21 per cent response rate, with responses coming from 18 different countries – including two from Russia, three from Turkey, one from Jordan and two from the US. In 2000, there were estimated to be around 62,000 'public benefit' foundations in Europe, so this is a minute sample, useful for gaining impressions rather than hard data.

[4] Luc Tayart de Borms, 'Supporting civil society – a dogma for our time?' *Alliance*, Vol 12, No 2, June 2007.

[5] Avila Kilmurray, 'Civil society in a divided society', *Alliance*, Vol 6, No 3, September 2001.

DIANA LEAT

17 Foundations and policy influence in Europe

For some, the idea that foundations have a role in influencing policy will appear strange – are foundations not about 'charity', filling gaps in government and market provision, and keeping out of 'politics'? Others may suggest that foundations, with their tiny resources relative to those of government, cannot possibly hope to influence policy. Yet others will argue that foundations as unelected bodies should not attempt to influence policy in a democracy.

This chapter examines these objections and illustrates the ways in which foundations in Europe can, and do, enhance democracy by contributing to policy debates.

Approaches

In Europe, foundations have not generally seen policy influence as a key role. The 21-country study of *Visions and Roles of Foundations in Europe*, coordinated by the Centre for Civil Society at the London School of Economics,[1] found that in general foundations in Europe most commonly described their roles in terms of innovation and complementing other sectors, including government. The majority of foundations did not see themselves as having much, if any, influence on social policy change. In part, this was attributed to politicians' lack of understanding and knowledge of foundations.

The conclusion was that between and within countries: 'Social and policy change, preservation and pluralism receive somewhat mixed assessments. In each case, these roles are rated as somewhat, but not very strongly, applicable by about half or more countries.'[2] However, as illustrated below, the exceptions are as interesting as the rule.

European foundations' engagement in policy change

Engagement in social and policy change	Country
Role pronounced/applies	Denmark, Hungary, Poland, United States
Somewhat	Belgium, Czech Republic, Estonia, Germany, Greece, Ireland, Netherlands, Portugal, Spain, Switzerland, UK
Less, not at all	Austria, Finland, France, Italy, Norway, Sweden

Source H K Anheier and S Daly, *The Politics of Foundations: A comparative analysis*, London and New York: Routledge, 2007.

There is, however, another important conclusion from the study. Despite the majority of European foundations' lack of current, explicit engagement with policy, some foundations saw greater policy relevance and involvement as one of their ideal roles in the future.

Foundations in Europe tend to define their roles in relation to the state, but they tend in general not to explicitly see their roles in terms of influencing policy.[3] So, what are the specific objections and barriers to greater explicit involvement with policy among European foundations?

Arguments against policy engagement

Foundations in Europe tend to employ a variety of assumptions and arguments to explain their lack of explicit involvement in policy. These include:

 – There is a clear dividing line between private 'charity' – providing services to the needy – and public policy; public policy is the preserve of government, private charity is the preserve of foundations.
 – Foundations do not have the moral/political right to trespass into the public policy arena.
 – Foundations should stay out of public policy because charity law prohibits involvement.
 – Foundations should stay out of public policy because it diverts resources away from providing immediate help.

- Public policy involvement runs the risk of raising the profile of foundations, attracting conflict, criticism and greater regulation.
- Public policy work is too difficult/too costly/requires long-term commitment/cannot be assessed and involves high overhead costs.
- Public policy formation is too complex for foundations to grapple with.

A changing context

So why and how do foundations in Europe overcome these supposed obstacles? In part the answer to the question lies in the changing context in which foundations in Europe are working. The *Visions and Roles* study revealed a number of elements in this changing context.

Concerns about how the 'rolling back' of European welfare states will affect foundations and widespread rejection of a state-controlled model
Foundations in a number of countries were facing increasing pressures to substitute for state services and the issue of substitution and relationships with statutory funding was for many foundations the most difficult current issue. 'The dilemmas and trends some foundations identify regarding foundations being reluctantly cajoled into assuming roles that are not their key priorities somewhat compromise assertions about independence and autonomy. The signs are that this will continue in the broader scenario of the restructuring of European welfare states.'[4]

Declining income
For some foundations the combination of issues of perceived pressure to substitute for government and to 'do more with less' (relative to demand) was leading to the consideration of new, more policy-oriented approaches, building on the foundation's existing knowledge base. Some foundations believed that, in this way, they could have more widespread and sustainable long-term impact.

Greater awareness of interconnected issues and pan-European issues
Foundations were increasingly aware that the roots of many of the most pressing problems they were addressing lay beyond national boundaries. Similarly, sustainable change was seen as requiring engagement with pan-European institutions.[5]

More generally, a growing number of foundations are realizing that old ways aren't working, governments are no longer prepared to pick up the tab, and problems have more complex roots. In the last half of the

20th century foundations generally worked on the more or less explicit assumption that their very limited projects and programmes would be taken up by (local) government. Government, having been shown the need and the way, would replicate and fund foundation-generated projects. In other words, foundations would influence policy by the back door of quiet example.

Today, that strategy is rarely available. Government has cast itself in the role of demonstrator and innovator; the role of non-profits is to implement government priorities. Foundations may 'demonstrate' all they like but demonstration alone is no longer enough to ensure wider change and impact.

This change in the environment in which foundations work is one of a number of arguments in favour of foundations' engagement with public policy.

The net result of these changes is that: 'One of the most salient challenges facing foundations in the context of the restructuring of welfare states concerns . . . how to "add value", whilst at the same time avoiding a wholly substitutive role. This is a challenge that resonates throughout each of the country studies. Foundations increasingly speak of the added pressures and responsibilities that have emerged as a result of broader public sector reforms'.[6]

Some seek to add value by exploring business metaphors and, closely related, capacity-building. But whereas businesses typically focus expansion efforts on organizational growth, foundations have other ways of achieving greater impact that involve letting go or spreading ideas rather than holding on to them. Businesses make money by retaining ownership of ideas and practices; foundations achieve impact by broadcasting ideas and encouraging others to take them up.[7]

Adding distinctive value

So how can foundations add distinctive value? What are their unique assets and capacities? What can they do that cannot be done by the state or the market? Arguably, the focus on foundations' wealth has diverted attention from their other, more important, distinctive attributes: their independence, knowledge and networks. In fact, of course, the wealth of foundations is tiny compared to that of government and the market.

What is truly distinctive about foundations is their relative freedom from the constraints of customers, shareholders, constituencies and goodwill of the general public as donors. This gives foundations a unique freedom to take risks and fail, to explore ideas and solutions that go against the conventional wisdom, and more generally to 'stand on the sidelines' by bringing diverse groups together across political and other boundaries. In addition, foundations have the capacity to have an overview of fields, drawing on their operational work and/or grantmaking, and networks.

These are the assets that make foundations truly distinctive and enable them to add unique value.[8] By acting as issue and knowledge entrepreneurs, risk-takers and convenors/brokers, foundations can make an invaluable contribution to public and policy debate, and enhance the quality of democracy.

Arguments for policy engagement

Foundations that see their assets in terms of independence, knowledge/ overview and convening ability believe that contributing to policy debate is a valid, feasible and effective way for endowed foundations to add distinctive value for wider public benefit. These foundations seek not merely to have impact on their immediate beneficiaries and grantees but to have impact that goes beyond those necessarily narrow confines.

These foundations make a distinction between policy and politics. Policy, or public affairs, is something in which foundations are inevitably engaged in the sense that there is no clear dividing line between private and public concerns in society today. Providing services to the needy and public policy are both processes of establishing social goals and distributing society's resources. Government is an instrument for shared public purposes and philanthropy has a role in increasing informed civic engagement and public participation.[9]

Foundations explicitly engaged with policy issues believe they have the same moral/political right to comment on and contribute to public policy as any other citizen/group in a democracy. Furthermore, foundation contributions to public policy processes may both enhance democracy by stimulating debate and contribute to the problem-solving capacity of society. Arguably, foundations have a moral responsibility to 'pay' for their lack of democratic accountability by enhancing democracy.

These foundations demonstrate that it is a myth that charity law prohibits contributing to public policy – there is ample space within the law in many countries for foundations to do so. They also argue that public policy involvement does not necessarily divert resources away from providing immediate help; by investing in policy debate, foundations can increase the impact of their investment in direct services.

More importantly, these foundations see involvement in public policy work as a way in which foundations, given their relatively small financial resources – individually and collectively – can create sustainable change with an impact beyond their immediate grantees. Without wider social change, the work of foundations is restricted to short-term benefit for a lucky few grant recipients.

Foundations explicitly engaging with policy issues may further argue that:

- Without wider social change, philanthropy runs the risk of sustaining the problems it seeks to solve; social change philanthropy seeks to reduce the demand for charity.
- Researching/knowing the causes of something does not necessarily lead to change. Change requires both feasible, constructive solutions and political will, which has to be built.
- Public policy work may be difficult, uncertain and slow but if it achieves wider, more sustainable change then it may be no more uncertain, slow and costly than year after year of grantmaking to achieve short-term assistance, which is constantly in need of renewal.[10]
- Public policy work is complex but, as various foundations demonstrate, there are skills and techniques to be learned and it is not beyond the capacities of even relatively small foundations.[11]
- Foundations have a moral responsibility to take a stand on public policy issues. If they do not, they 'risk coming under fire or, worse, becoming irrelevant'.[12]
- Today, it seems that engagement with public policy is coming back on to the agenda of foundations in both Europe and the US. In both cases we seem to be emerging from a phase in which foundations acted as though they could somehow ignore government, while at the same time implicitly relying on government to provide ongoing maintenance for projects fathered by foundations. For example: 'Foundations must finance long-range efforts that enable non-profit groups to understand that a strong government responsive and responsible to its people is essential to a strong civil society.'[13]

An important and feasible role

But what about the objection that foundations do not have the capacity to contribute to policy? A number of foundations, large and smaller, in Europe demonstrate that policy influence is an important and feasible role for foundations. Following are some examples. However, this list is not representative of the numerous foundations engaged in policy influence.

Joseph Rowntree Charitable Trust (JRCT)

JRCT, located in the UK, has a reputation for involvement in often contentious policy issues. A recent study of the Trust's work in support of the successful Campaign for Freedom of Information to incorporate the European Convention on Human Rights into UK domestic law, and the Democratic Audit, which aims to strengthen democracy and political culture in the country, suggests that it has indeed been effective in influencing policy debate.

The study concludes: 'By investing a comparatively small sum of money in the right place at the right time, the JRCT influenced policy debate, notably when Labour was open to reforming ideas in the early to middle 1990s. It enhanced the capacity of grant holders, helped them to push issues up the political agenda and enabled them to influence legislation . . . The JRCT is an important policy actor.'[14]

Bertelsmann Stiftung

The Bertelsmann Stiftung in Germany is one of the largest in Europe, primarily operating its own projects addressing key social and policy issues. One example is the Bertelsmann Reform Index, which seeks to identify and compare the need for reform in OECD Member States, as well as their ability to take action. The project's goal is to create a comprehensive data pool on government activity in OECD states. At the same time, its international comparisons are meant to serve as evidence-based input for national debates on reform.

King Baudouin Foundation (KBF)

KBF, based in Brussels, Belgium, works in a variety of ways including grantmaking, convening and operating. One of its projects, launched in 2004, concerned the training of imams. The decision to focus on the training needs of imams arose, in part, from their key leadership role within the Muslim community and, in part, from a perception in the media that imams were coming from the most radical sections of the Muslim community and were therefore 'dangerous'.

In fact, no one knew where imams were coming from or their degree of integration into Belgian society, their real roles, what knowledge and skills they needed, or what they already had. Although there was some sort of implicit consensus that 'something needed to be done', there were no clear suggestions for what or how; the Muslim community was itself divided and was not talking with government or with educational institutions.

By 2007, there had been change at a number of levels. There was solid information available about the training of imams in Belgium and other countries, and as compared with training of leaders of other religions. The key stakeholders from the Muslim community, education and government had been brought together and were continuing conversations. The issue was higher up the political agenda. The issues and the options had been clarified and there was acceptance that the Muslim community needed to take responsibility for agreeing ways forward. There were concrete propositions for moving forward. Two small experimental training courses had been developed at the University of Louvain and at CIFoP (the Inter-University Centre for Continuing Education); and there was wider international interest in developing training programmes recognized across countries.

In June 2007, the Walloon government recognized the first mosques, and the Flemish government did the same at the end of 2007. For each recognized mosque one or two imams are paid.

However, those involved see the overall aim as yet to be fully achieved. KBF brought people together, corrected misperceptions and created practical options for the future. But the case illustrates yet again that change is often slow, requires a favourable external environment, and often depends on the actions of others over whom the foundation has no control. KBF will continue to advocate on this issue with the Ministry of Justice.

Nuffield Foundation

The Nuffield Foundation in the UK has a long and illustrious history of effective influence on policy. For example, in 1991 it established the Nuffield Council on Bioethics as an independent body, jointly funded by Nuffield, the Wellcome Trust and the Medical Research Council. The Council's purpose is to consider ethical issues in new developments in medicine and biology, and it was created partly because government had decided not to establish such a body. Today, its independence from government is seen as one of its strengths.

The Council works by identifying a topic for consideration and then creating a multi-disciplinary group with the expertise to work on it. Reports are widely disseminated to, among others, policy-makers and other interested parties, and further debate is encouraged. Its first report on genetic screening, published in 1993, was regarded as very influential in setting the agenda for public and political discussion, and a number of its recommendations have been incorporated into policy.

The Nuffield Foundation also uses its resources to generate evidence and to encourage experiment with a view to stimulating knowledge and debate for change. It uses its reputation and convening powers to bring disparate, and sometimes conflicting, parties together. It also makes good use of its overview position, sometimes spotting connections and similarities between issues that would not be apparent to those immersed in their particular stream of work.

Körber Foundation

The Körber Foundation is one of Europe's leading policy-oriented foundations. According to founder Kurt A Körber, 'The purpose of foundations is to help shape the future of our society.' It is independent and without any commercial or political interests. It describes itself as a 'forum for new ideas', and 'designed to be used as a communication platform'.[15] More specifically, the Körber Foundation aims to involve citizens in discourses, further knowledge, identify problems and prompt additional activities.

Among other activities, since 1961 the Foundation has run the Bergedorf Round Table promoting international conversations among politicians, scientists, corporate representatives and journalists. Topics for the roundtables are suggested via Political Breakfasts. Over the years the roundtables have addressed key issues – often those where there were few other available settings for off-the-record, open conversations among people with very different perspectives. One example is the Körber Dialogue Middle East, a platform for multilateral, confidential discussion and formulation of recommendations on foreign and security policy among foreign policy experts from the EU, the US and the Middle East.

Dag Hammarskjöld Foundation

The Dag Hammarskjöld Foundation, based in Uppsala, Sweden, was founded following the UN Secretary General Dag Hammarskjöld's death in 1961 in a plane crash on a mission to the Congo. The Foundation searches for and examines workable alternatives and perspectives for a socially and economically just, ecologically sustainable, peaceful and secure world. By organizing seminars and dialogues in close collaboration with a wide and constantly expanding international network, it plays a catalysing role in the identification of new issues and the formulation of new concepts, policy proposals, strategies and work plans towards solutions.

Community Foundation for Northern Ireland (CFNI)
CFNI, based in Belfast, is a fundraising and grantmaking foundation
that is well known for its risk-taking and policy influence in very difficult
circumstances. One example is CFNI's work on reintegrating political
ex-prisoners into society after the paramilitary ceasefires of 1994. CFNI
continued this work with funding under the EU Special Support Programme
for Peace and Reconciliation from 1995 to 1999, work that was expanded
with the early release of political prisoners provided for under the Belfast
Agreement in 1998. Underlying CFNI's work in this area was the idea that
'if you are part of the problem, you must be part of the solution' and that,
whatever other views might be held, Northern Ireland could not achieve
genuine peace with a significant resentful and excluded population of
ex-prisoners and their families.

     Despite enormous difficulties, CFNI succeeded in contributing to
recognition of the issue of reintegration of ex-political prisoners as one
that had to be addressed; provided support to development of service and
support organizations; developed training and skills; created networks and
alliances; and encouraged understanding, dialogue and healing – basic
building blocks to reintegration and lasting peace.[16]

Jaume Bofill Foundation
Another foundation in Europe working to influence policy change is the
Jaume Bofill Foundation, based in Barcelona, Spain, which works to
promote Catalan national identity within a framework of promotion of rights.
An interesting point about this foundation is that although it asserts its
independence, it does not claim to be neutral about the major issues facing
Catalan society and the world.

Working together – collaborative programmes
One example of foundation collaboration around key policy issues is the
European Foreign and Security Policy Studies programme, designed
to encourage a transnational perspective on what are currently largely
national approaches to international security. Launched in 2004, it was
developed by Compagnia di San Paolo in Italy, Riksbankens Jubileumsfond
in Sweden and Volkswagen Foundation in Germany. The programme
seeks to influence policy by developing the next generation of leaders and
security experts. It gives European researchers and young professionals
opportunities to conduct research at European institutions and to build
networks and in this way hopes to influence wider policy debate.[17]

The Network of European Foundations for Innovative Cooperation (NEF) is probably one of the biggest forces for European foundation collaboration around key policy issues. NEF is not a membership organization but a 'platform' to enable joint projects to get off the ground. It involves 62 foundations participating in one or more projects, including work on integration and migration, deliberative democracy, and the future of rural areas. One of NEF's recent key programmes is concerned with religion and democracy. This has involved a roundtable with journalists, commissioning research papers prior to a conference, and stimulating youth debates. This combination of convening, research and participation is characteristic of the way NEF tends to work.

Methods and themes – rethinking roles

Policy influence is a real possibility for many foundations, but for many it will require a reassessment of all of their resources – financial and non-financial – and doing things in new ways to follow through the innovations they begin to achieve wider and longer-term impact.

Studies of foundations and policy change are remarkably consistent in their findings.[18] They suggest that to make an effective contribution to policy thinking and debate, foundations need to rethink their roles. Foundations that seek to achieve sustainable change with an impact beyond their grantees go way beyond conventional grantmaking for demonstration projects. They seek to contribute and effectively communicate new, informed perspectives on issues and problems, and proactively to encourage conversation and action by others.

Grantmaking is only the beginning of a usually long-term process and may be only one strategy in a complex toolbox. These foundations start with an outcome they want to achieve and the desired outcome dictates the strategy. Such foundations do not get stuck in conventional grantmaking or operating boxes; they are not afraid to do things themselves if necessary, but also recognize that grantmaking may not always be the best way of getting things done and reaching the outcome.

Foundations that seek to achieve impact beyond immediate grantees via wider policy change start with an outcome and think hard about how that could be achieved. They tend to accept that social change is a matter of iteration, not cataclysm, and is generally a slow, long-term process. These foundations work on an issue for as long as it takes to achieve the desired outcome – often ten years or more.

Moreover, they rarely see social change as either bottom-up or top-down, but more as a mix of both requiring work at various levels and with multiple strategies. As social change is not entirely predictable, these foundations usually maintain a degree of flexibility in programmes and strategies, and exploit opportunities as one of their tools. They see relationships as one of their key assets and work to build rich networks of different types at various levels.

Contributing effectively to policy thinking and debate involves focus and flexibility. To build reputation and credibility, develop sound knowledge and build rich networks in a particular field, these foundations must focus on a small number of priorities in a limited number of fields. But they must also accept that new ideas require flexibility to take advantage of unforeseen opportunities, new points of access and leverage for change. Perhaps one of the greatest differences between effective policy-oriented foundations and others is the significance attached to communication.

Communication is an essential element in these foundations' toolbox. The precise strategy follows from the theory of change, but goes way beyond the conventional publication of a report or an item in a newsletter or website. Because effective policy contributions addressing

12 practical tips for change

One recent study of foundations and policy influence[19] offers 12 practical tips for change:

1 Think about how widespread social change happens – who or what has to change and how that can be achieved.

2 Question assumptions that 'change just happens' and/or that change can always be achieved from the bottom up. Distinguish between rooting suggested change in the experience and views of those who are disadvantaged and leaving it to them to achieve change alone. Go to where the power to effect change lies.

3 Acknowledge that foundations have resources other than money and identify and build those resources. Invest time and effort in networks and convening; don't underestimate the power of the foundation invitation. Build up and on reputation.

4 Invest in research and evaluation to understand problems/issues, identify solutions and provide credible knowledge of what can be achieved; and make issues human – tell stories.

5 Invest in timely and tailored dissemination to ensure that messages reach those with the direct and indirect power to influence change; tailor messages and recommendations to provide policy-makers with what they need when they need it.

old and new problems often involve challenging the conventional wisdoms and experimenting 'outside the box', policy-oriented foundations accept that they have to take risks. Risk is an occupational hazard.

Making a unique contribution

Too many foundations in Europe are caught in conventional models of philanthropy that fail to do full justice to their true potential. Foundations have never been more important than they are today, in a European context increasingly dominated by short-term market considerations, values of competition and individualism, tensions between security and freedom and 'haves and have-nots'.

Foundations are unique in their capacity and freedom to offer genuinely alternative, wider and longer-term viewpoints free from political and market considerations. Paradoxically, it is foundations' very independence of particular constituencies that enables them at their most creative to make a unique contribution to the quality and quantity of democratic debate and the problem-solving capacity of European society.

6   Reframe issues by seeing things from a different angle and recruiting counter-intuitive supporters.

7   Keep the focus on the message not the messenger. Focus on policies not politics, build cross-party support.

8   Recognize the value of luck, and make luck by positioning; keep scanning the environment for debates and issues related to your work and be flexible enough to take advantage of opportunities; hitch rides on other related issue and policy bandwagons.

9   Stay with an issue long term if necessary – this is one of your unique advantages.

10 Recognize the importance of passion and charismatic individuals and facilitate ways of ensuring that they infect others. Recruit champions to spread the word and gain support.

11 Accept that success has many parents – don't expect to be a lone heroine; value the importance of small roles that may be crucial to the plot (or accept that although you can't make a cake with baking powder alone, a teaspoon or two of baking powder is crucial in making the cake rise successfully). Work collaboratively – begging and borrowing skills, resources and support.

12 Be prepared to take a leadership role if appropriate.

[1] H K Anheier and S Daly, *The Politics of Foundations: A comparative analysis*, London and New York: Routledge, 2007.

[2] S Toepler, 'Foundation roles and visions in the USA', in Anheier and Daly, *The Politics of Foundations*.

[3] Ibid.

[4] Anheier and Daly, *The Politics of Foundations*.

[5] Ibid. Also, L Tayart de Borms, *Foundations: Creating Impact in a Globalised World*, London: John Wiley, 2005.

[6] Anheier and Daly, *The Politics of Foundations*.

[7] See M Kramer, *Scaling Social Impact*, Foundation Strategy Group Perspectives for Private Foundations, Winter 2005.

[8] H K Anheier and D Leat, *Creative Philanthropy*, London: Routledge, 2005. Also, Tayart de Borms, op cit.

[9] See M Rosenman, 'Grantmakers Must Focus on Government's Role', *Chronicle of Philanthropy*, 2005, pp28–44.

[10] N Aron, 'Funding Nonprofit Advocacy: The increasing role of foundations' in R Cohen (ed), *The State of Philanthropy*, NCRP, 2002, pp79–81.

[11] J M Ferris and M Mintrom, 'Foundations and Public Policy Making: A conceptual framework', RP-10, May 2002, www.usc.edu/philanthropy

[12] Tayart de Borms, op cit, p76.

[13] M Rosenman, op cit. See also R A Heifetz, J V Kania and M R Kramer, 'Leading Boldly', *Stanford Social Innovation Review*, Winter 2004, pp21–32.

[14] J Davies, 'The Foundation as a Policy Actor: The case of the Joseph Rowntree Charitable Trust', *The Political Quarterly*, 75 (3), 2004, pp275–84.

[15] www.koerber-stiftung.de

[16] D Leat, *Just Change: Strategies for increasing philanthropic impacts*, London: Association of Charitable Foundations, 2007.

[17] Tayart de Borms, op cit, pp166–7.

[18] D Leat, 'Britain' in Anheier and Daly, *The Politics of Foundations*. See Tayart de Borms, op cit. See also R T Brousseau *Experienced Grantmakers at Work, When creativity comes into play*, New York: The Foundation Center, 2004.

[19] Leat, *Just Change*.

MAXIMILIAN MARTIN

18 Engaged philanthropy and market-based solutions

Private grantmaking foundations have significantly expanded in scale and visibility in recent years. Enthusiasm about a new golden era of philanthropy is widespread and contagious. The reasons are manifold. On the supply side of philanthropic capital, they include trends in growth and holding patterns of wealth, the demographic composition of wealth holders, as well as highly visible commitments from new philanthropists that 'up the ante' in the global philanthropic community.

The pool of philanthropic capital is substantial and growing. In 2006, high-net-worth individuals gave away US$285 billion globally; US foundations collectively held assets in excess of US$550 billion, and the top 50 European foundations had assets of €147.2 billion.[1] Moreover, the largest transfer of wealth in human history will take place by 2052, estimated by various authors to involve between US$25 trillion and US$41 trillion in the US alone, resulting in a huge new social investment potential.[2]

Due to their political independence and capacity to engage in the long term, philanthropic foundations are seen as highly effective intervention agents. Many philanthropists are ambitious and sophisticated. They ask how they can maximize the catalytic effect of their philanthropy. Given this quest, many view venture philanthropy, social enterprise and market-based mechanisms as exciting new conduits for social change.

This essay examines the prospects of market-based solutions for engaged philanthropy. It focuses on the two levers an impact-minded philanthropist can influence:

- The investment side: what are the options for philanthropists seeking to drive greater sums to be distributed towards social investment?

What about alternative investment strategies to raise financial returns or spending down more quickly? What are the prospects of aligning investment policies and philanthropic mission?
– The programme side: what are the options for venture philanthropists? What is the promise of engaged grantmaking and subsidizing self-scaling market-based social change programmes, taking them from initial concept to economic viability?

The 'inefficient market' hypothesis

Top philanthropic foundations – which in some cases surpass governments in the scale of their financial support – benefit from economies of scale and scope in their grantmaking processes and agenda setting. But this is not the case for the majority of charitable foundations. Civil society organizations and grantmakers alike follow a wide range of theories of change and impact assessment, allowing for little standardization. They operate in a fragmented resource allocation system with very high search and capital allocation costs. One study of the US non-profit sector puts the combined costs of grantmaking and fundraising as high as 22–43 per cent, compared to 2–4 per cent in the stock market.[3] Moreover, philanthropic funding decisions are often influenced by personal relationships and based on limited information. Compared to capital allocation processes in stock markets, the 'social capital market' therefore looks fairly inefficient – transaction costs are high as information flows are not robust. Take the case of social entrepreneurs. A recent global survey among 109 social entrepreneurs by SustainAbility revealed that, given the lack of efficient capital allocation processes, 72 per cent of those entrepreneurs considered accessing capital to be the main obstacle to growth (see Figure 1).

Figure 1 Challenges facing social entrepreneurs – respondents select the top two challenges they face in growing their organizations

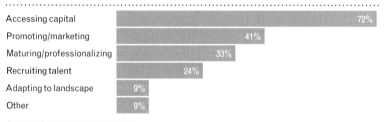

Accessing capital	72%
Promoting/marketing	41%
Maturing/professionalizing	33%
Recruiting talent	24%
Adapting to landscape	9%
Other	9%

Source SustainAbility Ltd, 2007.

These challenges can leave philanthropists frustrated as to how to make a difference. Not only is an individual looking to participate in the philanthropic sector faced with a bewildering array of players, but in many countries the processes of non-profit registration are complex, tax incentives discouraging and regulation stifling. Proponents of the 'inefficient market hypothesis' note that too little value-driven allocation takes place in philanthropy: social investors do not necessarily reward better performers with additional resources because grantmaking is not purely a rational choice, but also relationship-driven.

The emergence of new allocation opportunities

In the foreseeable future, a substantial portion of giving is likely to continue to be relationship-driven. But the relative importance of philanthropic capital seeking high returns is increasing fast, mirroring trends in mainstream investing. Globalization and geopolitical events increasingly drive capital towards under-attended populations. This creates opportunities to do good and do well at the same time.

We have entered a period of experimentation with blended social and financial returns. Emerging market funds are becoming more relevant. They are often theme-oriented, including sustainable development, environment, water, renewable energy, housing and small enterprise. Ethical funds, sustainable investments and socially responsible ventures – commonly aggregated under the umbrella term socially responsible investments (SRI) – have seen substantive growth in recent years. The market for SRI funds was estimated to be around US$2.2 trillion in the US alone in 2007.[4] A recent study estimated the market for SRI funds in Europe to be over €1 trillion, accounting for 10–15 per cent of assets under management and a real growth of 36 per cent (absolute growth was 106 per cent).[5] In Europe, there were an estimated 375 SRI funds in October 2007.[6]

In the foundation world, doing good and doing well at the same time is often referred to as blended-value or mission investing – investing (a part of) the endowment to achieve both financial and social returns. Conceptually, this is straightforward. If charitable foundations look holistically at expenditure and investment policies as complementary ways to further their mission, they can generate greater social impact. In addition to distributing 2–5 per cent of assets every year, a foundation could also invest some part of the other 95–98 per cent of its assets in investments furthering its mission, provided it can do so without sacrificing the financial returns on endowment assets.

The challenge consists of moving from concept to implementation. Many foundations and philanthropists still hold a binary view: as donors, they are happy to make grants that have no financial return.[7] By contrast, as investors they prioritize financially profitable investments, albeit deploying very conservative investment strategies when acting as foundation board members. From a social impact perspective, this preference is counterintuitive. In terms of market efficiency the optimal intervention in social and economic terms is a function of the issue the philanthropist seeks to address, and is likely to fall somewhere between these two binary opposites. Of course, some social investments may never provide a direct positive economic return, although they may contribute to positive change indirectly, for example through democratic development and upholding of human rights.

There are now clear signs of innovation in social finance. New allocation processes are coming on stream that leverage market mechanisms to efficiently target capital to address pressing social and environmental issues. Whether and how quickly these approaches will become mainstream is the sector's trillion-dollar question.

Leveraging financial investments for social change

Individual philanthropists and foundations have begun to explore to what extent capital markets and financial innovation can serve a philanthropic mission. This involves a two-part inquiry: how to obtain greater returns so that more money is available for philanthropic programmes; and how to increase the alignment of the social impact generated in the creation of economic value with a foundation's philanthropic objectives.

This inquiry can be powerful. For an endowed foundation, rather than focusing exclusively on the 2–5 per cent of the total endowment distributed in any given year, it implies focusing also on the remaining 95–98 per cent of assets. For a foundation board, this raises the following set of questions:

- Should we engage in 'limited-life philanthropy' by accelerating the rate of spending and aiming to spend down the endowment within a foreseeable timeframe?
- If we do not want to sacrifice the permanence of the endowment, how can the foundation generate higher risk-adjusted financial returns through investments in alternative asset classes?
- Finally, in the ordinary conduct of investment, how can the foundation invest a larger part of the endowment in assets that

create both risk-adjusted financial returns *and* a social impact that is aligned with the foundation's mission?

Done properly, all three potential routes of action – pursued individually or in combination – have the potential to significantly increase a foundation's ability to make a difference. All three require properly addressing challenges and handling risks.

Limited-life philanthropy

Spending down an endowment within a predetermined timeframe is an idea frequently considered. To assess the rationale, take the case of The Atlantic Philanthropies, established by one of the founders of Duty Free Shoppers, Chuck Feeney. Through the third quarter of 2006, Atlantic had awarded grants worth €2.5 billion. It adopted a spending policy to dispose of remaining assets of around €2.7 billion – and future returns on these assets – thoughtfully, stopping active grantmaking by 2016, ie, €233+ million per year for grants. The goal is to go out of business before 2020. Five points deserve consideration.

First, from a social impact perspective, spending down makes sense if the benefits of allocating much more money to a social issue today (or in the near future) substantially outweigh the benefits of a long-term stream of reliable lower levels of funding. In some issue areas, the opportunity cost of not spending more today is so high that the case for greater spending today is clear.

Consider the area of public health, where prevention is generally cheaper than treatment. For example, the fourth Millennium Development Goal (MDG) calls for the reduction of the mortality rate of children under five by two-thirds by 2015. Immunization programmes are critical to achieving this MDG, and much cheaper than treating common childhood diseases. Yet successful and comprehensive immunization remains an under-resourced challenge. The World Health Organization (WHO) estimates that 27 million infants have not received the DTP3 vaccine in 2003 and are not vaccinated against common childhood diseases, including diphtheria, tetanus, hepatitis B, yellow fever, measles and polio.[8]

Second, in many jurisdictions, foundations can be designed to operate in perpetuity. But this may not always be the most sensible strategy. If one looks at history, there are remarkable institutions surviving over long periods of time. For example, the largest grant-giver to London-only causes, the Bridge House Trust, dates back to 1097 (it was renamed the City Bridge Trust in 2007). The ability to operate in 'historical time' is an important motivator for many philanthropists. They institutionalize their giving in foundations to transcend the founder's biological lifespan.[9]

But foundations are constrained by the regulatory, political and socioeconomic contexts in which they operate. In European countries such as France and Germany, foundation endowments suffered tremendously at specific junctures during the past 200 years, when revolution and the consequences of war such as hyperinflation led to asset seizure by governments or destruction of endowments' monetary value in real terms.[10]

Third, because it is difficult to reverse, a spend-down decision is a pivotal moment in an organization's life. Such a decision needs to be carefully considered. Reflecting on the case of Atlantic Philanthropies, John Healy, its CEO from 2001 to 2007, remembers:[11]

> 'So we took care to make sure that every director was signed up to the policy to spend down. That was achieved without too much difficulty but the hardest person to bring to the point of finality was Chuck Feeney himself – the person whose reluctance to build an institution for the long term had got us to that point. Did he have last minute doubts about the course I was proposing? I do not think so. Chuck Feeney is the quintessential entrepreneur, and entrepreneurs prize flexibility above all else. They do not like to be put in corners from which they cannot escape. And there was something very final about this decision. Happily, once he had signed up to the spend-down decision Chuck Feeney became enormously enthusiastic about it.'

Fourth, spending very heavily over a short period of time implies that the typical grants will be larger than those made by the average foundation. Greater grant size requires more intensive due diligence. At the same time, the foundation must not turn due diligence into a process that stifles creativity and breeds excessive risk aversion, undercutting its ability to achieve the mission.

Finally, a decision to spend down has important implications for the investment policy. In the case of Atlantic, almost 50 per cent of the assets were in absolute return strategies in 2007, almost a quarter in private equity, about 12 per cent in the foundation's commercial interests, and the balance in conventional asset classes such as bonds. Time consistency between payout, investment and termination of positions needs to be factored into the investment policy.

Raising risk-adjusted financial returns

Limited-life philanthropy may be worthwhile under certain circumstances. But the bulk of endowed foundations seek sustainability and continuity.

Boards thus typically distribute an amount of the assets that will allow for the near perpetual existence of the foundation. Mandated to 'preserve and shepherd assets', and often not held accountable for maximizing risk-adjusted returns, foundation investment committees tend to adopt highly conservative investment policies. Many foundations determine annual distributions based upon a conservative formula often related to the anticipated return on investments in cash and cash equivalents. There is frequently little pressure to adjust the model.

Moreover, the fact that most European countries do not mandate payout rates removes structural incentives to seek higher returns.[12] As a result, the investment policies of European foundations are typically far less aggressive than those of their North American counterparts. Consider the typical foundation asset allocation comparing European foundations, US foundations, and US university foundations (see Table 1). This difference in asset allocation strategies could be attributed to a variety of 'investment cultures' based on different risk profiles. But a more plausible explanation is higher performance pressure from a minimal mandatory payout rate in the US.

Table 1 European and US foundations' asset allocation

	Pooled funds	Money market	Real estate	Alternatives	Affiliated companies	Fixed income	Equity
European foundations	11	9	5	6	25	20	24
US foundations	5	5	1	12	6	18	53
US university foundations	0	2	4	30	0	16	48

Source Watson Wyatt, 2006–07.

Compared to their US counterparts, European foundations hold much lower percentages of alternative asset classes such as hedge funds and private equity, and greater percentages of stock in affiliated companies. In terms of returns, the implications are substantial: lower returns imply lower payout rates – in 2006, the top 50 European foundations paid out €3.8 billion on assets of €147.2 billion, whereas the top 50 US foundations paid out €6 billion on assets of €133.1 billion (see Table 2).

Table 2 Payout vs total assets, top 50 European and US foundations, 2006

	Aggregated assets (€ million)	Total charitable spending (€ million)	Payout ratio (%) Aggregate	Average	Median	St. Dev.
Top 50 Europe	147,212	3,804	2.6	3.4	2.2	4.6
Top 50 US	133,086	6,009	4.5	4.6	4.6	1.9

Source Watson Wyatt, 2007.

Even if external pressure is lacking, raising the average annual return on the total endowment remains a valuable strategy for greater impact. Funding a foundation's programmatic work today without compromising its ability to pursue such work in the future requires that the endowment generate sufficient financial returns. Consider the impact of, say, 2 per cent added return on the foundation's overall long-run capacity to distribute and fulfil its mission!

In practice, evidence suggests that higher risk-adjusted returns cannot be achieved without investing in alternative asset classes, such as private equity or hedge funds. In alternative asset classes, however, empirical evidence shows a wide variety of performance between top-decile, top-quartile and other funds.

For foundations, the ability to access top-performing funds is critical to obtaining higher returns. Large endowments can more easily afford to develop in-house the expertise needed to access top-decile funds and to meet the minimum investment required when allocating an appropriate percentage of the endowment in alternative asset classes. By contrast, smaller foundations often face structural barriers in accessing such funds when they act on their own, and need to look for pooling solutions.

There is still a great potential for European foundations to raise the risk-adjusted returns on their endowments. Thus far, the combined effect of structural factors driving risk aversion of board members and scarcity of effective alternative asset pooling solutions for foundations means that many foundations have not yet maximized returns. But this is now changing.

According to philanthropists Daniel Schwartz and Rafael Meyer, proactive boards must address three potential traps undercutting the commitment to maximize risk-adjusted returns:[13]

'Making money is what is done outside of the foundation, and when it comes to discussions of investment and endowment management, too often we hear "Do not embarrass me," "Do not surprise me" dominating the instructions given to those handling the investments of the endowment. Foundation boards and investment committees fall into a few common traps. One is adopting an ultra-conservative approach to investment management motivated by the correct and honorable desires to preserve assets. Another trap is to treat the endowment's management as a reward to a trusted family member or friend, or to keep a high concentration of assets in a related company or entity, and in many cases without a comprehensive portfolio analysis including risk-adjusted return. While reputable banks and advisors can elucidate the risks and downsides of the second trap, avoiding the ultra-conservative "no surprises" "no embarrassments" investment strategy is much more challenging. Inertia is another trap. Why should any of the involved parties be an active agent for change? Who wants to be the banker, board member, investment committee member, or senior staff member who was responsible for any section of the portfolio that underperformed investment returns on the safest investments?'

Aligning investment and mission

To date, mission investing is still a cottage industry. Foundations seeking to invest in social enterprises with such 'hybrid' returns face a specific set of challenges, which are largely regulatory and transaction cost-driven. For example, under US tax laws non-profit foundations can make programme-related investments (PRI) in profitable organizations that advance the foundation's mission. PRI investments are beneficial to a foundation as they count as part of the required 5 per cent payout and are not booked as part of the endowment. This means they do not count towards calculation of the next year's 5 per cent payout requirement and any capital gain is not included in the excise tax. So PRI investments, unlike regular endowment investments, are an 'off-the-books' investment to be dealt with only when they earn income or are sold. Even then, rules are simple: any income or gains must be given away or reinvested in another PRI within the same year in addition to the 5 per cent already allocated for that year.

Notwithstanding, PRIs remain the exception. A recent study on US foundation mission investing identified 1,030 mission investing intermediaries and 92 foundations that have mission investments. Collectively, approximately one-third of these 92 foundations committed no more than US$521 million.[14] Interestingly, many of the emerging social ventures in the US continue to be largely grant-financed and fairly small. A recent study of emerging US for-profit ventures – defined as under 30 years old – targeted more than 200 CEOs and top managers of for-profit companies based in the US who identified their companies as 'social

282 PHILANTHROPY IN EUROPE

ventures'. The study found that of 155 respondents, 72 per cent of social
ventures reported revenues below US$1 million, including a quarter of
the sample with no revenues. The median revenue was US$100,000 to
US$250,000.[15]

In Europe, there is also considerable interest in mission investing.
But in most European countries, the scene is even less developed than in
the US. In some cases, the regulatory hurdles are considerable because
no equivalent of the PRI process exists and foundations need to seek
approval from regulators. The results are therefore meagre. A recent study
of foundations involved in mission investing lists only a few European
foundations, for example the Canopus Foundation (40 per cent of assets,
mainly in wind parks), the Esmee Fairbairn Foundation (loans to non-profits,
under 1 per cent of the endowment) and the Shell Foundation (socially
targeted venture capital-type investments in East Africa).[16]

Framework conditions are improving in some countries, creating
new asset allocation opportunities. For example, in 2006 the UK established
a new limited company type, the Community Interest Company (CIC).
CICs must conduct a business or other activity for community benefit,
and not purely for private advantage. Through certain qualification tests
(community interest test) and an 'asset lock', regulations ensure that the
CIC is established for community purposes and the assets and profits
are deployed accordingly. However, a CIC can have both non-profit and
for-profit ownership, potentially opening it to investors across the spectrum.

Leveraging grantmaking for social change

Re-examining how financial investments can be leveraged for social
change is a powerful option for foundations seeking greater social impact.
However, grantmaking remains the bread-and-butter activity for most
philanthropists and foundations. Significant innovations are taking place in
this domain as well.

Predating the wave of innovation in foundation finance, a more
engaged approach to philanthropy is gaining ground more generally. The
emergence of venture philanthropy in Europe is accelerating.[17] To date, in
many European countries, there are still only a few venture philanthropy
organizations and they are small compared to traditional charitable
foundations.

But various efforts to nurture this new, albeit small-scale movement
are under way, and some are very promising. Europe has seen a particularly
successful effort through the creation of the European Venture Philanthropy
Association (EVPA) in 2004. The EVPA, a membership organization,

promotes the expansion of venture philanthropy in Europe.
It had 62 members in January 2008, up from only 39 members in
December 2006.[18]

Engaged grantmaking

The majority of venture philanthropy organizations (VPs) practise what
can be called 'engaged grantmaking'. They carefully select grantee
organizations and, beyond money, provide a range of value-added
services to enable grantees to achieve greater scale, effectiveness and
sustainability. A recent survey of 35 VPs provides the following picture:[19]

- **A focus on start-up philanthropy** VPs focus overwhelmingly on
  supporting early or expansion-stage civil society organizations.
  In the sample, 86 per cent of the respondent organizations focus
  on growth, 63 per cent on early stage, 46 per cent on established
  organizations, and 14 per cent on mergers (multiple priorities
  possible).
- **Micro-size** Most supported organizations are very small. Over half
  have only one to five staff.
- **Some involvement in governance** VPs take a less interventionist
  approach than venture capitalists, but they tend to be more
  involved than 'traditional' foundations. In the sample, 15 per cent
  of respondents report a board seat as a requirement for funding,
  whereas 24 per cent do not get involved at board level; 61 per cent
  reserve the right to take board places in individual cases.
- **Mainly traditional financing instruments** Grantmaking remains
  the preferred means of financing target organizations, but there are
  some interesting innovations: 83 per cent of the respondents make
  grants, 63 per cent make loans, 43 per cent take equity, and 26 per
  cent engage in mezzanine financing. Given the strong interest in
  financial innovation, new tools are likely to become significant in the
  medium term.
- **Involvement beyond financial instruments** Many funds
  contribute services related to strategy, governance, financial
  management, fundraising and access to networks. Such services
  are delivered either through in-house capabilities or by third parties.

Subsidizing the emergence of market-based solutions

Given the right recipient, engaged grantmaking can add substantive value.
From a social impact perspective, one subset is particularly exciting:
potentially profitable social investment opportunities that require a kick-off

subsidy, but are ultimately self-scaling and profitable. Such organizations are often referred to as 'social enterprises'. As they are typically too small and risky to be considered as financial investments, it makes sense to treat them as part of a foundation's programmatic activities.

Distinguishing opportunities from bottomless pits requires understanding sustainability in the emerging social investment landscape. 'Social enterprise' and 'social entrepreneurs' serve as umbrella terms used in many ways.[20]

In a nutshell, grants are the most effective form of financing for social entrepreneurs whose activities cannot reasonably be expected to become financially self-sustaining because they provide social rather than economic benefits. Applying economic theory, we can refer to them as public-good social entrepreneurs.

By contrast, some small and medium enterprises, microfinance institutions and social entrepreneurs provide 'private goods'. They create a substantive economic benefit for their constituents. These organizations should be able to monetize a part of the benefits created to cover costs. This is the idea behind microfinance. Indeed, some microfinance institutions have returns on equity equivalent to, or higher than, some successful large banks. Experience shows that a mix of capacity-building grants and for-profit investments is the most effective way to support such private-good social entrepreneurs. We can thus divide potential social investment targets into four sub-categories (see Table 3):

- Small and medium enterprises with a demonstrated social impact. These are real-sector for-profit companies that create both social and economic benefits[21] – for example, by offering jobs in depressed areas or producing goods and services that carry positive externalities in sectors such as healthcare.
- Social entrepreneurs that provide private goods. These are mission-driven real-sector for-profit or not-for-profit organizations that create both social and economic benefits.
- Social entrepreneurs that provide public goods. These are mission-driven, real-sector, not-for-profit organizations that create mainly social benefits.
- Microfinance institutions. Microfinance institutions work in the financial sector and create both economic and social benefits. Ranging from very small non-profit associations to large commercial banks, they serve the poor by extending very small loans and other products to the unemployed, poor entrepreneurs or others living in poverty. Such organizations can have a variety of

legal statuses, including as foundations, cooperatives, credit unions, non-bank financial institutions or fully-fledged banks.

Table 3 Disaggregating social enterprise investment opportunities

Category	Sector	Type of benefit	Investment solution	Opportunity
Small to medium enterprises	Real	Economic and social	Equity or loan deals	Theme funds
Private good social enterprises	Real	Economic and social	Loan deals and technical assistance	Loan funds (eg irrigation, housing)
Public good social enterprises	Real	Social	Grant and technical assistance	Donor collaboratives
Microfinance institutions	Financial	Economic and social	Equity or loan deals	Second tier funds

Applying the tools of investment banking can reduce the transaction costs of capital allocation. Consider, for example, the creation of funds with various tranches of target returns and risk exposure and collateralized debt obligations: a wide range of investment instruments above or below risk-adjusted market returns is conceivable.[22] An important constraint to drawing additional financial resources into financing private good social entrepreneurs is the challenge of identifying, characterizing and qualifying pools of possible investments and then aggregating them into sufficiently large capital pools to meet the minimal size requirements for the financial services industry.

From a fundraising perspective, defining risk-return characteristics that are attractive to philanthropically minded investors is also critical. For loan funds, LIBOR plus x type formulas (the interest rate banks charge each other for inter-bank loans) offer a greater alignment with general interest rate conditions than do low fixed-interest rates.

Given that such funding mechanisms are new in the field of social enterprise, a look at financial innovation in the field of microfinance can provide a sense of their potential future relevance. In the sizeable and growing microfinance market, the sophistication of funding mechanisms has progressed substantively in the past ten years. The 2005 Microcredit

286 PHILANTHROPY IN EUROPE

Survey acknowledges more than 3,164 microfinance institutions reporting over 92 million microenterprise clients worldwide, of which over 70 per cent are among the poorest.[23] Its 2000 survey reported market data at one-third of its current size. Many specialized fund management boutiques and fund advisers have emerged, offering various tailored products for specific groups of investors. Some global banks have also started their own funds. Innovative transactions include taking first-loss positions in collateralized debt obligations and securitizations or guaranteeing bonds and local debt loans. Social enterprise investment vehicles are the likely next wave of innovation.

Market-based solutions – *quo vadis*?
There is strong evidence that an inefficient social capital market has burdened the non-profit sector with high transaction costs and constrained its growth, producing fragmentation of initiatives. This is well documented in the case of the US, where fewer than 0.1 per cent of non-profits founded in 1970 or after had reached an annual turnover of US$50 million or more by 2003.[24] However, the status quo is now changing. Partially inspired by the enormous success of some US university endowments, foundation boards and philanthropists are becoming more ambitious on the investment side, seeking to allocate a larger percentage of the endowments in alternative asset classes such as private equity or hedge funds.

Mission investing makes sense conceptually but is still at an early stage in Europe. To emerge on a massive scale, it will require the emergence of a liquid market for mission-related investments. But market-based solutions are advancing. Innovative capital market transactions such as the International Finance Facility for Immunization Bond serve as a source of inspiration, providing a solution for frontloading resources needed for scaling up immunization efforts. Over the next few years, it is likely that financial innovation in the social enterprise field will create exciting new opportunities for leveraging philanthropic resources. By funding first-loss tranches or issuing guarantees, philanthropists and foundations can bring additional commercial capital to the table.

Realism is nevertheless required. Challenges remain concerning the design of specialized financial products. They include cost-effective due diligence processes, the identification of a critical mass of reliable deal flow, technical challenges regarding product design, and achieving alignment with social investor preferences. The experience of microfinance shows that to operate at a reasonable scale and risk characteristics, most for-profit social investment opportunities require some philanthropic capital for a considerable amount of time, be it in the form of technical assistance and capacity-building grants, or of first-loss commitments or loan guarantees that transform junk paper into investment grade.

Let us also keep in mind that creating market-based solutions for engaged philanthropists and foundations is not merely a technocratic exercise. Designing mechanisms for minimizing transaction costs for philanthropic capital is an important challenge, but it can be solved only if we do not neglect the experiential dimension of philanthropy. The philanthropic impulse comes from the heart. Scalable solutions are likely to provide an effective combination of the relational element in philanthropy with sophisticated financial engineering.

[1] *World Wealth Report*, Capgemini/Merrill Lynch, 2007, p 21; *Foundation Yearbook*, Foundation Center, 2006; *European Foundations: Report on Top 50 ranking and database*, Watson Wyatt, 2007.

[2] J J Havens and P G Schervish, *Millionaires and the Millennium: New estimates of the forthcoming wealth transfer and the prospects for a golden age of philanthropy*, Social Welfare Research Institute, Boston College, 1999. See also M Zesbaugh, *Discovering the American Legacy: Findings from a landmark study on boomer/parent relations and the $25 trillion issue*, Allianz, 2005.

[3] W F Meehan, D Kilmer and M O'Flanagan, 'Investing in Society', *Stanford Social Innovation Review*, Spring 2004, p35.

[4] Data from 2007, SiRI Company.

[5] *European SRI Study*, Eurosif, 2006.

[6] Source: Forma Futura Invest.

[7] A Wood and M Martin, 'Market-based Solutions for Financing Philanthropy', *Viewpoints 2006*, UBS Philanthropy Services, 2006.

[8] In 2006, an estimated 2.1 million people around the world died of vaccine-preventable diseases, including 1.4 million children under five. Many more fall sick, miss school and become part of the vicious cycle that links poor health to continued poverty in adulthood. See www.who.int/mediacentre/factsheets/fs288/en/index.html. Borrowing against future grant pledges through a capital markets transaction, the GAVI Alliance (formerly known as the Global Alliance for Vaccines and Immunization) was able to tackle a time-critical public health issue – immunization – prior to the actual disbursement of the funds by donor governments. See Matrix Group paper 'F4F – Finance for Foundations', *UBS Philanthropy Services, 2007*.

[9] See M Martin, *Strategic Legacy Creation*, 2004.

[10] Only two of the large US foundations were founded before the depression in 1929 (Rockefeller and Carnegie). Many well-known European foundations were already in place in the 1920s. In several countries, they had to absorb the trauma of hyperinflation, which destroyed the real value of the endowment, which thereafter had to be rebuilt completely. In this context, it is not surprising that in many European countries, legislation allows foundations to own majority stakes in companies (which was forbidden in the US in 1969). A high spending rate could jeopardize the longevity of the company and thereby also (often) the only asset of the foundation.

[11] John R Healy, 'Giving while Living: The implications of limited-life philanthropy', *Viewpoints 2008*, pp84–7. UBS Philanthropy Services, 2008.

[12] In the US, 5 per cent of foundation assets minus administrative charges have to be paid out every year to qualifying charitable recipients for the foundation to retain charitable status.

[13] Matrix Group paper 'F4F – Finance for Foundations', UBS Philanthropy Services, 2007.

[14] M Kramer and S Cooch, *Aggregating Impact: A funder's guide to mission investment intermediaries*, FSG Social Impact Advisors, November 2007, p5.

[15] C Clark and S Ucak, *For-Profit Social Entrepreneur Report, RISE*, March 2006, p26.

[16] See M Kramer and S Cooch, *Investing for Impact*, Foundation Strategy Group, 2006.

[17] Currently, there are several competing definitions of what venture philanthropy is or should be, and how it relates to venture capital.

[18] In January 2008, EVPA had 17 full members, 42 associate members, and 3 honorary members. Among the 17 full EVPA members listed in the website, 5 are from the UK, 3 from France, 2 from Italy, 2 from the Netherlands, 1 from Estonia, 1 from Germany, 1 from Hungary, 1 from Ireland, and 1 from Spain.

[19] The data comes from R John, *Venture Philanthropy: Evolution and opportunities*, presentation at the WINGS Forum 2006 on Emerging Patterns in New Philanthropy, Bangkok (www.wingsweb.org/forum06/documents/Track2_emerging_John.pdf) and personal data from the author.

[20] See M Martin, *Surveying Social Entrepreneurship*, University of St Gallen, 2004; M Martin, *Investing in the Emerging Social Enterprise Landscape, Giving*, 1/2007.

[21] The 'real sector' refers to economic activity in the primary (agriculture), secondary (industry) and tertiary (services) sectors, except financial services.

[22] M Martin, 'Aggregating Demand, Targeting Impact', *Viewpoints 2007*, UBS Philanthropy Services, 2007.

[23] S Daley-Harris, *State of the Microcredit Summit Campaign Report 2005*, Microcredit Summit Campaign, 2005.

[24] W Foster and Gail Fine, 'How Nonprofits Get Really Big', *Stanford Social Innovation Review*, Spring 2007.

GERRY SALOLE

19 The importance of there being a European foundation statute

Algy: **Do you mean you couldn't love me if I had a different name?**
Cecily: **But what name?**
Algy: **Well . . . Algy, for instance.**
Cecily: **I might respect you, Ernest, I might admire your character, but I feel that I could never give you my undivided attention.**
Oscar Wilde, *The Importance of being Earnest*

It feels slightly odd to be writing the concluding chapter in a book that is attempting to capture the flavour, dimensions and history of the myriad European foundations and having to virtually plead for foundations to be taken more seriously by European politicians, journalists, pundits and the general public. There has been a disturbing tendency in some quarters to adopt the term 'foundation' to evoke the image of probity and benevolence that it conveys, and apply it to obscure, less noble causes such as commercial enterprises that are, in fact, very thinly disguised self-serving efforts to protect and hold on to assets.

But if anything, the very strength and resilience of philanthropic impulse and agency in Europe have actually contributed to a rather droll situation where it appears that many Europeans hold a vague instinctively positive and generally trusting attitude to the notion of 'foundations' while simultaneously being blissfully ignorant and confused about what precisely a foundation is and what it does – something that we trust this book will contribute to redress. The irony of having the EU institutions increasingly requiring assistance and resources from foundations, while simultaneously pointedly failing to respond to, even dismissing, foundations' exigencies from the European treaties, is marked.

Currently, there is a vital element missing from the landscape of European philanthropy. EU citizens are at liberty to travel, study and work in other EU countries and set up transnational European companies, but the rapidly growing foundation sector does not enjoy the same cross-border freedoms. As Europe tackles disaffection with the EU project, one might imagine that the EU would be anxious to offer its citizens a way to pool their expertise and financial resources for projects of public benefit and European interest. However, there is a notable absence of such anxiousness, which is why the European Foundation Centre (EFC), strongly supported by our members, has in recent years been pressing for a European foundation statute at national and European level.

The European foundation statute would ideally be a new, optional, public-benefit legal tool governed by European law and complementing existing national laws. To avoid any risk of ambiguity, it is important that we constantly stress that there is no desire whatsoever for the statute to circumvent existing laws in EU Member States. We want the statute to reflect a European mortar that will cement existing bricks of national legislation to form a coherent environment conducive to foundations' work at both local and cross-border levels. The eventual statute should, however, not become an aggregate 'lowest common denominator' of national foundation laws.

A feasibility study

As recently as November 2006, Internal Market Commissioner Charlie McCreevy dismayed advocates of a European foundation statute by saying that he was 'not yet convinced about the ability of a European foundation statute to respond to the specific needs of foundations', which showed a disappointingly low level of enthusiasm, and was seen by some to suggest that the European Commission's avowed plans to adopt such a statute might be shelved. EFC and its members reacted immediately by expressing their disappointment to the Commissioner, particularly given that McCreevy had previously announced that the Commission would launch a feasibility study on a European foundation statute in 2007.

Fortunately, the feasibility study has since gone ahead, following the strong reaction to the Commission's spring 2006 consultation on future priorities in European Company Law & Corporate Governance, a process in which we are proud to say that many EFC members and national foundation networks participated. In fact, nearly a third of all those who replied were foundations, all of whom unanimously urged the Commission to carry out the study. They emphasized that an optional statute would foster cross-border activity and cooperation between foundations and funders, and would help achieve several of the EU's own objectives.

The feasibility study began in autumn 2007. Run by the Max Planck Institute for International Private Law and the Centre for Social Investment at the University of Heidelberg, it aims to provide an overview of the main regulatory differences as affecting foundations across the

Member States, as well as an inventory of the main internal market barriers impeding foundations, and an estimation of the costs triggered by such obstacles. It will also assess the critical mass of the foundation sector and its economic footprint, as well as the impact a statute would have on Europe's philanthropic sector and the EU's economy as a whole. The study will contemplate various options for overcoming obstacles to cross-border activity and the consequential necessary regulatory measures, including the development of a European foundation statute.

Reasons for optimism

In addition to the current feasibility study, on the political side Members of the European Parliament have recently lent their support to the European foundation statute cause. In July 2006, the European Parliament called on the Commission to continue work on a statute. Speaking at EFC's conference in June 2007, Manuel Medina Ortega, a Spanish MEP and member of the EP's Committee on Legal Affairs, said that a European foundation statute is needed because 'we have to develop European [structures], and one way of developing European [structures] is through foundations . . .' And in October 2007, the office of the EU President, Jose Manuel Barroso, wrote to me stressing that the Commission was 'fully aware of the benefits such a statute would bring to foundations in the internal market'.

In December 2007, the EU's Science and Research Commissioner, Janez Potoçnik, went into greater detail on the benefits the European Commission believes that a European foundation statute may provide. He stressed that the feasibility study on the statute will provide a comprehensive overview of the European foundation sector's role and importance, taking into account information on existing barriers to cross-border cooperation. It will analyse how these barriers might be eliminated, and will assess the potential impact of establishing a European foundation statute. On the fiscal side of things, over the last couple of years the Commission and European Court of Justice have also taken an encouraging step of initiating work on ending discriminatory tax treatment of public-benefit organizations across the EU.

The growth of philanthropy in Europe

The foundation sector is expanding dynamically and already makes a significant contribution to Europe's sustainable economic growth and development. Recent history reflects a number of developments. Approximately one-third of foundations in the largest EU countries, including France and Germany, have been established since 1990. By 2000, there were approximately 62,000 public-benefit foundations across the EU, which works out at roughly one foundation for every 7,000 people.

How can this accelerated growth be explained? It is in large part due to escalating levels of private wealth both within and outside Europe. In 2004, there were more than 27,000 foundations with assets of €174 billion, based in just eight EU countries. Their combined spending was approximately €51 billion. As a sector, foundations also play an important role as employers. Each of the 10,500 plus foundations which have their headquarters in seven EU countries employed an average of 18 staff, which accounts for nearly 200,000 jobs in those countries alone.

Foundations also give grants or capital support to activities that generate employment, creating and sustaining initiatives in their respective fields. The phenomenon of the privatization of Italian savings banks to create some 85 foundations is being mimicked and augurs well for further privatizations of savings banks elsewhere in Europe. Norway is just one example of this trend.

Looking a few years ahead, we expect to see the philanthropically inclined 'baby-boomer' generation transferring a large slice of the wealth they have amassed from new industries such as information technology and bio-science to the kind of activities for the 'public good' which coincide substantially with the areas in which foundations have expertise.

Barriers preventing international cooperation

The foundation sector in Europe is not only growing in terms of numbers but also in its outreach. In particular, cross-border and multilateral work has experienced a boom. In 2007 two-thirds of EFC's members were working beyond the borders of their home country – a dramatic change from the situation just a few years ago when this was very much the exception. Individual and corporate donors are also becoming more mobile, increasing their assets or investments in several countries. But the framework of laws that ought to be facilitating foundations' attempts to reach beyond national borders has simply not been keeping up with the needs of philanthropists.

One striking example of this growing international mindset is the Rural Investment Support for Europe (RISE) Foundation, a new initiative to promote investment in rural conservation and renewal, and to advance private property and cooperation between landowners and rural communities in Europe and beyond. The Foundation aims principally to operate across all 27 EU countries and thus faces the challenge of supporting transnational projects, and dealing with 27 different legal systems. During the Foundation's establishment, considerable thought was devoted to the best way of inserting what is essentially a transnational, primarily trans-European, philanthropic player into national legal systems in view of the current absence of any European framework to help the Foundation attain its objectives. The Foundation decided to base itself in Belgium but stressed that it would adopt the European foundation statute as soon as the option became available. Its Executive Committee Chairman, Corrado Pirzio-Biroli, has expressed his dismay at the increasing absurdity represented by ignoring the need for a European foundation statute in a single market.

The RISE Foundation is just one example among countless others related to the ongoing struggle foundations are facing when engaging internationally. Unfortunately, the barriers to cross-border work are numerous. One obstacle is that it is difficult to ensure that national authorities recognize the legal personality of foreign-domiciled foundations. There is also an unhelpful climate of legal insecurity over achieving national recognition of the 'general interest' nature of resident foundations' work outside the borders of that country of residence. The parochial and, dare we suggest, at times even xenophobic nature of what constitutes the 'public good' all too frequently does not extend across international boundaries.

A further barrier is the plethora of rules and regulations with which foundations are obliged to wrestle. Not only do they have to accommodate to the various national laws of all the countries in which they are active, they must often, especially in federal states like Germany, or Spain's network of autonomous communities, also satisfy regional laws. Suffice to say, this is a far cry from what would ideally be a sort of 'one-stop shop' allowing foundations to register just once, subsequently liberating them to operate elsewhere.

Not so. Instead, foundations are obliged to set up multiple branches in different countries in order to carry out their transnational work, and are met with a considerable extra administrative burden and unnecessary increased costs, which together erode the sum of money available to spend on their target beneficiaries – Europe's citizens. This means that creative new European initiatives can often be delayed simply because the appropriate legal tools are lacking. Who can doubt that Europe's laws ought to be allowing foundations to pool their resources in funding public-benefit projects?

The current unimaginative and obstructive state of affairs smacks of inertia and scarcely embodies the EU's vision of a Europe without frontiers. Finally, there are barriers that take the form of 'user-hostile'

294 PHILANTHROPY IN EUROPE

fiscal environments. Considerable sums that would otherwise benefit public-interest causes are leached away by tax laws that often treat foundations more harshly than commercial companies. Non-resident bodies can also suffer from additional discrimination where national laws favour locally domiciled operators to the detriment of foundations based elsewhere.

Impediments to collaboration
The establishment of bodies such as EFC, the Network of European Foundation for Innovative Cooperation (NEF) and Donors and Foundations Networks in Europe (DAFNE) has proved that a strong instinct for initiative and for ever-closer relationships exists in this sector. But, frustratingly, we cannot justifiably claim that there has been a similar degree of effort from officialdom at the EU level.

How exactly does the current tissue of national laws cause disillusion among Europe's foundations which are working creatively and with initiative to promote the role and development of civil society across the continent? Perhaps it helps if we understand that the current mishmash of laws is based on a fundamental contradiction. Despite the much-vaunted concept of a common European citizenship, EU nationals cannot exercise the full range of EU-wide citizens' rights to which they are theoretically entitled, such as the right to set up European foundations. It's possible to establish pan-European companies, but the equivalent opportunity for philanthropic organizations is denied to those who work in the civil society sector. Until a statute and a more tax-friendly environment for cross-border funding becomes a reality, the foundation sector will remain obliged to develop work-around and cumbersome, albeit creative, fix-it solutions to operate across borders.

Take for instance the EUSTORY Foundation, also described as the History Network for Young Europeans, an initiative led by the Körber-Stiftung and a consortium of other European foundations, which decided to set up a pan-European foundation. The EUSTORY network seeks to explore European history from the grassroots level and recognize the diversity of experiences. The network has brought young people together to discuss such historically pivotal episodes as the holocaust, anti-Semitism and the legacy of dictatorships in Europe and has so far involved more than 90,000 participants and some 40,000 research papers with a total budget of €11 million. This type of project would benefit immensely from the backing of a European foundation. It would be strengthened by pan-European structure and funding, which could also potentially ensure that endowments were balanced in a sustainable manner, spending on short-term needs, and thus making this type of organization financially much sounder. As we have stressed, these are obvious reasons for the statute to be embraced.

Positive by-products

We have attempted to outline the nature of the complex web of national laws that is currently frustrating many foundations' cross-border aspirations. It is clear that funders need to have the freedom to work throughout Europe, aided by a minimum of constricting red tape, a goal we believe a European foundation statute would achieve. However, a statute would also bring with it other positive by-products as it would, for instance, inherently address the manner in which foundations are governed and the transparency and accountability of cross-border work and financing. Such issues are particularly relevant given the current climate of concern over the covert financing of international terrorism.

At the European level, the foundation sector has already been advocating key elements of general standards for foundations' conduct, so some of the necessary groundwork for a European foundation statute has already been done. Foundations have been discussing codes of conduct, principles of good practice and self-regulation at European level since the 1990s.

The driving forces in this debate range from the focus on enhancing foundations' governance, a serious and concerted set of efforts to look at efficacy and outputs, a desire for enhanced professionalism and efficiency, and, of course, the tremendous and robust examples of increased collaboration and cooperation between European foundations. There is clear understanding that self-governance is urgently needed and there are efforts to develop a mutually beneficial and transparent relationship between partners, funders and beneficiaries.

Many forms of governance-strengthening vehicles – principles of good practice, ethical codes, charters, quality marks and frameworks – have already been developed by national associations of donors and foundations in Europe. By 2006, 11 of these 17 associations had developed codes of practices or standards; seven of them were drawn up over the last three years. The EFC Principles of Good Practice also address such issues, and are designed to apply to diverse cultures and jurisdictions and a wide range of foundations in the EU and elsewhere in Europe.

It is always good to declare one's biases. My favourite by-product of the statute will be its ability to help demystify foundations to the European body politic and public. We can all play a part in wrestling with the problem caused by the cultural differences between countries, as 'foundations' can be interpreted differently, depending on who is defining them. However, we should agree that the term 'foundation' is certainly one worth defending. One would be correct in assuming that the term 'foundation' as it is used in Europe is infinitely more ambiguous and confusing than, for example, in the United States. The word is often used as synonymous with 'NGO', 'charity', 'think-tank', 'institute' and countless other terms, and it is therefore not surprising that people get confused about what precisely they are talking about. There are thus 'foundations' that have nothing to do with public benefit, some that have no resources of their own, and others that are essentially parastatal entities. A statute, we hope, would begin to address these issues of vocabulary.

The adoption of a pan-EU statute would thus be of immense conceptual help in clarifying the terms by which we define foundations and the underlying concept of how they work (by stressing, *inter alia*, that they must have their own independent resources and governance structure). More importantly, it would contribute to eradicating the unfounded defamations that are tarnishing the sector's reputation. It is high time that the very term 'foundation' was appropriated by the philanthropic sector and legally defined across the continent in a single and mutually comprehensible way. This would have an enormous impact on the sector and would – one would hope – safeguard matters so that any organizations using the label 'foundation' would be unequivocally deploying private resources to ensure public good. To paraphrase Bob Dylan: may you have a strong 'European' foundation when the winds of change shift!

Benefits for European citizens

Francis Charhon, Executive Director of Fondation de France and a founding member of the EFC, has said that he believes the statute would not only address the needs of foundations but would also ultimately address the needs of European citizens, a sentiment echoed by all advocates of the statute. This would be achieved both by providing an effective way for citizens to contribute to the European public good and by reinforcing democratic accountability in the EU.

It would also help channel the burgeoning private wealth from newly emerging sources, such as the philanthropically inclined newcomers. Furthermore, foundations would be better placed to support the objectives of the EU and provide funding for key policy areas. Among the recent initiatives that contribute to the goal of benefiting EU citizens and policy is the European Forum on Philanthropy and Research Funding, a new EFC-led initiative supported by the European Commission and individual funders.

The Forum aims to help underpin philanthropic funding for research by exchanging experiences and best practice, developing cooperation on research funding, and promoting a favourable environment for foundation and private philanthropy undertakings. This sort of project also makes, in my view, an essential contribution to initiatives like the 'Lisbon strategy', inaugurated in 2000, which seeks to allow the EU to compete with other major world players and become, by 2010, 'the most competitive and dynamic knowledge-based economy in the world, capable of sustainable growth with more and better jobs and greater social cohesion'. The Lisbon strategy embraces areas such as research, education, training, internet access and online business.

Commissioner Janez Potočnik expressed the European Commission's growing belief in the 'distinctive and important role that foundations and "charitable giving" can play . . . Private entities serving public goals will add value to European research activities and thus to the European Research Area. Foundations not only increase the volume of available funding, but also bring competencies and unique characteristics that contribute to the pluralism of European research and development funding. Government funding is often taken for granted, and is often accompanied by slow and bureaucratic procedures, albeit to ensure the effective use of taxpayers' contributions . . . Foundations and trusts demand excellence and quality on behalf of their donors, but have no expectations of monetary returns. Rules and procedures can be less cumbersome, allowing faster action and more flexibility. Beneficiaries are thus responsive, giving this sector a small but powerful influence on the direction, nature and quantity of research in Europe.'

We should not lose sight of the crucial role that foundations are already playing in this arena and how much more they could do if only a European foundation statute existed. It is not unreasonable to assert that having a statute would be likely to bolster the EU's overall competitiveness in the world market, not least in those sectors that focus on the knowledge society, research and innovation. Let's bear in mind that the work achieved by education and research foundations affects virtually all areas of our lives. Another gain would almost certainly be the promotion of sustainable socioeconomic development and territorial cohesion in the enlarged EU. Similarly, we could expect there to be an advance for the European public good and citizenship, and freedom of capital and establishment for all activities that assist the EU's objectives, regardless of who carries them out.

What we stand to lose

We are aware that this chapter has criticized the shortcomings of the current European environment for foundations, and extolled the likely benefits of having the much-desired statute, but in conclusion it is perhaps also worth examining the impact of not pushing for the statute. If we did nothing, we could expect to see donors and foundations continuing to struggle with restrictive laws that ignore the transnational nature of so many foundations' activities, and the poor value for money that inefficiently structured cross-border activity represents. Large sums would continue to go down the drain in counter-productive taxes, and we would be missing a vital opportunity to channel growing sources of private wealth.

Nor ought we to run the risk of causing Europe's privately held wealth to migrate elsewhere to places where it would receive a warmer and less bureaucratic reception. A prime example of a more welcoming large economy is the United States, which is a fully integrated single market, and in many respects has a more favourable legal environment. Just as transferring philanthropic funds from Connecticut to California is currently done without having to invent alternative and duplicative structures, we should be emulating this process in shifting assets from Stockholm to Seville.

If we retain the status quo, what other damage would it do to the internal cohesion of the EU and how would it deprive its citizens? Without a foundation statute, we would be de facto allowing official discrimination against foundations to persist, in clear breach of the spirit and goals of having a single European market. Arguably, this could contribute to a further decline in trust in the EU's institutions, which is already amply demonstrated by its citizens. Surely it makes good sense to create this new mechanism to support the European public good and encourage active participation by EU citizens.

National governments and EU institutions alike are struggling with the challenges that result from social discontent, whether it is the escalating flow of migrants from less prosperous countries and the resulting tensions, the major threat to people's safety and livelihoods that climate change represents, or the perennial need to keep pace with society's expectations of healthcare provision, particularly as more of us live longer. Foundations are ideally placed to act as pressure valves and to help produce solutions to these and other causes of discontent and instability. We have no doubt that a European foundation statute would help to achieve even greater impact from this sector.

Why we cannot sit on our hands

We must certainly hope that the outcome of the feasibility study later in 2008 will favour foundations. But even if the study conclusions support the case we have been making so emphatically and find that a European foundation statute would bring added value, we would not be entirely out of the woods. There would still be a risk of political inertia, and we need to be cognisant of, and prepared for, this looming danger. For there to be any further progress in implementing the study's recommendations, the Commission would then still need to draft a European foundation statute regulation for the European Parliament and Council to review.

It is our responsibility and intent to keep this issue on the boil. We cannot wait passively, naively hoping for the best and imprudently assuming that the feasibility study will turn out the way we would like, with all its recommendations magically resulting in a foundation statute tailored to our demands. There is still work to be done and ground to be covered in the form of information-sharing and advocacy, as well as scrutiny for us all to engage in to ensure that potential decision-makers are reliably briefed and that whatever undertakings they may give are acted on to the letter. We would be foolish to be complacent. It is imperative that we miss no opportunity to keep this vital issue fully before the public gaze and constantly present in the minds of Europe's legislators, in Brussels as well as in national capitals.

Decision-makers must also be persuaded about the next steps they must take and the vigour with which they need to pursue the last and most critical stage of this initiative. We are confident that only by making the case strongly will we be able to achieve the final push that will see the merits of our case acknowledged, and the EU's leaders definitively accepting the logic of creating a European foundation statute. The phenomenal growth of foundations, coupled with the more unified meaning of the word foundation that would be achieved by the statute, may allow the sector as a whole to receive the 'undivided attention' that it deserves, a privilege not granted to Algy by Cecily in *The Importance of Being Earnest*.

About the contributors

Filiz Bikmen is an Istanbul-based foundation professional, speaker and writer. She has recently been appointed as the Manger of Institutional Development and Programs at the Sabancı Foundation and as an Adviser to the Board at TUSEV (Third Sector Foundation of Turkey), where she was previously the Director for five years.

Anna Cantaluppi is the Head of Historical Archives at Compagnia di San Paolo, Turin, Italy.

Caroline Hartnell is Editor of *Alliance* magazine.

Wilhelm Krull has been the Secretary General of the Volkswagen Foundation since 1996 and is currently the Chairman of the European Foundation Centre.

Diana Leat is an academic and consultant specializing in issues related to philanthropy and grantmaking. She has written widely on the topic of philanthropy; her latest book *Just Change: Strategies for increasing philanthropic impact* is available from the Association of Charitable Foundations, London.

Norine MacDonald QC is president of the Gabriel Foundation, managing director of the Mercator Fund, and president, founder and lead field researcher of the Senlis Council and Senlis Afghanistan.

Maximilian Martin is Global Head, UBS Philanthropy Services, and serves as Visiting Professor at the University of Geneva. Andreas Ernst and

Lukas Stuecklin's very helpful comments are gratefully acknowledged, as well as excellent research assistance by Andrei Gidkov.

Dianna Rienstra is the Director of Phoenix Ink Communications, a Brussels-based consultancy. She specializes in writing, strategic communications advice, media and presentation coaching, as well as moderating and reporting on conferences.

Gerry Salole is Chief Executive of the European Foundation Centre.

Hildy Simmons has been involved in the philanthropic community for more than 25 years. She retired as head of the Global Foundations Group at JPMorgan Chase Private Bank and now works out of New York as in independent consultant advising select clients on their philanthropic activities.

Luc Tayart de Borms is managing director of the King Baudouin Foundation in Brussels, Belgium and chair of the Network of European Foundations for Innovative Cooperation.

António José Teixeira is a Lisbon-based journalist and political analyst. He is also the director of SIC-Notícias, a news television channel.

Gottfried Wagner has been Director of the European Cultural Foundation since January 2002. He was previously the Director of KulturKontakt Austria, a non-profit organization for educational and cultural cooperation with Central, Eastern and South-east Europe. He has also worked for the Austrian Ministry of Education, Science and Culture, with responsibility for educational cooperation with Central and Eastern Europe.

David Watkiss is an associate with Phoenix Ink Communications, a Brussels-based consultancy, where he works as a writer and consultant. Prior to moving to Brussels in 2006, he practised law in the United States for nearly 30 years. At Harvard Law School, he served as an editor on the *Harvard Law Review*.

Index

The index contains the names of people and organizations referred to in this book.

Albergo di Virtù (Hostel of Virtues) 57

Amato, Giuliano 48

Anna Lindh Euro-Mediterranean Foundation for the Dialogue between Cultures 71

Anna Lindt Foundation 14

Aristotle 45

Ashoka 179

Association for Cancer Research 90

Association of Charitable Foundations 248, 257

Association of Leaders of Local Civic Groups 28, 30

Atlantic Philanthropies 277, 278

Austwick, Dawn 253

AVINA 180, 185

Aydın Doğan Foundation 229, 233

Barnardo, Syrie 209

Barreto, António 128

Bart, Cécile 94

Báthory, Stephen 24

Batko-Toluc, Katarzyna 31

Beat 140

Berg, Dieter 42, 49–50

Bernard van Leer Foundation 197–200

Bernard van Leer Stiftung 189, 193–5

Bernhard, HRH, Prince of the Netherlands 69, 70

Bertelsmann Stiftung 265

Biedenkopf, Kurt 48

Bloch-Lainé, François 87

Borgen, Erling 109, 110

Borsinger, Nicholas 252

Bosch, Christof 42

Bosch, Robert 13, 37–42

British Venture Capital Association 135

Brugmans, Hendrik 69

Bund der Erneuerung des Reiches (Federation for the Renewal of the Empire) 40

Burroughs, Silas 207

Business Council on Sustainable Development 175, 178

Calouste Gulbenkian Foundation 115–28

Canopus Foundation 282

Carnegie UK Trust 248, 249, 252

Casa del Deposito 57

Casa del Soccorso (House of Relief) 57

Central European University 238

Centre for Civil Society, London School of Economics 259

Centre Français des Fondations 89

Charhon, Francis 85, 88, 96, 296

Charles Stewart Mott Foundation 22, 48

Christian Children's Fund 199

Churchill, Winston 117

City Bridge Trust 277

Civic Development Forum 27

Collegio Carlos Alberto 64

Collegio dei Nobili Convittori (College for the Young Noblemen) 57

Commercial Union of Poland 22

Community Foundation for Northern Ireland 256, 268

Compagnia di San Paolo 12, 48, 53–68, 239, 268

Consorzio Collegio Carlo Alberto 54

Council on Foundations 161

Creasy, William 213

Curie, Marie 22

Dag Hammarskjöld Foundation 267

Dale, Henry 208, 210

Daros 179

Dawson, Stephen 13–14, 129–42

de Rougemont, Denis 69

Debré, Michel 85

Democratic Voice of Burma 107–8

Deutsch, Martin 193

Deutsche Bundesstiftung Umwelt (German Federal Foundation for the Environment) 246, 251, 255

Deutsche Liga für den Völkerbund (German Federation for the League of Nations) 40

Diana, Princess of Wales Memorial Fund 137

Die ERSTE Österreichische Spar-Casse Privatstiftung 48

Disegni, Dario 65

Donors and Foundations Networks in Europe (DAFNE) 294

Dracopoulos, Andreas 149, 156

Dufton, Robert 250, 251

Educatorio Duchessa Isabella 60

Egmont Foundation 249

Elion, Trudy 212

Elkana, Yehuda 239

Emergency 65

Emerson, David 248

Erichsen, Bente 109

Esmee Fairbairn Foundation 253, 282

Essayan, Kevork 121, 126

Essayan, Nevarte 116, 124

Etherington, Stuart 248

European Commission 76

European Cultural Foundation 12, 65, 69–84, 233

European Foreign and Security Policy Studies 64

European Foundation Centre (EFC) 7, 14, 75, 88, 161, 230, 232, 237, 249, 257, 290, 292, 294

European Fund for the Balkans 48

European Union Institute for Security Studies 30

European Venture Philanthropy Association (EVPA) 130, 135, 283

EUSTORY Foundation 294

Evens Foundation 249, 255

Fairburn, Christopher 215

Federation of Polish Private Employees 27

Feeney, Chuck 277–8

Fidalgo, Manuela 124

Figueiredo, Maria Rosa 124

Fondation de France 12, 74, 85–97, 296

Fondazione Cassa di Risparmio di Cuneo 250, 255

Fondazione per l'Arte 54, 65

Fondazione per la Scuola 54, 64

Fondazione San Paolo di Torino per la Cultura, la Scienza e Arte (San Paolo Foundation for Culture, Science and Art) 62

Ford Foundation 22, 245

Ford, Henry 117

Frang Hoyum, Nina 106

Free Word Centre 110

Fund for Central and East European Book Project 72

FUNDES 176, 184

Gaberman, Barry 245–6, 253,254

Gastaldo, Piero 63, 66

German Institute for International and Security Affairs (SWP) 30

German Marshall Fund of the United States 48, 152

Gerstberger, Günter 46

Gibbs, Sir Roger 212

Giolitti, Giovanni 59

Goerdeler, Carl 41

Gulbenkian, Calouste Sarkis 11, 13, 115–28

Gulbenkian, Sarkis 118

Hahn, Dr Olaf 46

Hammarskjöld, General Dag 267

Hamsun, Knut 105

Hand in Hand Center for Jewish-Arab Education 199

Hauge, Jens Christian 101

Healy, John 278

Heidehof Stiftung 45

Heuss, Theodor 38–9

Hitching, George 212

Holl, Steven 106

Hollingsworth, Rogers 241

Holloway, Adam 135

Home-Start International 150

Human Genetics Foundation 55

Human Genome Project 213

Hüsnü Özyeğin 229

Ihsan Dogramaci Foundation 228

Impetus Trust 129–41

Innsikt (Insight) 109

Institusjonen Fritt Ord (Freedom of Expression Foundation) 11, 99–113, 246, 250

ISIS Equity Partners 135

Istituto Case Popolari 61

Istituto di San Paolo di Torino, Credito e Beneficenza (Credit and Philanthropy) 60

Istituto Superiore Mario Boella 54, 64

Istituto Superiore sui Sistemi Territoriali per l'Innovazione (SiTI) (Advanced Institute for Territorial Systems of Innovation) 55

James, Robert 211

Jaruzelski, Wojciech 22

Jaume Bofill Foundation 268

Jerusalem Film Center 197, 201

Joseph Rowntree Charitable Trust 251, 256, 265

Jüdische Mittelstelle 41

Keyfund Federation 140

Kilmurray, Avila 256

King Baudouin Foundation 48, 245, 255, 265

Kluk, Neville 255

Koç, Vehbi 228

Kolade, Wol 135

Kollontaj, Aleksandra 100

Körber Foundation 267

Körber, Kurt A 267

Kwasniewski, Aleksander 34

LabforCulture 72

Landmine Survivors Network 151

Leap Confronting Conflict 132, 136–40, 142

Legal Clinics Foundation 28

Lemaistre, Dominique 92

Liggins, Graham 214

Lutnes, Elin 251

Malraux, André 85

Masisa 177

Massé, Pierre 87

Maung Win, Khin 107

McConnell, Charlie 249

Médecins Sans Frontières 65, 156

Medina Ortega, Manuel 291

Meyer, Rafael 280

Miller, Doug 135

Mission Enfance 156

Monnet, Jean 74

Monte di Pietà 57–8, 60

Mother Child Education Foundation (ACEV) 230

Mother Child Literacy Foundation 167

Mullin, Henderson 111

Narvesen Kioskkompani (Narvesen Kiosk Company) 101

National Council for Voluntary Organizations 248

Naz Project London 140

Network of European
Foundations Cultural
Cluster 65

Network of European
Foundations for Innovative
Cooperation (NEF) 16,
66, 75, 233, 269, 294

Niarchos Prize for
Survivorship 151

Niarchos, Spyros 154

Niarchos, Stavros
11–13, 143–56

Nobel Fredssenter (Nobel
Peace Centre) 108

Nordlie, Jens Henrik 101, 103

Norwegian House of
Literature Foundation 106

Nuffield Foundation
249, 256, 266

OC&C Strategy
Consultants 133

OECD 66

Open Society
Institute 22–3, 33

Opere Pie di San Paolo
(Charitable Institutions
of Saint Paul) 59, 61

Özyeğin, Hüsnü 165

Pacaçioğlu, Hüsnü 160

Pamboukian, Kevork 118

Paul Hamlyn Foundation
250–1, 256

Perdigão, Azeredo 122, 126

Perse, Saint-John 122

Pirzio-Biroli, Corrado 293

Pittam, Stephen 251

Pomey, Michel 86

Potoçnik, Janez 291, 297

Pro Victimis
Foundation 249, 252

Project for Early Childhood
Education 195

Retinger, Joseph 69

Ribeiro, António Pinto 120

Riksbankens
Jubileumsfond 239, 268

Robert Bosch Stiftung
13, 22, 37–51

Roberto Cimetta Fund 71

Rogall, Dr Joachim 45

Rogers, Jenny 132, 136–9

Roving Caregivers 199

Rozicka, Anna 23–28, 30, 33–34

Rudeng, Erik 102–3

Rui Vilar, Emilio 124

Rural Investment
Support for Europe
(RISE) Foundation 292

Russo Perez, Nicolò 64

Sabancı Foundation
11–12, 157–71, 228

Sabancı, Güler 160, 170

Sabancı, Hacı Ömer
157–60, 170

Sabancı, Sadıka 159

Sakharov, Andrei 103

Salole, Gerry 7, 249, 257

Saroyan, William 121

Satrapa-Schill, Dr Almut 44

Schmidheiny, Stephan
13–14, 173–87

Schuman, Robert 69–70

Schwartz, Daniel 280

Sejerstad, Professor
Francis 100, 109, 112

Setkova, Lenka 248, 252

Shell Foundation 282

Silvestri, Andrea 250, 255

Sira Myhre, Aslak 107

SiTI 64

Skedsmo, Finn 102

Sloane, Nat 131, 136

Soros Foundation Network 72

Soros, George 13, 22, 238

Sparebankstiftelsen
DnB NOR 249

Speaking Up 140

St Giles Trust 140

St Sarkis Charity Trust 119

Stanley, Henry 208

Stavros Niarchos
Foundation 143–56

Steel, Sir David 212

Stefan Batory Foundation
11, 13, 21–35

Stevens, Franco Grande 67

Strong, Maurice 178

Stuttgart Technical
University 39

Sulston, Sir John 213

Suu Kyi, Aung San 108

Tall Ships Youth Trust 147

Tayart de Borms, Luc
245, 247, 253, 254

Tchamkerten, Astrig 118

TEMA 230

TESEV 230

Theiner, Dr Peter 45

TOG (Community Volunteers
Foundation) 230

Trust for Civil Society
in Central and Eastern
Europe 22, 246

Tschol, Dr Ingrid Wünning 44

TUSEV (Third Sector
Foundation of Turkey)
161, 230, 232

Ufficio Pio (Pious
Office) 55, 57

van Gendt, Rien 197

van Leer, Bernard 13, 189–203

Van Leer Foundation
Group 189–203

Van Leer Jerusalem
Institute 197, 200

van Leer, Oscar 189, 194

van Leer, Wim 190

Vehbi Koç Foundation 228–9

Verein zur Abwehr
des Antisemitismus
(Association against
Anti-Semitism) 41

VIVA Trust 180, 185

Volkswagen Stiftung 239, 268

Walesa, Lech 103

Walport, Dr Mark 216–17

Walz, Hans 41

Weatherstone, Sir Dennis 147

Wellcome, Sir Henry S
13, 205–13

Wellcome Trust 205–19

Wellcome Trust Sanger
Institute 213

White, Nick 213

Williams, Peter 212

Witte, Ulrich 255

World Business Council on
Sustainable Development 178

ZEIT Foundation 112